The
Art
of the
Psychotherapist

BOOKS BY JAMES F. T. BUGENTAL

*The Search for Authenticity: An Existential-Analytic Approach
to Psychotherapy*

Challenges of Humanistic Psychology (Editor)

*The Search for Existential Identity: Patient-Therapist
Dialogues in Humanistic Psychotherapy*

*Psychotherapy and Process: The Fundamentals of an
Existential-Humanistic Approach*

A NORTON PROFESSIONAL BOOK

The
Art
of the
Psychotherapist

JAMES F. T. BUGENTAL, Ph.D.

W· W· NORTON & COMPANY · *NEW YORK* · *LONDON*

Library of Congress Cataloging-in-Publication Data

Bugental, James F. T.
  The art of the psychotherapist.

  "A Norton professional book."
  Bibliography: p.
  Includes index.
  1. Psychotherapy. 2. Psychotherapists. 3. Humanistic
psychotherapy. I. Title.
RC480.B75   1987   616.89'14   86-31072

ISBN   0-393-70032-1

W. W. Norton & Company, Inc., 500 Fifth Avenue, New York, N.Y. 10110

W. W. Norton & Company Ltd., 37 Great Russell Street, London WC1B 3NU

1 2 3 4 5 6 7 8 9 0

ALVIN A. LASKO, Ph.D.
1916–1983

This book is lovingly dedicated to Al Lasko, my friend and colleague of 35 years, whose loss I still find painful and unbelievable. Together we grew up in clinical psychology even as clinical psychology was itself growing up in its astonishing blossoming after World War II: the first of the post-war trained, clinical psychologists to become faculty members at UCLA, venturing into private practice to the disapproval of our academic brethren and medical colleagues, founding a group practice which continues today, developing our own training program, exploring new areas—group dynamics and therapy, residentials for patients, depth therapy, psychoanalyses, psychedelics, existential theory.

We shared so much: chess and shuffleboard, endless "shoelacing" arguments over theories (shoelacing because we continually switched sides), vacations, discoveries of new books, new places, new theories, new jokes. We shared our new families, our children's growth to maturity, the ends of our marriages, entering into our older years.

And we shared much that is in this book under my name but to which he was the never-failing contributor.

I will remember always, Alvin.

James

CONTENTS

PREFACE

ART AND SCIENCE ARE two extremes of the polarity from subjectivity to objectivity, a dimension which permeates all human enter-
prises. Adopting a subjective perspective on life contrasts with and
complements focusing on objective aspects. Both, always present,
create a dynamism in whatever is undertaken. Psychotherapy mani-
fests this duality in many ways, and the artistry of master therapists
shows in their ability selectively to blend the subjective with the
objective, their art with their science.

The subjectivity of patients is the site of the most important, most
demanding, and most threat-arousing work of life-changing psychotherapy. Concentrating work in this area distinguishes therapists
more deeply engaged with their patients, just as it challenges them
with the most difficult and personally confronting issues. Because
much of this realm is implicit rather than explicit and because in this
realm we rely heavily on our own subjectivity, therapists need to
season awhile before attempting to work in depth with patient subjectivity.

Other therapeutic goals (e.g., adjustment, symptom reduction) are
well served by objective means, but life-changing psychotherapy requires major attention to the subjective. This recognition does not
permit depth therapists to ignore the objective aspects of their art;
rather, they must use the full continuum in fostering their clients'
inquiries into and reconsiderations of their own subjectivity. This
book talks about perspectives which aid therapists in attaining that
greater range. Each of these vantage points is to some degree objective, and each seeks to disclose some aspect of patients' subjectivity;
thus, they serve as bridges between the two realms.

THE EMERGENCE OF THE SUBJECTIVE

In earlier times mariners' maps showed vast blank areas which
were labeled, "Terra Incognita," unknown land. Between the familiar
world and terra incognita lurked sea monsters waiting to devour
unwary sailors. Today's geography has few zones of unknown land,
and the sea monsters have gone the way of the unicorn and the
Minotaur. But the subjective is a psychological terra incognita,
guarded by monsters of anxiety and pathology which threaten those
who venture there.[1]

ix

The realm of the true subjective has been neglected by Western culture and science for at least three centuries. Much investigated by Eastern spiritual disciplines, it has—until recently—been dismissed by our parochial epoch as superstitious nonsense or proof of dim-wittedness. "Until recently" recognizes that this chauvinist prejudice is receding to such backwaters as academic positivism, political conservativism, or religious fundamentalism, three curiously but frequently related points of dogmatic certainty.

Depth psychotherapy has largely abandoned Freud's early dream of psychology as a nineteenth century natural science. Instead many of us have come to realize that the absolute determinism, linear reasoning, and dependence on explicit formulation characteristic of such scientistic pretensions do not accord with the reality of human subjectivity, the ultimate domain of our endeavors.

This book is, obviously, dedicated to the proposition that life-changing psychotherapy requires therapist and patient alike to give high priority to the subjective—the patient's first of all, the therapist's nearly as importantly.

PSYCHOTHERAPY AND THE SUBJECTIVE

Psychotherapists are as diverse a breed as any, and the arts they practice are, if anything, even more widely contrasting.[2] Nevertheless, those who over many years practice "intensive" or "depth" therapy often come to be more similar to each other in their ways of conducting therapy (if not in their theories about therapy) than to those who share their clan names and academic histories. This book tries to distill some of this commonality into forms which will aid those who want to move more quickly into such work.

My purpose is not to create a new psychotherapeutic system or methodology. I want to aid therapists of various orientations who intend doing depth, life-changing work to extend the range and power of their own perspectives and styles. From these pages I hope they will draw support for their own artistry and potency.

There are three stages in the development of therapists[3]:

1. They learn the rudiments of conducting therapeutic interviews.
2. They develop increasing sensitivity and skill in helping patients move from everyday kinds of conversations to deeply invested disclosures of subjective experiencing.
3. They come to appreciate the living experiences which underlie systematic views of personality, pathology, and therapy.

This book is addressed to the second phase. There are many good books for the first and the third and their relation to each other.

For those wanting to extend their powers in that second phase, here is an opportunity to experiment with a variety of perspectives. Here therapists may find those aspects which best serve their unique temperaments and skills, adapt others, and discard what is not compatible. Only in this way can there be any valid sharing of what is always and inescapably a highly individual art.

It follows that no volume, no one perspective, and no teacher can possibly be sufficient to the diversity of therapists and of patients. Certainly the materials brought together here cannot be so. These dimensions have grown out of the soil of intensive individual psychotherapy. They have been cultivated by working with clients from a wide range of backgrounds with quite varied investments in their therapy. They have been further developed by interactions with psychotherapists of all the major professional disciplines and of contrasting prior (and subsequent) theoretic persuasions.

TO WHOM THIS BOOK IS ADDRESSED

In writing this book, I have three groups of therapist-readers in mind:

- Principally, experienced therapists who seek ways of broadening or deepening their sensitivities and skills.

  The complete neophyte to this art is very apt to find much that follows incomprehensible or unbearably demanding. When the first self-consciousness about being a psychotherapist drains down to livable proportions and the uses and limitations of one's initial complement of techniques have been repeatedly experienced, then the dimensions in this book will open fresh perspectives and opportunities for the dedicated therapist. Each person will have to assess his own readiness, of course, although caring and sensitive instructors, supervisors, and colleagues can certainly help.

- Instructors and supervisors will find this collection of ways of looking at therapeutic interchanges aids in communicating with trainees about subtleties that are often noted but hard to identify.

  In the same way they may find it useful to assign certain exercises. The trainer can point out those patterns to which a developing therapist especially needs to become more sensitized or in which the therapist must develop greater skill.

  A repeated difficulty in teaching and supervising neophyte therapists is their preoccupation with "What do I say?" and "What should

I do?" The following chapters provide avenues for pointing such therapists beyond the explicit and helping them with the difficult task of learning to sense the implicit. One cannot teach that skill directly, but having ways of orienting the person to that realm gives the best chance for refining perceptiveness.

• I hope that researchers seeking to get into the subjective more fully will find these dimensions suggestive of avenues for their purposes. None of these is a ready-made instrument, but all are clinically proven pointers to areas of demonstrated significance.

SOME NOTES ON THE STYLE OF PRESENTATION

The gender matter. I systematically alternate using one gender for therapist and the other for patient. This makes for an absence of same-sex therapeutic teams, which is, of course, unrealistic. The only exceptions to these two conditions occur when I am quoting from previously published case material in which I am identified as therapist. People in general take the same gender as does the patient/client.

"Patient" or "client." I don't like either of these terms. "Patient" suggests an inert object on which the doctor practices. I cannot readily imagine a more contrary suggestion to the kind of therapy this book describes. On the other hand, "client" smacks of commercialism to such an extent that I have heard the term used for those served by midwives, prostitutes, and morticians! Once again choosing the routine of compromise (I save my ammunition for the important battles), I systematically alternate these two terms but in a pattern which keeps them from always being tied to gender.

Abridged excerpts. I liberally insert illustrative interview excerpts. These samples of the work are misleading in two ways: The work moves ahead more rapidly and effectively than it ever does in real life. To show all the long periods in which no apparent impact is evident, to repeat all the starts and stops of normal conversation, or to set out all the repetitions, detours and returns, and confusions on the parts of both participants that are part of all psychotherapy would transform this volume into a cure for insomnia.

The second unreality is that the need for concise presentation dictates that I confine excerpts largely to illustrating the particular point being presented. This loses many contextual indications for and side-effects of interactions. In an effort to restore some of these, I carry the same hypothetical case through several passages when that is possible. The reader may judge what success that stratagem has achieved. All names, except mine, are fictitious, and I do not hestitate to create fictional dialogue to make a point as clear as possible. If any of my fictional therapists or patients have your name, my apologies are tendered and my hope that you will be in no way troubled.

A PSYCHOTHERAPIST'S JOURNEY

Under this heading in each chapter I practice what I preach: disclosing some of my own subjective experience and opinions. These, deriving from nearly a half-century of working with people, are meant to directly supplement the main presentation by letting the reader get some sense of its personal and subjective roots.

Writing this book is a culminating effort for me. I have been invested in trying to find ways of communicating what hundreds of patients have taught me about how we humans frame our being, how we express our questing, and how we—wittingly and unwittingly—defeat some of our own best efforts. I have been developing the idea of semi-objective avenues to the subjective for longer than I knew that was what I was doing.

In calling this a culminating effort I don't mean to say I've reached a summit beyond which no progress can be made. That is just not so; I'm not even sure I'm on much of a plateau. This is just the place I am at this point in my life, and I want to set it down for myself and others now. (I am 70 now, but I intend to write at least ten more books in the coming years, so this is not a swan song either.)

My work as a therapist has been richly rewarding, often upsetting, frequently confusing, continually challenging, and the greatest thing that ever happened to me. I hope these ideas in these pages will communicate some of that excitement and stimulation to you who read what I have written.

ACKNOWLEDGMENTS

FIRST AND FOREMOST, I must express my gratitude to my most numerous and most persistent teachers, my patients. I wish that I could have been more what you needed, but I am happy for the ways in which we joined forces to do our work together as well as we did at the time.

Then I want to say to my students and supervisees: Thank you for your trust in me, for your questions, and for your eagerness to grow and learn. You have contributed much to the work which I am reporting here.

I find genuine pleasure in acknowledging the contributions of a particular group of friends—the supervisors, interns, and associates of Inter/Logue, our nonprofit training and service center. They have been generous with their stimulating responses, thoughtful suggestions, and sustaining encouragement: Nancy Bertelsen, Tom Cushing, Roberta Goldfarb, Carole Firestone-Gillis, Dennis Glick, Susan Goyton, Pat Poe, Roger Rose, Jeff Scannell, Adele Schwarz, Molly Merrill Sterling, and Eileen Sullivan.

Professor Tom Dorsel of Western Carolina University offered helpful suggestions and supportive encouragement.

Four other people have been particularly important in their contributions to this book:

John L. Levy, busy as he is, took time to painstakingly read the entire manuscript with an eye that is critical in the very best sense of that often misused term. His discernment, judgment, and support made a difference objectively—and, even more, subjectively.

Carole Lang, secretary, administrative assistant, gofer, collator, duplicator, advisor, encourager, and friend. She came in when needed—ignoring Sundays and other days off. Her hand is everywhere in these pages.

David Young, busy completing his own doctorate, was there when I needed him to do every manner of task from repairing a toilet seat to discerningly commenting on chapter drafts.

And then there is my one special person whose gifts to me I want to publicly acknowledge: my wife, colleague, and buddy, Elizabeth K. Bugental. She contributes in ways past counting, and her loving support gives added meaning to my belief in the primacy of the subjective for all of our human endeavors.

James F. T. Bugental
Santa Rosa, July, 1986

SECTION I

Introduction

CHAPTER 1

Life-Changing Psychotherapy
and the Subjective

We in Western culture are only now beginning to discover the primacy of our subjectivity. Yet life-changing psychotherapy is psychotherapy that engages the patient's subjectivity, and in that focus is its greatest difference from other psychotherapies. This focus calls for continual attention to the patient's inner experiencing, and it recognizes that the prime instrument needed for that attention is the therapist's own subjectivity.

In this chapter I describe the nature of life-changing psychotherapy, what is involved in bringing about major life changes, and how subjectivity is conceived. This leads to thinking about the implicit image of the person involved in this work and how that work is conducted.

With this background, we survey the 13 dimensions which constitute this book. These are identified as ways of fostering greater depth and scope for therapist's own subjectivity. The chapter concludes by pointing out how integral to a true grasp of the concepts presented are the practice exercises which are provided for many of the dimensions.

LIFE-CHANGING PSYCHOTHERAPY is a unique human invention whose characteristics, necessities, outcomes, and implications are only beginning to be appreciated. It is frequently and erroneously lumped with other therapeutic forms which serve valuable but different purposes and have importantly different necessities and implications. To make generalizations—"therapy is usually successful (or unsuccessful) with borderline conditions" or "psychotherapy is more (or less) effective than medication with depressives (or some other category)"—is as sensible as to make such statements about all transportation—"transportation is too slow (or rapid)."

Life-changing psychotherapy, more than most other forms of therapy, demands that we recognize the patient's subjectivity as the true site of our endeavors. The tide of objectivism that has been running

3

for the past two centuries in Western culture has pushed us to extremes that approach the ludicrous. Increasingly, science, philosophy, government, education—even art and religion—have been swept up on this inhospitable shore. We have come to react with repugnance or shame to that which is labeled "subjective" and to confuse the term with sentimentality, undisciplined permissiveness, and moral "softness."

Our subjectivity is our true home, our natural state, and our necessary place of refuge and renewal. It is the font of creativity, the stage for imagination, the drafting table for planning, and the ultimate heart of our fears and hopes, our sorrows and satisfactions. For too long we have dismissed the subjective as ephemeral and of little consequence; as a result we have lost our center and been magnetically drawn to the shallow harbors and arid beaches of unrelieved objectivity.

If one seeks fundamental change in his experience of being alive, that quest must, beyond question, take the seeker into the depths of his subjectivity. No amount of objective manipulation can do the job for him. The wording of that assertion is quite deliberate. "Fundamental change in the experience of being alive" is the goal sought by many who enter psychotherapy but achieved by a lamentably smaller number. This distressing result is due, in appreciable degree, to the overemphasis on the objective in the training, supervision, and practice of many therapists. From this same source arise the abnormally high rates of alcoholism, divorce, and suicide among psychotherapists. Confronted with challenges for which they are ill-prepared but endowed with a sense of reponsibility and caring for those who come to them for help, some therapists find their work disappointing and, ultimately, destructive of their careers and lives.

Abstract theories of personality, heavy emphasis on perceiving overt symptoms, preoccupation with diagnoses and technique combine with a suspicious attitude toward the therapist's own inner promptings to produce an impersonal, mechanical, and detached attitude in the therapist—and soon thereafter in the patient—an attitude which foredooms the whole enterprise.

Life-changing therapy gives primary attention to the patient's subjective experiencing and does so by making the therapist's own subjective experiencing central to the work. This is not a parochial definition, for it includes practitioners from perspectives as diverse as Jungian analytic psychology, neo-Freudian psychoanalysis, Gestalt therapy, object-relations and ego psychologies, and existential and humanistic psychology and psychotherapy. None of these labels will distinguish those who practice in this subjectively oriented way. A better cue is apt to be the completeness of therapist's dedication to intensive and extensive work aimed at assisting patients in making major life changes. However, even that criterion is quite fallible, for not all who aim in that direction choose or are able to engage themselves as fully and personally as that work requires.

An aside: I do not say that theory, technique, and the processes of objective approaches to psychotherapy are without value. To do so would be manifest nonsense. Clearly they importantly contribute to the lives of many who seek that aid; certainly also, they offer much that is useful to therapists who work at all levels on the objectivity-to-subjectivity continuum. In brief, in many of the engagements of limited-goal psychotherapy, the objective approaches are both necessary and sufficient. For major life changes, they are only necessary; they are not sufficient.

ELEMENTS OF LIFE-CHANGING PSYCHOTHERAPY

What Are "Major Life Changes"?

Note: The following section provides a first summary answer to this question.[1] Later chapters will expand on this conception. The "Notes and Comments" section provides citations to more complete treatments of these matters.

Each person must in some way answer the basic questions life puts to us all: "Who and what am I? What is this world in which I live?" We answer these questions with our lives, with how we identify ourselves, how we use our powers, how we relate to others, how we face all the possibilities and limitations of being human. We collect the materials from which to form our answers from our parents, our brothers, sisters, and other family members, our teachers and age fellows, from our reading, including fiction in all its forms, from our churches and our memberships in various organizations. Throughout our lives we collect these materials, form and revise our answers, and continually carry this process up to the final question, which we answer with our deaths.

Of course, not all the sources we use for our answers are of the same importance to us. Some elements are superficial and transitory, some deeply invested and literally defended with our lives. The more central to our being an element, the more tenaciously we resist its being challenged or altered. This is the source of the deepest "resistances" with which life-changing psychotherapy is concerned (Chapter 10 describes this work in greater detail).

Life-changing psychotherapy is the effort of patient and therapist to help the former examine the manner in which he has answered life's existential questions and to attempt to revise some of those answers in ways which will make the patient's life more authentic and thus more fulfilling. Obviously this is much more than an explicit and consciously conducted enterprise. Instead, the more fundamental the elements of one's way of being which are being reworked, the more deeply into patient's subjectivity the work must go.

> Gloria came from a deeply religious family in which all standards of conduct were based on interpretations of the Bible. She grew up to feel mistrust of her own impulses and dependence on the teaching of her church. As she matured and went away to college, she found herself in an emotionally wrenching conflict between a view of the world in which "good" and "bad" were sharply contrasted and a more relativistic view to which her intelligence was leading her. Relinquishing the traditional guide to her life seemed tantamount to "giving in to the Devil," but trying to live by that tradition became increasingly constricting.
>
> She came to therapy with complaints of unexpected bouts of temper, sleeplessness, and fear of suffocation. It was many months before the underlying conflict was evident to Gloria—and, of course, that conflict was only one of the more salient issues of her whole life situation. Working out a resolution to the contradictions in which she was enmeshed involved great anguish and struggle. Eventually she arrived at a way of being that gave space for her intellect's seekings while preserving some measure of value for her background.

> Kate,[2] due to repeated times of feeling abandoned by her parents, taught herself to need no one, to try to be totally self-reliant, and to rigidly control her emotions, since they were apt to undermine the other intentions. She came to therapy because she found her ability to work at her profession being continually disrupted by unwanted thoughts and by periods of depression. In therapy she had to confront the futility of her tight, limited way of being and her long-suppressed hunger for relationships. Facing these was a terrifying process for Kate. In the long run, Kate was able to redefine herself in more flexible terms, although she retains a pattern of being unusually invested in whatever she undertakes.

What Is Subjectivity?

Subjectivity is that inner, separate, and private realm in which we live most genuinely. The furnishings or structures of this realm are our perceptions, thoughts, feelings and emotions, values and preferences, anticipations and apprehensions, fantasies and dreams, and all else that goes on endlessly night and day, waking and sleeping, and so determines what we do in the external world and what we make of what happens to us there. Significantly for psychotherapy, subjectivity is the closer bank on which must be founded the bridge of relationship to others and to the world. To change the metaphor, subjectivity is the seedbed of the concerns which impel us to undertake therapy, and it is the root system of our intentionality, which must be mobilized and focused if our therapeutic quest is to succeed.

Having said all this, I am still missing the key significance of subjectivity. The simple but profound truth is that we are subjects rather than objects, actors not the acted-upon, and this sovereignty is the essence of our subjectivity. Therein lies the ultimate meaning: It is the autonomy of human beings which escapes the cages of objective determinism and which resides in our subjectivity.

What Is the Image of the Person?

The subjective perspective holds as primary the conviction that a person, the patient, is a autonomous being. This is assumed, not for moralistic, idealistic, or democratic reasons alone, but as a consequence of realistic, clinical experience. That learning can be summarized in this fashion: Although all humans share many more or less objective characteristics, the more we know them as individuals, the more we recognize how each is ultimately unique. Yet the more we know a particular individual, the more we realize he cannot be fully known by anyone (including himself). This final unknowability arises from the reality that we humans are not empty containers filled from the outside only. We are, in ourselves, sources of phenomena (ideas, feelings, perceptions, relations, etc.) which alter expected sequences and upset predictions.

This crucially important characteristic of humans is a product of and is manifested in our unique capacity for reflexive awareness. Because we are always in some measure self-observing, a "wild card" is thrown into the human enterprise. We respond not only to outside stimuli — as the objectivists insist — but to our own responses, including our perceptions of ourselves and the situation. Thus there is the infinite regression, an endless sequence of subjective interactions, quite beyond the reach of any objective containment. Thus arise the truest subjectivity and the inexorable unpredictability which are the essence of the human.

All of this can be summarized by recognizing that in their deepest nature, human beings are causes; not simply caused. Thus there is a crucial difference between the subjective and the objective views of humans. Table 1.1 makes exaggerated contrasts as it summarizes some of these observations in terms of their implications for psychotherapy.

What Are the Characteristics of Life-Changing Psychotherapy?

I would be foolhardy indeed to try to lay down a set of specifications for all life-changing psychotherapies. What I can do is briefly characterize some of the distinguishing characteristics of the way I work, having confidence that other depth therapists agree on some, if not all, of these.

As I work I am indebted to the methods of psychoanalysis, the grandfather of this kind of work.[3] I have had the advantages (and to a lesser extent, the handicaps) of a classical analysis for myself and of some training in analytic methodology. Additionally I have had a number of further training experiences and have read in the psychoanalytic tradition. With the years, my work has evolved away from that base, but it still draws significantly on it in certain regards, as the list below will make evident.

- I believe that patient process needs to be the main focus of my attention, with content not unimportant but definitely secondary (see Section III).
- I find the recognition of levels of consciousness valuable clinically, although I recognize that the usual divisions—conscious, preconscious, and unconscious—have certain conceptual limitations.
- The central importance of work with the resistance (see Chapter 10) seems to me to be a hallmark of genuine life-changing therapy.
- The inevitability of transference and countertransference phenomena and the great values in working with them are almost as manifest.
- The necessity of frequency of contact is something I insist on less than formerly, but I still believe that twice a week is minimal, with only rare exceptions.
- Emotions are inevitable, valuable clues and to be respected, but I do not see them as central, in themselves, to our work.

TABLE 1.1
Contrasts Between Objective and Subjective
Perspectives on Psychotherapy

Objective		Subjective
adjustment	*Therapeutic goals*	life change
behavior	*Focus of attention*	experience
explicit	*Communication mode*	implicit
reinforcement	*Agency of change*	increased awareness
relation aids but is secondary	*Role of alliance*	transference/ countertransference
short-term (weeks)	*Time expectation*	long-term (years)
behavior modification or adjustment counseling	*Typical approaches* *	psychoanalysis or existential therapy
causality	*Explanatory model*	intentionality
consensual	*"Reality" assumption*	evolving, individual

*Not limited to these examples.

- Intentionality, the directionality of persons' lives, is a much more meaningful and therefore powerful explanatory notion than is causality. The latter, unthinkingly or unwisely carried over from objective physical science, misses the very essence of the human experience.
- The goals of the kind of therapy with which this book is concerned are aiding patient to experience himself as larger and more potent in his life, and thus as having choice, where formerly he experienced compulsion. Symptom reduction or problem solution may or may not occur as such. The disruptive effects of symptoms and problems, however, are markedly lessened when our work goes well.

What Is the Central Focus of Therapeutic Work?

Whatever the theoretical perspective of a depth psychotherapist, she must continually maintain some awareness of the patient's inner flow of experience. The most exquisitely crafted interventions are futile—and often countertherapeutic—when advanced with timing and form that fit poorly with where the patient is in his subjectivity. The wild card effect of human reflexive awareness must be taken into account by therapists as best they can when they seek to influence their patients' inner processes.

An example of the problem. Viewed in one way the work of therapy is an effort of patient and therapist to understand how the laatter's life is presently structured, what it is he seeks to do, what he wants to avoid, and what meanings reside in his experiences (e.g., events of his life or dreams). Yet this effort is futile if it is judged only in terms of *arriving* at answers to these questions. Paradoxically, the pursuit itself is the only thing that can be pursued.

Let's make all this more concrete: On January 5th, John Smith, a patient in long-term therapy, reports a dream which, after some joint effort, he and therapist come to see depicts his ambivalence about his mother's influence on his marriage. Two months later, current issues remind John and his therapist of that earlier dream. Now it is soon evident that the dream expresses John's apprehension about losing control of his anger. Then in June another dream recalls to the therapeutic partners the January images. Now their work results in seeing how that earlier imagery disclosed John's underlying but unconscious yearning for his father's love.

The "same" dream—three different interpretations. Was the January understanding wrong? Was the March? Is the "real" meaning of January's dream what the June work brought out? No to all of these questions; of course not. The meaning of the dream is not a fixed, single matter. It is an evolving process, due to the reflexive nature of subjectivity. Interpretation, by either therapist or patient, is always set within a particular time-affect-relations matrix. Thus, it changes as each of those elements is varied and as the superficially "same" material evokes new wild cards.

Summary

We have examined some of the most obvious contrasts between the objective and the subjective perspectives and some of the significances of the latter for understanding human psychology and the workings of depth psychotherapy. Now we need to consider ways in which we develop bridges between these two realms, bridges which aid therapists and patients in gaining access to the inner worlds of those who are committed to self-knowledge and greater actualization of their potentials.

EXTENDING THERAPIST SUBJECTIVE
CAPACITIES

There is a crucial difference between attending to patient reports of subjective experience and actually coming into immediate intersubjective communication. That phrase does not *necessarily* imply extrasensory contact; it does mean being open to intuitive sensing of what is happening in the patient back of his words and, often, back of his conscious awareness.

What the therapist must bring into action — in degrees which vary from patient to patient, even from session to session — is an appreciation for the patient's immediate experiencing, for the intentions implicit in his participation, for the ways he structures his own life, and for his accessibility at any given moment. This is the normal sensitivity that all of us have in relating with others, but it is that normal sensitivity carried to greater than normal acuity.

Training Therapist Intuition

What we are talking about, of course, is usually termed intuition.[4] A therapist must develop her intuitive capacities, continually seeking to become more sensitive and skillful in using them to sense where the patient is and what is possible and needful at any given point in the work.

This book offers aids to the development and refinement of therapist intuition. The dimensions which follow have two uses. First, they are similar to those used implicitly by many experienced and successful therapists. Thus, they can be adapted by those with sufficient background to use them in the career-long project of continual self-development.

The other use for these dimensions is to expedite therapists' coming to greater sensitivity to their patients' inner living. In this capacity, these dimensions are avenues to increased familiarity with the subjective realm. They are ways of entering into awareness of some of the most therapeutically significant processes likely to be going on in patient.

This does *not* mean that one should try to take one or more of these dimensions into the consulting room during actual work with patient. To do so would be to introduce contamination in the immediacy of relating with patient. There is much to be gained from familiarizing oneself with these dimensions when not with patients and then allowing them to emerge from one's preconscious and illuminate our perceptions in the actual contact hours. But that emergence needs to be uncontrived and spontaneous.

Dimensions for Therapeutic Artistry

The deepest subjective levels are the concern of a variety of therapeutic viewpoints — psychoanalysis, ego analysis, analytical psychology, psychosynthesis, transpersonal therapy, and existential psychotherapy, for examples. Since these schools of thought are specialized perspectives, rather than modalities shared by many views, they lie outside the domain of this book.

It may be helpful if I say again what I see as the domain of this book. Each of the therapy orientations listed in the previous paragraph is the fountainhead of a considerable literature which treats of personality formation, the vicissitudes of life which produce pathology and health, the sorts of depth or unconscious structures and processes which must be dealt with by psychotherapy, and the kinds of interventions to be used in these deeper levels to achieve the outcomes that viewpoint sees as desirable.

This book cannot attempt to synthesize all of these perspectives. Its program is more modest: I hope that, whatever the reader's theoretical orientation, he will find the dimensions in the following chapters useful. These are conceived as vehicles to take therapists who have become familiar with the basics of patient interviewing from that point to such competence in working with patient subjectivity that they can then use the literature of their perspective more adequately.

Basic Conversational Arts

- *Communication level* (Chapter 2) is a way of referring to how fully present and deeply immersed in the conversation the participants are.
- *Therapist presence and the alliance* (Chapter 3) deals with the reciprocal effects of therapist involvement, both its desirability and the qualifications that need to be made as to its form and content.
- *Interpersonal press* (Chapter 4) consists of the many ways in which

one person may influence another so that the other will feel, think, speak, or act differently.

Subject Matter Guidance

- *Topical paralleling* (Chapter 5) refers to the degree to which therapist and patient talk about the same subject matter.
- *Feeling paralleling* (Chapter 6) directs attention to the amount of attention each speaker gives to the patient's feelings about what is being discussed.
- *Frame paralleling* (Chapter 7) looks at how abstractly or concretely the subject matter is handled by the speakers.
- *Locus paralleling* (Chapter 8) has to do with where a speaker's comments focus—on the patient, on herself, or on some interactional pattern.

Getting Greater Depth

- *Objectivity-subjectivity ratio* (Chapter 9) characterizes the extent to which a speaker confines himself to detached, impersonal statements, as contrasted with expressing more emotional and uniquely personal elements.
- *Basics of handling resistance* (Chapter 10) offers a view of therapeutic resistance which has limited allegiance to any one orientation and is a practical, clinically tested sequence of therapist interventions for working with it.

Intrapsychic Processes

- *Concern* (Chapter 11) is a name for the gestalt of patient feelings and intentions which must be mobilized if true life change is to result from therapy. Complementing aspects of therapist concern are also identified.
- *Intentionality* (Chapter 12) is recognized as a principal patient process which must be influenced if the patient is to find more satisfying ways of having his life.

The Therapist's Own Being

- *Commitment* (Chapter 13) is essential to living authentically and for therapists engaged in effective life-changing psychotherapy.
- *Artistry* (Chapter 14) is a way of characterizing the matured therapist's dedication to her craft, her continually evolving sensitivities

and skills, and her inner fulfillment from expressing her own life in this enterprise.

GENERAL OBSERVATIONS

The 13 dimensions just described share certain important characteristics which are summarized below.

Eye of the beholder. The enterprise in which I am engaged is that of picking out constellations, not identifying stars or galaxies. Stars and galaxies exist in space; constellations exist, like beauty, only in the eye of the beholder. This does not mean that constellations are false or not to be trusted. Indeed, even that science of ultimate precision, astronomy, finds use for these constructions. It does mean that the particular grouping which we call by one name could be grouped otherwise by a different observer. The test is a pragmatic one: What gives us a helpful way of making our observations and conducting our work? Each reader will need to make his own judgments on the constellations I offer.

Suggestive, not exact. These dimensions are not fully objective, nor can they be stated precisely. Each points in a general way to an observable or semi-observable aspect of the therapeutic interaction. Each identifies an aspect important to artistic, effective therapy. Yet, by their nature, all are still ambiguous as well as both objective and subjective.

Overlapping. The dimensions are not independent of each other; there is necessarily and desirably a significant degree of overlap — "desirably" because this permits important processes to be viewed from several angles.

Bilateral. The greatest gain from attention to most of these dimensions comes from using them as frameworks for studying patient responses, guiding therapist actions, and making comparisons between the two. As one becomes more familiar with them and more experienced as a therapist, she will see additional significant applications.

Nonverbal and verbal.[5] Most of the following descriptions concern verbal aspects of conversations since these are the most readily available ways of pointing to the ways one person relates to another. It is important to recognize, however, that the nonverbal dimension is nearly always of equal importance.

Hazards in using. It is countertherapeutic to let any of these dimensions come into the foreground of therapist's consciousness during actual therapeutic interviews. To do so is to foster a kind of countertransference in which the patient is made into an object upon whom one is practicing a skill. To avoid this it is recommended that the therapist study and practice with these dimensions outside the actual consultation times; then, when she is with patients these refinements of perception and skill, having been incorporated into her subconscious, will take their natural places in her total awareness.

Premature attempts to use these dimensions. This book can be harmful to developing therapists who have had too little exposure to the work of the consulting room to be able to *perceive* appreciatively the frequently subtle dimensions as they are played out in the hour. The key word here is *perceive*. Any reasonably intelligent person can *understand* these processes, will even find some of them familiar, but understanding is quite another matter from appreciative perceiving. To perceive genuinely is not only to recognize the idea of the dimension but simultaneously to recognize (re-cognize) *with a sense of familiarity* the manner in which these dimensions have been subtly playing their parts in the conversations therapists have already been having with their patients.

The danger for the embryonic therapist is that understanding will be substituted for perception, with the result that enactment (of the processes) will take the place of intuitively meaningful selection from among them. This forced performance, resting on a too little subjective foundation in the therapist, will be sensed by patients as therapist inauthenticity. In turn, this will lead to patient responses which give the therapist misleading feedback as to the effects of the dimensions she has attempted to use. Learning, as a result, will be delayed and contaminated.

On the other hand, when there is *familiar recognition*, a basis is provided for aiding apprentice therapists as they increase their grasp of the subtle dynamics of therapeutic interchanges. From this gain they will be able to enrich and extend their work, to bring more power into the interactions, and to draw out the healthy potentials of their patients.

Using This Book

The next 13 chapters describe these dimensions, extending the definitions given above, providing examples from therapeutic interactions, and, where appropriate, proposing continua along which one may use them. Also, I offer suggestions for selecting responses and comment on alternative ways of handling various situations.

The practice exercises. Learning will be greatest and use of these dimensions more skillful and sensitive when therapists move from passive reading to active practice and experimentation. To facilitate these steps, readers will find in the appendix exercises which can add depth to understanding and prepare them for applying these insights in their therapeutic work.

Summary

Long experience with many patients teaches the aware psychotherapist many things, only some of which can be reduced to explicit formulation. Yet for the dedicated therapist who has moved past that first self-consciousness and is now able to focus on her art, those difficult-to-formulate aspects are precisely the things she wants to learn. Knowing how much she has already moved beyond early awkwardness and ineptitude, knowing there is much more to learn, she is eager to shorten the learning period, and she may have a nagging sense of something still not mastered.

In this book, I am trying to bridge that gap between competence and mastery in some measure, knowing I can do so only incompletely. I take some of the aspects to which experience teaches us to attune our awareness and translate them into moderately explicit or objective dimensions. Inevitably, in the process of doing this I make the dimensions more tangible, more orderly, and more systematic than they are—or than they ought to be. So far as I can see, there's no help for it. Communicating these matters requires a degree of objectification, even though our goal is to enrich the therapist's subjective sensitivity.

Thus, I can only do half the job. Each reader-therapist must pick up the task where I set it down. If she will do so, she will grasp in a fully experiencing way what each dimension is about. Then she will practice, developing her sense of its operation. In that practice she will gradually let the name of the dimension fade out as she makes her own unique integration of the perspective involved. Finally, having incorporated the dimension, she will let her preconscious take over the sensing and utilization of the now altered and personalized process. In this way, and only in this way, will these teachings be transmitted as both the writer and the reader-therapist truly want.

A PSYCHOTHERAPIST'S JOURNEY

I think I may have been born to be a people watcher. People always fascinated me. Watching them, watching myself, I wondered. Somehow they seemed so many mysteries among whom I dwelt. Certainly I was a mystery to myself. Always each person seemed to be or to have something more than I could get ahold of. Then I got to college and took my first course in psychology, the study of people. Now, at last, I would get a line on that something more. But, in fact, I was disappointed—and barely squeaked through with a "D." Where I'd been fascinated by people, by the something more that the people I watched continually presented, the psychology course made people something less.

Later, in graduate study for a master's degree, I felt as though I were getting closer, but still something eluded me. Psychological experiments, psychological testing, psychological theory—they all were fascinating, gave me a sense of new power, taught me much that was *about* people, but never really brought me to know others—or myself.

Yes, there was always still that something more. Something more than the people I interviewed and tested could tell me. Something more than the tests could disclose about them. Something more than the mysterious Rorschach and other new projectives with all their strange probing could bring to the surface. Something more than my developing intuition could reveal. Always something more.

For that matter—Great God!—there was always something more right here in me. More than I could always control. More than I could think of. More than I could write down or speak out. More than my analyst or later my therapist could discern. More than my midnight sweating and anxious breath could reach. More than my deepest wish to, effort to, prayer to, urgent effort to could plumb. Always something more.

And today I still ask, what is this elusive essence? In *The Agony and the Ecstasy*, Stone[6] has Michaelangelo ask again and again,

"Where do thoughts come from?" When I talk with someone enthusi-astically or haltingly, where do my next words come from? When I write does this sentence that I'm putting down right now so that you can read it right now (although at a totally different "right now")—where are these words coming from? Always something more.

Sometimes such questions seem nonsensical, the stuff of which madness or alienation is compounded. Sometimes they seem the most fundamental queries the human race can possibly put forth. How can we go on to any other matter when we cannot even say from whence we draw our living thoughts in this moment? Always something more.

Are we but dolls, manipulated and given words and actions by some inconceivable children playing on a late afternoon? Are we but the robots of chance collections of molecules, or amino acids and oxygen compounds? Are we but . . . ? It all comes back to the same question. What is the something more?

Religion and spiritual systems attempt to answer these questions. God, the Higher Self, Atman, the Cosmic Mind, the collective un-conscious—most of these are capitalized to demonstrate a certain humility toward that which is so evidently so much more than we. Is that the something more that is always there? Or are these just other ways of asking the same question?

What does it mean to be the author of something—this book, for example? I write the words down—for the first time, we assume. So where do I get the words? From the study of psychology and many other subjects, of course. From many years of conducting psycho-therapy, to be sure. From teaching and supervising such work. From writing other things. Yes, yes, of course, but . . . some place else, something more.

Others study those subjects, others practice and teach and super-vise and write. Others have written—at this very moment (whichever very moment that is, yours, mine, or theirs) are writing other words for other books on the same general subject. How can that be? Where do their words come from? Always something more.

Some years ago, vacationing for a month in Puerto de Pollensa, Majorca, an idyllic spot, I practiced a ritual: Each morning for at least an hour I sat at the typewriter (since I was able to be most spontaneous in that mode) and let my fingers write whatever they chose with as little intervention from my conscious intent as I could manage. A kind of automatic writing—to give it a name. What happened? I did not know from day to day what to expect, although gradually I was drawn into what came through and the extent to which I could be detached lessened markedly. Still, I held to my purpose as best I could.

"What came through" mostly were, to my surprise, episodes in a suspense novel. Episodes that jumped about in their time sequence. Some days a different content came through: short stories of a bizarre and slightly off-color turn. These were unrelated to the novel and related to each other only in their general tone. Where did these come from?

"What came through" is a way of characterizing the subjective experience of being a channel, not an author. I know the feeling of authorship—mysterious enough in its own right—of conceiving an idea, watching it develop and working out sequences and illustrations and all that goes into putting it into book or article form. On these mornings I had that feeling only fleetingly. Instead I felt as though I was receiving dictation. Sometimes, as my fingers found the assigned keys, I would laugh aloud or feel an emotional pang at what they wrote, but I didn't laugh or feel that pang with any sense that I had evoked it. I was simply the first person to read it.

Always something more. The familiar miracle. The invisible miracle. Invisible because so familiar.

As a psychologist I should know about such matters as this. Either I or the priest. Some priests think they know; I know I don't. And I don't find their answers satisfying.

In this book I tell about some of the ways in which we can move between the familiar world of the objective and point-at-able to another, less familiar world. The other world is one in which there is always something more.

The world of something more is the subjective world, a world about which we know so very little. We have many theories about it, of course, but it mocks our theories as it continually is revealed to extend far beyond them.

The amazing fact is that our homeland is that same mysterious world of something more. Ultimately we take all that happens in the outer world back to the caves of our innerness—there to taste it, chew on it, reject some parts, digest others, and try to make it all fit together.

From that inner world issue all our thoughts and inspirations, our creativity and destructiveness, our hopes and fears, our goals and apprehensions, our depths of relationship, faithfulness of commitment, choices and decisions, cruelty and benevolence, and all else that gives meaning, color, and value to our being. We need, as individuals and in our collectivity, to be more aware of that inner world, of its dimensions and powers, of how we can be more at peace within it, and of how we can draw more from it to renew our daily encounters in the outer world.

This book will have few answers to the questions which confronting the something more poses. Instead, it will point to tools one may use in seeking more understanding and in aiding others in their searches, while that always tantalizing something more draws them and us onward and onward.

Basic Conversational
Skills

CHAPTER 2

Communication

Level

Clients vary tremendously in how fully they bring their receptivity and willingness to be truly known to the consultation room. When they are in distress, they are likely to be fully engaged, but many other times they are distant, reporting on themselves rather than genuinely revealing their own being in the moment. This failure to be fully present is the most overt and pervasive way clients avoid bringing their subjectivity into the therapeutic work.

Unwary therapists can easily slide into preoccupation with content, symptoms, and clues to psychodynamics, thus missing the fact that the client is not present as a whole person. This oversight may make the most meaningful interpretation impotent, reduce the therapeutic alliance to a speculative debate, and yield a fund of knowledge about client without producing any real therapeutic gain.

This chapter deals with this crucially important matter of presence, defining five levels: formal relating, contact maintenance, standard conversations, critical occasions, and intimacy. Familiarity with these alerts the therapist to needed steps to aid the client to the deep immersion which is a necessity of truly life-changing psychotherapy.[1]

WE BEGIN BY LOOKING in on a therapy session which is a parody of the sin of non-presence:

Segment 2.1
Client: Betty Stevens; Therapist: Carlton Blaine
CL-1: (Breathlessly drops into the big chair and wheezes out an apology) Sorry to be late. Just couldn't get away from the office, you know.
TH-1: (Nodding reassuringly) Well, Betty, I'm sorry too, but I started without you.
(Barring some sort of extrasensory perception, this response is nonsense. How can a client's therapy begin when client is not here? That's a good question, and one that too few therapists ask themselves.)

23

CL-2: (Not noticing the absurdity) Well, that's good, Dr. Blaine. I wanted to tell you about what I've been thinking since I left here last time, . . . but I've been so busy, I'm not sure I can remember it now. Oh, yes, it was about something you said just before we ended. Let's see, what was it now? Do you remember what you said? Oh, well, never mind. I've been such a rattle-brain lately, I don't know what. . . . Well, anyway I want to tell you I'll probably have to skip our next session because my mother will probably be coming to visit me. Oh, and I forgot to say that. . . . "

    (Betty talks for five minutes in this way, obviously trying to make up for lost time. She barely looks at Dr. Blaine as she rattles off item after item from the list in her head. None is dwelt on or developed. So is Betty here now?)

My example is extreme, of course, but many an unwary therapist has let his client go on at length without noting that she is acting as a reporter on herself rather than as a concerned person seeking greater awareness into her own life. The mere transmission of detached information is not therapeutic; indeed, it is likely to be counterthera- peutic. This untoward result can occur when the client feels en- couraged to focus on content, on collecting data about herself, and — by implication — on "solving the problem" of her life.

THE EVOLUTION OF PRESENCE

To get a better appreciation of the importance of presence let's follow another client from her first interview until she is well settled into the therapeutic routine some months later. From this span we select five descriptions of herself that she offers the therapist. Thus we can see how her presence evolves.

Segment 2.2
Client: Donna Davis; Therapist: Bert Graham
    Client sits anxiously in the stiff waiting room chair, mentally rehears- ing what she will say to therapist. Her first self-description is to herself as she imagines talking to the therapist.)
CL-1: I have these times of feeling so frightened that I can't concentrate on my work, and I'm afraid that my boss will know something's wrong, and then I'll be in trouble . . . (pauses, glances around the empty room). Then I'll be in trouble . . . uh . . . just like I was always in trouble with my father. . . . Well, no, not always, but then . . . (again pauses). What will it be like to talk to a *psychotherapist*? I don't like that word; it scares me. Maybe I should be just seeing a *counselor*.

What's the difference? No, Dr. Graham was recommended by my own doctor, and he would know. But he is a man. I really ought to see a woman; a woman would understand better how . . .

TH-1: Mrs. Davis?

(The voice breaks in on her thoughts. When did he open the door? It unnerves her, as though she's been caught doing something wrong. She starts to her feet, dropping the unread magazine from her lap; as she stoops to pick it up her glasses almost fall from her head. She must look like a real psycho to the doctor. He is coming toward her. Clumsily she settles her glasses on her nose, drops the magazine on the coffee table, and turns toward him.

CL-2: Yes, that's me. I mean, I. (That sounded so childish. Damn it, I'm not usually such a klutz; why am I acting so much like one now?)

TH-2: Good. I'm Dr. Graham. (Smiles, indicates the door behind him) Why don't you come in so we can talk?

(With this beginning, let us imagine that three times during the ensuing conversation, Mrs. Davis tells Dr. Graham about what brings her to therapy. Here are segments of each of those self-descriptions.)

CL-3: (Second description, first few minutes) Well, you see, I haven't been able to work. . . . I mean, I can work all right most of the time, but. . . . It's just that sometimes I feel kind of . . . well, you know, not really able to do all that. . . . It's not a major problem, really, but. . . .

CL-4: (Third self-description, ten minutes into the conversation) I think that I let things bother me too much. I mean, I have a tendency to worry more than I should. I think it's probably something my mother did, and I probably copied her without quite knowing it. It is upsetting, you know, and I'd like to find out why I do it so I can stop it and. . . .

CL-5: (Fourth description, 35 minutes into the conversation) The panics come on me at the worst times. I've tried to think what might make them happen, but whatever it is just eludes me. I'm worried; I mean, I'm really worried. My boss—he's a lot like my father was—my boss is very critical, and he's sure to notice. . . . I'm afraid he'll think I can't handle the job, and then I don't know. . . .

(Now we skip ahead four months and look in on Donna's therapy in her 32nd interview—she comes twice a week. Here is the way she gives her fifth self-description.

CL-6: I'm feeling tense and anxious right now. I don't know why, but I do know it's happening here while I'm talking to you. I feel as though I want to run someplace and hide, like I'm going to get caught and hurt.

I never thought of it that way before: "Like I'm going to get hurt!" Hmmph! These feelings just block out what I was just talking with you about a minute ago. I hate them! I really hate them. I want to stop feeling them and to. . . .

Donna Davis is telling about her troubled inner life. In these five different self-descriptions, she demonstrates the difference between a shallow, distant report and immediate immersion in the experience which is distressing her. Notice also that her first account, the introspective one which was not spoken aloud, is in many ways more like the fourth or fifth telling than the way she described herself to therapist at first. The attempt to do therapy at the level of the second account is doomed to be shallow and without much lasting effect. On the other hand, the fourth and fifth accounts show Donna to be much more genuinely in the room, into the work, and caught up in the very emotions which trouble her. Thus, psychotherapeutic forces can be brought to bear directly on these disturbances as they occur. If the client is limited to detached reporting, therapy becomes an exercise in abstractions. Such therapy produces clients who know a lot about themselves but experience little lasting change in what they do or how they feel in their lives.

Developing a scale. Looking back over Donna's five self-descriptions we can observe several ways in which they are distributed along a scale. Here are some of the most evident dimensions of that range:

- From distant to immediate.
- From concern about how therapist will see her to focus on expressing what is going on within herself.
- From replays of familiar material to self-discovery for Donna herself.
- From detached reporting to emotional concern about her experiences.

A summarizing notion that includes all of these is the concept of *presence*.[2] It calls our attention to how genuinely and completely a person is in a situation rather than standing apart from it as observer, commentator, critic, or judge. Donna Davis is much more authentically in the work of therapy in the last description than in any of the prior four.

The effective psychotherapist is sensitized to note how genuinely his client is present, and he is prepared to devote significant efforts to aiding that client to increased involvement in the work. This focus on presence is a major cornerstone of the therapeutic art.

Presence is a name for the quality of being in a situation or relationship in which one intends at a deep level to participate as fully as she is able. Presence is expressed through mobilization of one's sensitivity—both inner (to the subjective) and outer (to the situation and the other person(s) in it)—and through bringing into action one's capacity for response.

We will recognize two facets of presence: accessibility and expressiveness. As we define them, it will be evident that they overlap; yet there is value in recognizing both. Oftentimes one or the other will be more manifest, and attention then needs to be directed to the less available part.

Accessibility designates the extent to which one intends that what happens in a situation will matter, will have an effect on her. This calls for a reduction of our usual defenses against being influenced by others; thus, it involves a measure of commitment. Opening oneself to another's influence is significantly investing in that relation.

Expressiveness has to do with the extent to which one intends to let oneself be truly known by the other(s) in a situation. This involves disclosing without disguise some of one's subjective experiencing, and it requires a willingness to put forth some effort.

Presence and its subsets, accessibility and expressiveness, are all ranges, not either/or processes. They vary continually in relation to the persons involved, the situation and its purpose, the material being discussed, and many other influences.

The degree to which the client is genuinely *in* the interview, ready to be affected and willing to make herself known is one of the most influential factors determining whether a genuinely therapeutic impact will result from the work.[3] For this reason we will examine different levels of presence as they occur in therapeutic conversations.

THE CHIEF CONVERSATIONAL LEVELS

Very likely Salome was not the first striptease artist, but she certainly is one of the best-known. Her *Dance of the Seven Veils* has lingered tantalizingly in our imaginations for millenia, perhaps in some part because we recognize in ourselves her layered veils of protection. Figure 2.1 illustrates how these cover us.

In Figure 2.1 the relative size of the bands roughly suggests the extent to which each of these levels of presence is evident in ordinary conversations. It is also important to recognize that the point in the center is very likely the source of all that is displayed. The idea of a

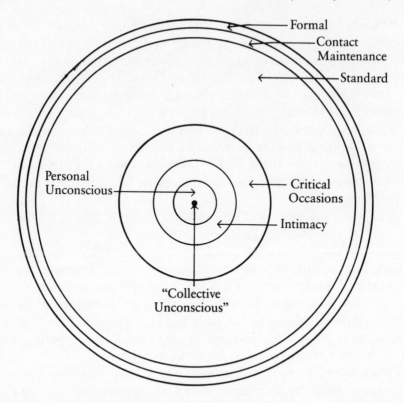

Figure 2.1.   The Seven "Veils" or Levels of Conversational Presence as They Occur
in Everyday Talking.

"collective unconscious," as proposed by Jung, suggests that underlying all of our experience is a species-wide bond of archaic but unconscious perceptual material. This is a useful conception, even though one need not accept all that is attributed to it. It is manifest that we share a common heritage in varying degrees and that this issues forth in the various phenomena of our conscious living. Graphically to represent it accurately is impossible; thus I have chosen to use the central point.

In the same way, it is impossible to do more than guess at the size of the personal unconscious, which I see as that subjective accumulation of preverbal, repressed, and suppressed perceptions which each of us brings to every moment of our lives and which is evidenced in the values, expectations, and apprehensions with which we meet each moment.

As I describe the five levels and show their significances in the work of depth psychotherapy, it will be useful to refer to Figure 2.2, which illustrates the relative importance of these levels in depth psychotherapy. Here, it will be apparent, there is much greater emphasis on immersion in the work than is true for conversations in general. The differences between Figures 2.1 and 2.2 show why therapists need to develop refined communications artistry far beyond the ordinary.

Level One: Formal Occasions[4]

When a client comes for the first interview, when all is newness and, often, seeming threat, when there is no backlog of experience with the therapist, the client will use our culture's folkways for dealing with such times. These are patterns which we use with those in authority, with those who look only at our outer surfaces, with those whom we seek to impress or whose favor we seek.

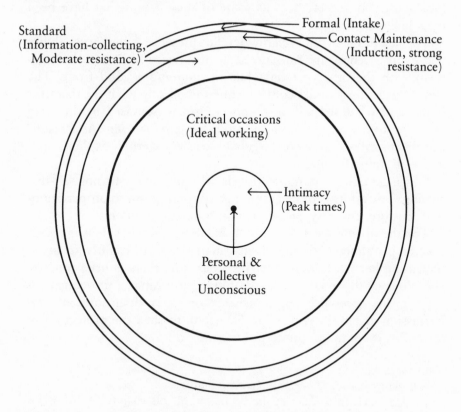

Figure 2.2.   The Seven "Veils" or Levels of Conversational Presence as They Occur in Effective Psychotherapeutic Conversations.

Formal communication is relating between the objective aspects of persons: "Carlton Blaine, Doctor of Philosophy in Psychology, Graduate of the Leland Stanford Junior University, Diplomate in Clinical Psychology of the American Board of Professional Psychology. . . . " All of the panoply of position is, at least implicitly, confronting client. Small wonder that many clients find themselves shoving aside their concerns to try to match what they are encountering: "I am Elizabeth Franklin Stevens. My father was Doctor Edward Franklin, no doubt you've heard of him, and I am the wife of Mr. Kenneth Stevens, and. . . . " Others may announce, "I own my own business, and, if I do say it myself, it has been unusually successful in its field. . . . "

Sometimes the matching is disguised: "I never believed much in this psycho stuff, but the wife insisted and so. . . . " "I'm not sure I really need to be here, you know; it's just that I thought I ought to take a look with your expert help at some of these issues that have been troubling me."

The key to the formal relating level of presence is that accessibility and expressiveness are constricted in the service of limiting engagement with the other person while maintaining a good front. The client keeps things under control while she sizes up what the therapist is like and what she will do. This control is exercised by directing attention to her *image* and away from her *experiencing*. As a result, the client's talk is apt to be largely objective, external, explicit, and, above all, impersonal.

Image-centered communication is self-conscious but not self-disclosing. The effort is to be correct; attention is given to proper grammar, posture, courtesy. Spontaneity is minimal or absent.

The therapist must seek a useful balance: On one side it is necessary to go along with the client's maneuvers sufficiently to avoid increasing her fearfulness. On the other side, there is need to draw client out of this relatively sterile mode. Too rapid a movement toward greater presence (e.g., insisting on early disclosures of embarrassing material), with its implicit pull to shed the protection of formality, is apt to be counterproductive.

Segment 2.3A
Client: Betty Stevens; Therapist: Carlton Blaine
   (Betty, whom we met at the beginning of this chapter, is not a new client being seen on intake. It was her self-consciousness about being late that moved her to fall back into the formal level. After several

minutes of Betty's trying to say everything at once, Dr. Blaine interrupts.)

TH-11: I hear you trying to make up for lost time by pushing yourself to say
quickly as much as possible.

CL-11: Yes, I know. That's silly, isn't it? But I just thought if you knew what
I'd been thinking before I came here today, and. . . . Well, not just that
but how it's been at home. You see, Ken and I . . .

TH-12A: Why don't you pause just a minute now, and take a deep breath or
two, and check inside to find out how you really want to use your time
here today?

CL-12A: Yes, I'll do that, but first I must tell you about . . .

TH-13A: (Interrupting) First, the breathing, Betty (firmly).

CL-13A: Oh . . . (catching herself, quieting, breathing a bit more deeply).
Yes, you're right. I do get so caught up. (Sighs) I guess I just felt like a
bad child coming in late, and . . .

Of course, with a new client this approach would probably be too
strong. In such a situation, the therapist might test the client's readiness as was done here (TH-11), but if the client showed no readiness
to use this help (CL-11), he would not go on so quickly to the breath
suggestions (TH-12A), and he would be even less likely to insist as
Dr. Blaine does (TH-13A).

For the less prepared client a different pattern can be illustrated.
The purpose here is to help the client focus attention and reduce the
pressure to perform. This is illustrated by revising the interaction:
The first two therapist responses and the first client response above
are the same, but then we'll imagine that a different direction is taken,
due to client's different response at CL-12B.

Segment 2.3B

TH-11: I hear you trying to make up for lost time by pushing yourself to say
quickly as much as possible.

CL-11: Yes, I know. That's silly, isn't it? But I just thought if you knew what
I'd been thinking before I came here today, and. . . . Well, not just that
but how it's been at home. You see, Ken and I . . .

TH-12: Why don't you pause just a minute now, and take a deep breath or
two, and check inside to find out how you really want to use your time
here today?

CL-12B: I really don't think that will do any good. I'm all right now, and
besides I need to tell you some things that I've been thinking.

TH-13B: What sorts of things?

CL-13B: Oh, just that maybe I shouldn't see a local therapist since my
husband is so prominent in the community. I mean, he has to think

about the way people will see him. And then . . . but I suppose I shouldn't really worry about that, should I? It's like when we were living in Palo Alto. Do you know that area, Doctor? I liked it, and yet there was something . . .

TH-14B: (Interrupting quietly) What other thoughts did you have about whether to come to see a therapist?

CL-14B: Well, I guess I was kind of wondering whether I make too much of little things, you know. I mean, I have had these times lately of crying without any reason. I know it's silly of me, but . . .

(In this way, client is helped to move to a deeper level.)

Level Two: Contact Maintenance

When the first newness of the situation passes, some clients can readily move into the third level, "standard" relating. Others, however, need an intermediate step. These latter clients may appear relaxed and ready to talk about their concerns; yet it soon becomes evident that they are exercising a great deal of restraint. This holding back may take the form of shallowness in their participation, of their responding only with factual content, or it may simply be a manifest lack of real subjectivity. For such clients a transition step is indicated. This is the place for the contact maintenance level.

In this mode, needed factual information can be collected (age, address, telephone numbers, availability of insurance coverage),[5] while therapist watches for signs of emotional reactions signaling readiness to move to a deeper level. When those are not forthcoming, therapist impatience should not result in pushing insensitively for deeper involvement. Instead, alertness to client presence will often indicate where it may be helpful to invite the client to give some familiar information (e.g., a typical day, how she came to her work, educational history). With such matters the client may begin at a superficial level but is likely soon to display some greater involvement. The tuned-in therapist will sense when this movement is occurring and how it can be reinforced.

This alertness is even more important when collecting data about topics likely to be therapeutically significant (e.g., family status and members, employment issues, persons significant in the client's life); thus, this step often is best postponed until the client is ready for greater openness. Otherwise important opportunities may be lost.

Outside the therapeutic office, contact maintenance conversations typically are those we have with people we see regularly but for very limited purposes—the man who sometimes cleans the windshield at the service station, the supermarket checker, the mail carrier, or the starter at the golf course. Such talk tends to be brief, offhand, and focused on the matter at hand or on simple greetings. While the formal level's concern with image is much less present, there is little self-disclosure. Some ritualistic jocularity may occur, but it is all impersonal.

Ms. A: Hi, Bob, fill it up please.
Mr. Z: Okay, sure, Helen. How's the family?
Ms. A: Great. How is it with you?
Mr. Z: Can't complain.

Indeed, for the most part they could be talking gobbledegook:

Ms. B: Caf tee dob gril?
Mr. Y: Yug, dobby gif lumper.

Of course, sometimes a bit of information is exchanged:

Mr. Z: Oil okay?
Ms. A: Yes, think so. You checked it last week.

But except for a narrow band of concerns, the answers would very likely be the same even if Bob's wife were ill or Helen's son in trouble.

In the therapist's office, as already indicated, second level talk is largely transitional—between formal and more standard communication.

Sometimes, when highly emotional work has been going on and the client needs to decompress before leaving, the transition may be in the opposite direction. In this latter instance, the therapist moves to this level as a way of aiding the client's preparing to face the outer world again. Here is an example of how this might be done:

Segment 2.4
Client: Jessica Thomas; Therapist: Lester Brown
CL-1: . . . I'm just reeling with the realization of what all that I've just been uncovering has meant to me. It seems unbelievable how long I've been seeing things in such a confused way and even more unbelievable how much it's hampered me. (Pause) Oh, damn it, I've got to get out of here in a few minutes, and I feel so shaky I'm not sure I can even stand up. (Client is clearly at the critical occasions or fourth level.)

TH-1: Take it slow, Jess. You've done a lot of important work today, and you need to make your transition gradually. Where do you go from here today?

CL-2: How do you mean? Where do I go on the things I've been working on? (Confusion due to therapist's changing levels)

TH-2: No, I was thinking more literally: Where do you go after you leave here now?

CL-3: (Obviously collecting herself) Well, I have to go into my office for a few minutes to pick up messages. (Third level, standard communications.)

TH-3: How's your work going these days? .

CL-4: Okay, I guess. Usual headaches, but nothing big. (Second level, contact maintenance.)

TH-4: You're pretty much on top of it, eh?

CL-5: Yeah, I think so. Well, I guess I better hit the road now.

Contact maintenance can, of course, represent a form of client resistance to taking responsibility for self-exploration: "Hell, Doc, I don't know what's bugging me so much lately, but you just ask the questions, and I'll give you the answers. You and I can lick the damn thing, I know." This apparently cooperative invitation, if delivered in an offhand, uninvolved manner, would clearly indicate the same avoidance of true engagement.

This second level of presence is a narrow band, and if a conversational partner breaks the ritual, they change levels:

Mr. Z (the gas station attendant): How about you and your husband coming to dinner Saturday?

Or:

Ms. A (the gas customer): Bob, can you loan me $10 till Friday?

Definitely not second level!

Notice that a response to this latter request might occur at any of the first three levels:

Mr. Z: I'm sorry, Ms. A, but our policy here is not to engage in any personal financial relations with our clients. (Formal relating)

Or:

Mr. Z: Sure(laughing), and how's about making it a million; I haven't any small change. (Contact maintenance through treating the request as a joke)

Or:

Mr. Z: I'd be glad to, Helen. Here you go (handing her a ten dollar bill). (Standard conversation)

Level Three: Standard Conversations

"Standard" is a word that suggests the usual or expected, and that is my intent in employing it here. As Figure 2.1 indicates, this level of communication is by far the most widely employed in everyday talking. When it is having its greatest impact therapeutic communication depends significantly less on standard engagement, but it is still important in the consultation room. (Note its size in Figure 2.2)

Standard conversations provide the balance point between concern for one's image and involvement in expressing one's inner experiencing. Figure 2.3 illustrates how these conversations usually are most taken up with the content being exchanged, the *what* of the conversations. Thus they typically include genuine but limited personal involvement, may be repetitious but are not ritualistic, and generally contain little conflict.

If one, as an outsider, visits an office or shop in which people work together regularly and there is an easy flow of talk, it soon is evident how different these exchanges are from the stiffness of the first level or from the deeper, more emotional tone of the fourth and fifth levels. Standard conversations characteristically use lots of slang and in-talk, which is directed toward current activities and issues. People can and do both talk and listen at the same time without apparent difficulty, and they readily mix personal and work talk as their needs dictate.

Mr. B: Hey C, give me three four-twenties, will ya?
Mr. D: B never gets a full hand, does he?
Ms. C: (to B) Yeh, sure. (to D) Aw, don't give him a hard time; he's probably hung over.
Mr. B: (simultaneously with D) Look who's talking! Why last week he couldn't even find his docket key (laughs).
Mr. D: Don't I just wish I'd had that kind of weekend. Let me tell you it was the pits. Where's the 502 file? We went to the beach with the kids. Wow! What a zoo! Oh, thanks (to B, who has handed him the file).

Therapists use this level to collect factual and semi-factual information (e.g., identities and characteristics of family members, client's

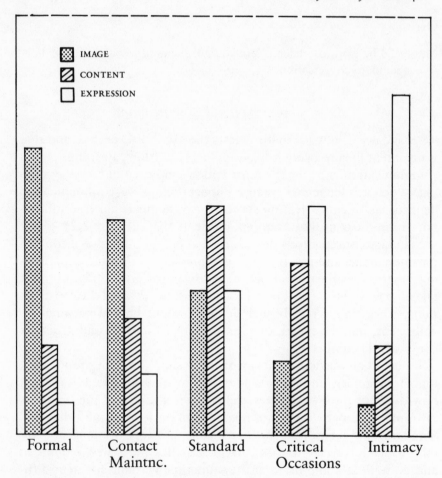

Figure 2.3.   Contrasts in Attention to One's Image, Concern with Content, and
              Urgency to Express Inner Experience in Relation to Degree of Presence
              or Immersion in the Therapeutic Conversation.

educational and vocational history, previous therapeutic experiences). While gathering these data, the therapist is alert to clues to
deeper feelings and conflict, although attention may or may not be
directed to such indications at this time. When such leads are followed up, there is the likelihood that work will move to the fourth
level.

Segment 2.5
Client: Donna Davis; Therapist: Bert Graham
TH-11: What does your husband do?
CL-11: He's manager of the Stevens Street Market.

TH-12: How does he like that work?

CL-12: Oh, okay, I guess. I wouldn't like it, but he seems to get on okay.

TH-13: You wouldn't like that kind of work, eh?

CL-13: No, I sure wouldn't. Having to please so many different kinds of people and riding herd on the incompetent clerks is for the birds.

TH-14: "Different kinds of people"?

CL-14: Oh, you know what I mean. People who you have to watch all the time or they'll rip you off. You know, people who don't want to go out and work but just live off food stamps.

At this point, therapist has the choice of following up on an apparent area of prejudice with its hint of personal implications for the client or of continuing to collect information.

For another example we return to the tardy client whom we met at the start of this chapter and again in Segment 2.3.

Segment 2.6
Client: Betty Stevens; Therapist: Carlton Blaine

TH-21: What was your family like when you were young?

CL-21: The usual. Father, mother, sister. No brothers. Always wished I had had an older brother. My sister was two years older than me, and that was nice.

TH-22: How did you get along with them?

CL-22: Oh, all right, I guess. You know how families are. We had our ups and downs.

TH-23: Would you say there were more "ups" or more "downs"?

CL-23: That's hard to say. About like usual, I guess.

TH-24: You don't sound very sure.

CL-24: Yes, well, I guess I'm not real happy about my family. I wasn't very close to them.

TH-25: To any of them?

CL-25: Well, to my sister (uneasy shifting of posture), but not to my Dad.

TH-26: Want to talk more about how it was with your Dad?

Here therapy has been proceeding at a standard level (shown in highly abridged fashion in responses 21 through 26), but as the sensitive area of the client's family relations is entered, clues to deeper feelings are disclosed (the qualifiers "I guess" in CL-22 and CL-23). Clearly the client is hesitating about getting into loaded material. The therapist reflects this back (TH-24), and the client becomes more open (CL-24), which makes possible an invitation to change level (TH-26). Since this is still fairly early in the work with this client, the therapist offers the option of pursuing the subject rather than pressing more strongly.

Level Four: Critical Occasions

If therapy is to result in significant life changes, much work needs to be done at the critical occasions level. Only when the client makes herself truly accessible to the impact of these conversations, only when the client seeks truly to express to the therapist her inner experiencing, and only when the therapist genuinely meets the client in this depth — only when these essential conditions are met can one reasonably expect lasting changes and growth to occur.

This flat assertion rests not only on long clinical experience but also on the manifest logic that clients who cannot make a major investment in the therapeutic enterprise are in fact withholding the very stuff of the way their lives are being conducted. To illustrate this, we can imagine that the conversation we've just been following continues in this way:

Segment 2.7A
Client: Betty Stevens; Therapist: Carlton Blaine
TH-26: Want to talk more about how it was with your Dad?
CL-26A: Not really. It's all over now anyway.
TH-27A: You don't sound as though it's all over.
CL-27A: Well, what's happened has happened, and it doesn't do any good to dwell on it.
TH-28A: Do you really want to push it all away from you?
CL-28A: Yes, I do. I'd like to talk with you more about what I'm going to do about my son. He's been acting very strangely lately, and I . . .

Here the client is determined to avoid the emotions and their associated memories and other feelings; yet ironically, what she is in effect doing is insuring that their disturbing influences on her life are going to continue. Her avoidance of the deeper engagement of the critical occasions level is not, of course, beyond therapeutic recourse, and we will discuss the handling of this resistance further in this and other chapters.

"Critical" means making a difference. When I speak of "critical" occasions, I am directing attention to the times and the conversations that *can make a difference.* The word *crisis* denotes a turning point, a stage in a sequence of events at which future outcomes will be influenced for good or ill or in some other significant way. Conversations which go on for some time at the critical occasions level will result in genuine changes in the thoughts, feelings, words, or acts of one or both of the participants.

After a conversation at this level, client will be different than she would have been had that talk not occurred. If therapist is also at this level—a highly desirable state—he too will experience some impact, and the effects on the client will be even greater. (The next chapter addresses the relation of therapist level to client level.)

Let us see how this level of emotional investment may bring the client toward such changes. We will use the same situation as in our last example, but now we will imagine that the client is ready to respond positively to the therapist's invitation.

Segment 2.7B
Client: Betty Stevens; Therapist: Carlton Blaine
TH-26: Want to talk more about how it was with your Dad?
CL-26B: Yes, I guess so (pause). Well, there's not a lot to tell. We just never agreed about much after I got to be a teenager. It seemed like he was always so tired and so angry. He . . . (face changes, saddens) . . . used to be so different when I was younger.
TH-27B: It was different then.
CL-27B: Oh, yes. When I was seven, Mom and Dad gave me a big birthday party, and he was so nice. You know, he played a clown for the party, and he . . . he . . . gave me a pendant that I still have (tears start).
TH-28B: It makes you sad right now remembering the difference between those days and the way it's been more recently.
CL-28B: (weeping) Yes, it does. Why did he change? What did I do? I can't seem to do anything right for him anymore.

Typical of the fourth level is emotionality in the moment rather than only recalled (contrast CL-22 and CL-23 or CL-27A and CL-28A with CL-27B and CL-28B). Similarly the candid description of past (CL-26B) and present (CL-27B) inner experience, and the self-questioning (CL-28B) are familiar evidences of deepened involvement.

Other characteristics of the level. As Figure 2.3 shows, clients engaged in critical occasion conversations are more concerned with expressing their inner experience than with creating or preserving an image to impress the therapist. Their talk is more varied in form, tempo, and emotional toning. For example, a typical pacing would be prompt and fluid as a cluster of percepts is brought out and then slightly hesitant as new material comes into consciousness. Typical also are manner and intonation that betoken an inward focusing of awareness in which the therapist is not forgotten but is only part of the background for what is being said.

As inner experiencing becomes more available and more immediately alive, the client often uses more adjectives and adverbs in an effort to convey the texture and colors of that experience. Slang, exclamations, profanity, and obscenity are frequent. Bodily posture may become more relaxed and open, although body language will change in keeping with emerging feelings.

A word of caution: These generalizations about overt behaviors typical of greater client involvement must not be taken as invariable. People vary widely in how they manifest intense immersion. For example, some become physically rigid, some show utter limpness, and a few go into physical contractions which cause them to contort their faces and bodies. Only the therapist's intuition can sort out the genuinely immersed from those who are trying to appear so or to force themselves to a level they are not yet ready to attain.[6]

In general, the person working at fourth level is caught up in the expressive side of the presence coin. Accessibility may be somewhat reduced, as attention is strongly focused on the inner flow. There are, of course, important occasions when the client is quite accepting and receptive in the fourth level, receiving therapist instruction, questions, or response without usual screening.

The change potential of this level. These conversations are crossroads talks from which one or both participants are likely to emerge with some difference in perspective, attitude, or emotion. The client we have just been following is coming to an implicit but unconscious choice point: If she continues to explore the sad (and resentful) feelings about the change in her father's feelings, she will very likely emerge with a different sense of her relation with him. It may be improved, or it may be worsened, but it will be affected. If she chooses to pull back from this level of involvement or from further exploration of this topic, she may avoid such a change. In general, psychotherapy assumes that greater awareness results from such explorations and that greater awareness, in turn, yields increased understanding and choicefulness.

Getting to the critical occasions level. In the next chapter suggestions will be given for ways of aiding clients to deepen the level of their therapeutic work; however, it will be useful here to cite clues to client readiness to move from standard communications to this more powerful plane. Here are some of the most frequent and obvious:

Client . . .

- repeatedly returns to one topic or feeling despite apparent efforts to move away from it.
- frequently repeats a word or phrase, often without apparent awareness.
- seems unable to recall something one would expect to be well known to her.
- abruptly switches away from a topic or feeling in which she has been involved.
- inexplicably loses the train of thought.
- becomes physically restless or unusually immobile.

We can see some of these operating as we return to the client who was describing her husband's work (Segment 2.5, page 36):

Segment 2.8
Client: Donna Davis; Therapist: Bert Graham

CL-21: Like I say, I wouldn't like his job and the creeps—uh, the people he has to deal with. I'm more the introspective type, I guess. I mean, I like people and all, but . . .

TH-21: But?

CL-22: But if there are too many people around, I can't really concentrate. In my work, I've got to be able to concentrate. If I get distracted, my ideas just go up in smoke. (Pause) I don't know how he puts up with some of those creeps that come into the market. Well, that's his headache. I'm sure glad it's not mine.

TH-22: You find yourself coming back again and again to the fact that you wouldn't like that kind of work.

CL-23: Yes, I do (pauses, considers). Well, I don't know, but I do know I sure wouldn't (pauses, seems distracted). How'd we get on this? I can't remember why I'm talking about . . . (short, humorless laugh). What were we talking about?

TH-23: You were talking about your husband's job and how you wouldn't like to have to deal with the kinds of people he has to put up with.

CL-24: That's for sure. In my field, we have to do a lot of intense thinking before we get what we're looking for. If some old creep comes around, pretty soon blooey; nothing gets done.

TH-24: The "creeps," as you call them, that he deals with would really mess up your concentration.

CL-25: You'd better believe it! I suppose I shouldn't call them "creeps," but really. . . . Why just last week he had this crazy old dame come in and demand that he take a bunch of out-dated food coupons. Said she'd call the cops or write to the President about him if Bob didn't. You know, he was so good-natured about it. I sure wouldn't have been. I'd have told that impossible woman and her stamps off quick enough, believe me.

TH-25: Donna, these people that your husband has to deal with are in your thoughts a lot, aren't they?

CL-26: No, I . . . well, sort of. Anyway, what I really want to talk about is this thing that's happened at work.

TH-26: You want to drop the topic of Bob's job, huh?

CL-27: Sure. He can handle them all right; so why don't I just skip it and get back to what I'm here for?

TH-27: Evidently because they're in some way related to what you're here for, I imagine. Give yourself a minute just to reflect on that and see what comes to mind.

CL-28: Well, I don't see any connections to the problems I need to talk to you about. I think I . . .

TH-28: Wait, Donna, you're just answering off the top of your head. Give yourself a better chance than that. For some reason the oddballs Bob has to deal with keep coming into your thoughts today. At some level there's a good reason for that. Just let yourself be open to see whatever comes up; don't try to figure it out.

CL-29: (Silent for 30–40 seconds; body tensed up) Yeah, uh . . . well, I . . . I don't know. I don't get any new ideas, but I do feel kind of uneasy, like I'd rather not talk about this anymore. Maybe . . .

TH-29: No, don't "maybe." Just stay with the uneasy feeling.

CL-30: Uh-huh. (Silence; arms crossed, hands squeezing arms tightly) I really don't like this feeling (silence). I think of that old woman with her damned food stamps. . . . Oh, I don't know (impatiently). I won-der . . . I wonder what she felt like when Bob turned her down. Oh, damn, I don't see any good in getting into all that stuff.

TH-30: You want to break out of what you're getting into, but it's clear there's some really uncomfortable feelings in there. Can you hang in with yourself, and see where they take you?

CL-31: Yes, I think so. (Pause) So . . . I think of my mother, you know. (Face rigid) Don't want to think about her . . . about where she might be or what she might be doing . . . or whether she . . . whether she needs anything . . . (face contorted, anger or pain).

Level Five: Intimacy

For most of us the word *intimacy* has meanings beyond the diction-ary's view. It suggests intensity and emotionality, the sensual and sexual, nudity and intercoursing. It suggests the private, even the secret. These implications accurately express the quality of this level of human interaction. For this reason, some therapists avoid it. Breuer, Freud's early associate, withdrew from further work in devel-oping psychoanalysis because of his Victorian distaste (fear?) of the intimacy involved.[7] Today, Breuer's successors similarly regard inti-mate relating as inappropriate or even unprofessional.

Saying it bluntly, I believe that psychotherapy which does not involve intervals of genuine intimacy may be helpful but will never lead to the depth of confrontation necessary for major life change.

Characteristics of the level. When two people relate at the intimacy level, there is maximum accessibility and/or expressiveness between them. In the therapeutic setting this means that the client is so caught up in the expression of inner experiencing that she has little or no concern about maintaining an image (see Figure 2.3) and is readily receptive to what the therapist may say or do. The therapist, in parallel, is receiving in a total fashion what the client expresses. His sensing is maximal, and his intuition is fully engaged. Instances of what may be considered extrasensory perception or telepathy may occur.

The mutuality of intimacy is one of its most distinguishing features, but this mutuality does not take the same form in both partners. While the client is open and expressive of feelings, thoughts, and inner processes, the therapist is apt to be less verbally open. Instead, the therapist, in addition to being maximally receptive, is allowing his human responsiveness to be played upon by the client's experiencing—and often is allowing that impact to be evident to client.

In such engagements, I have wept, laughed, felt deep dread, experienced exaltation, ached with knowledge of loneliness and despair, grown tense with anger or sexual excitement, and fallen silent in appreciation of my client's courage and latent wisdom.

Out of times of intimacy comes the potential for confrontation of lifelong patterns, comes the hope for reorganization of one's way of being alive, comes the vision of more authentic being. These are far more than simple verbal formulations. In moments of true intimacy, the subjective being of the client is vitally involved in inner recognitions which lead to lasting consequences.

It should be noted that I am not saying the time of intimacy in itself is the change agent. That is not the case. Rather, only if the client persists in her efforts when the magical moment has passed will those moments of intimacy provide the increased vision which is the true change agency.

An instance of intimacy in therapy. Betty, who mourned the change in her father, continued to work on the pain that change has caused her. Now, some time since the last interview (Segment 2.7B, page 39), she is returning to this topic. As the excerpt begins, she is moving from the third (standard) level to the fourth:

Segment 2.9

Client: Betty Stevens; Therapist: Carlton Blaine

CL-41: I know I keep coming back to that pendant my father gave me when I had my seventh birthday party, and I don't know just what it means to me, but it's been in my thoughts again today.

TH-41: Uh-huh.

CL-42: I wore the pendant today. See? (It is hung about her neck and she pulls it forward toward therapist.)

TH-42: Yes. It's very nice.

CL-43: It's just a child's present, I know, but . . . (weeps).

TH-43: But?

CL-44: But it means so much to me. (Still weeping) It . . . it . . . it's as though . . .

TH-44: Mmmmm.

CL-45: . . . as though he . . . (sobs)he loved me then. He loved me then; I know he did (crying strongly).

TH-45: He loved you *then*.

CL-46: Yes, he loved me then (crying eases; voice drops, becomes more reflective). But then I . . . but then I . . . what did I do? I did something so that he stopped loving me and was angry all the time. What did I do? (Crying again, a protesting tone)

TH-46: (Tone low, intent) What you did made him stop loving you?

CL-47: (Crying stopping, eyes unfocused, searching inwardly) Yes . . . (deeply seeking). Yes, what was it? What did I do? Oh!

TH-47: (Silent, waiting)

CL-48: I think I know (fresh sobs, face miserable). (Pause, hardly aware of anything but inner thoughts and feelings).

TH-48: (Silent, breathing slowed)

CL-49: I know (quietly, firmly, resignedly). I know: I became a woman!

In that moment a door opened inside of Betty, and she became aware of so much that she *had known but not let herself know* for so very long. That awareness within her was so much larger than she could ever reduce to words. In that enlarged inner vision is the healing/growth dynamic. In that recognition there was no need for words for several moments. Therapist and client were very close emotionally; their heads and bodies bent toward each other; they did not touch though they might well have. A time of true intimacy.

Other occasions of intimacy

Eric,[8] having been repeatedly confronted with the superficiality of his participation, angrily announces he will not be badgered in that way; it is too reminiscent of his father's hectoring. The therapist once

again points out his need to avoid, and that increases Eric's aggrava-
tion. In rapid fire they exchange charges and confrontations. Both are
intense; the atmosphere is explosive. But no untherapeutic explosion
occurs; instead, the client comes to a new awareness about his inner
processes and emotions.

Another client, Laura, an attractive woman, comes in a skimpy
shorts and halter costume. She wants her male therapist to admire her
beauty, comment on her sexual desirability. She hints of wanting actual
sexual contact with him. The therapist acknowledges her attractive-
ness, makes explicit her implicit messages, and insists that she is using
these to prevent further work on her need to please and to keep subtle
control of the situation. She grows more provocative, suggests she may
remove the halter. The therapist grants that this is exciting and challenges Laura to use the same courage in dealing with her life issues. She
breaks into tears and wants to be held. The therapist holds her hand
but says he won't embrace her in her near nudity because he wants to
maintain perspective. This is at once a tribute and a restriction. The
client is visibly relieved. Her crying quiets, and she gradually lets
herself recognize that the only part of herself that she believes could be
really valued by desirable men is her sexuality.

Jerry, a newly widowed older man, has been busily making contacts
and attempting to be sexual with several different women, with some
but not complete success. The therapist points out how casually the
client describes his adventures and how much he dodges dealing with
his new aloneness. After several sessions on this pattern, Jerry admits
his panic at being alone and becomes locked in a kind of agony of pain
and fear. The therapist expresses some of his parallel feelings and the
two sit for some time in silent unity. At the end of the hour, the client
quietly embraces the therapist, saying, "I was too tired to run after all
those chicks anyhow. It'll be a relief to quit it."

Intimacy is a sharing of deep and immediate experiencing. It is not
expressed in the content of what is said but in the depth of the client's
inner awareness and the readiness to make that awareness open to the
therapist and in the therapist's deep openness and resonance to the
client's immediate inner living as it is expressed in any way.

Intimacy is not a lasting condition of relating. Moments of intimacy come; sometimes they last most of a therapeutic hour, but inevitably they end. If the work goes well, others will follow until the time
when the client takes this newly acquired inner knowing out of the
consultation room into his life at large.

A PSYCHOTHERAPIST'S JOURNEY

Looking back now, it is surprising to me how long I overlooked the fundamental importance of presence to therapeutic work. It is even more surprising to me how many therapists and therapeutic systems also overlook it. All too often, therapists seem to be so attentive to the content of what is being said and to their prior conceptions about client dynamics and needs that they don't notice the distance that exists between themselves and their partners.

That oversight has at least two likely roots: It is part of the legacy from nineteenth century scientism which Freud and many others passed along. The notion of the impersonal, objective, and scientific doctor treating his "patient" who needed do nothing but *be* patient and provide needed information was the ideal of that time, and incredibly it still exists in many quarters.

The other source also resides in the endemic objectification of ourselves and our clients. One of its most virulent forms is what I think of as the "who-dun-it" school of psychotherapy. In this view the conditions (neurosis, problems, symptoms) that bring our clients to us are seen as some kind of lack of information which it is our job to correct by doing a skilled job of detection. We must find the historic roots of these issues, must trace how they are bringing about the present misery, and then disclose all this to our clients, who should then be cured.

Of course it doesn't work that way, but still many therapists concentrate on the content, the history, the information from and about the client. They bring their theories to the consultation room and seek to find where each client fits into the niches of their system. When they have that information, they start teaching it to the client, and they treat any client objection as "resistance" which must be overcome—as though the client were a bad pupil who must be disciplined into learning her lesson. In all this, there is no place for attention to how fully caught up in the work the client may be. That scarcely matters.

Well, I've parodied some therapists, I'm sure. Many would by no means fit that extreme description. It is certain that sensitive therapists have always noted and worked with presence or its lack. Still it is surprising how little attention the concept has received in the literature of our field.

Of course, all along therapists have assumed that "rapport with the patient" is the same as presence. It is not; rapport is quite a different matter, having to do with the relation between therapist and client but not directing attention to the client's own immersion within her own subjectivity. Similarly, "client motivation" has been addressed by many writers and teachers; yet a motivated client is not necessarily a truly present client.

Even more dismaying is the frequent lack of attention to therapist presence and the encouragement of "objectivity" and "therapeutic detachment." Indeed, there are those who take the attitude that the full presence of therapist is a form of countertransference! "Therapeutic detachment," standing at an aseptic distance from the client has been—and for some still is—an ideal, countertherapeutic as it is. The fear of involvement that such doctrines convey makes one wonder what motivated their exponents to undertake careers in a field whose core is relationship.

Objectivity was the unquestioned paradigm for all disciplines who aspired to be recognized as sciences. Well, they gave it a try for nearly a century; now it is time for a new paradigm.

I believe that the new paradigm—for psychotherapy, for psychology, for science, for society, for our times—is (and must be) recognizing the centrality of subjectivity. Subjectivity means all that goes on individually, privately, and only partially consciously within each of us.

So conceived this paradigm puts at the center of our concern in all of our various perspectives—personal, communal, social, scientific—such matters as intention, courage and dread, how we confront contingency and death and spirit.

What else can we say about this new paradigm? It maintains:

- Human beings are the locus of any knowledge.
- Knowledge is not an "out-there" *thing*, but an "in-here" experience.
- Out-there is always an inference, a selection from the much more that is potential, and thus what we say of the out-there is always a partial statement.
- Therefore, to learn about the out-there, we must learn about the in-here.
- And whatever we learn about the out-there must be qualified by the in-here instrumentality of its discovery.

It is possible to propose some corollaries of these assertions:

- The primary reality is in-here reality.
- We cannot study the in-here with out-there methods. (That's been the futile effort of the last 100 years.)

- In-here knowledge is fragmented, conflicting, and ultimately incomplete.
- It is important not to apply out-there standards to the in-here realm. Certainty, completeness, freedom from ambiguity or conflict are out-there criteria which may or may not be appropriate to the in-here.

This paradigm in no way invalidates out-there science or knowledge; it simply recognizes how very incomplete that knowledge is and must always be. It is likely that if we develop better in-here knowledge, we can then discover how that fits with the out-there.

CHAPTER 3

Therapist Presence
and the Alliance

The therapist must bring her own subjectivity into the work if she is to be sufficiently sensitive to the client's efforts to reach the critical occasions level of presence. Thus, the therapist's own presence is needed continually to develop an effective therapeutic alliance.[1]

In this chapter the ways in which the client can be helped to attain greater subjective depth are reviewed, and the nature of the therapeutic alliance is illustrated by examining how the therapeutic partners need to become open to immersion in their common enterprise.

The therapeutic alliance is the powerful joining of forces which energizes and supports the long, difficult, and frequently painful work of life-changing psychotherapy. The conception of the therapist here is not of a disinterested observer-technician but of a fully alive human companion for the client. In this regard my view is in marked contrast to the traditional notion of the therapist as a skilled but objective director of therapeutic processes.

LOOKING AT Figure 2.2 (p. 29), we see how much of the work of psychotherapy needs to be done at the "critical occasions" level. Therapists need to bear in mind that this immersion is often not easily attained or maintained. Patience with oneself and one's clients is necessary. Some of the highest forms of the therapeutic art are called for in this task.

GETTING GREATER DEPTH OF
THERAPEUTIC ENGAGEMENT

While much of the best therapeutic work occurs at the critical occasions (fourth) level, one cannot expect to go directly to that mode; instead, important preparatory talk often is required at the standard (third) level. Of course, there is little value in lingering at the formal (first) and contact maintenance (second) levels, unless clients are so anxious that any deepening of the engagement is likely to be disruptive of their life management. (In such instances, one may question whether life-change therapy is an appropriate venture.) At the other extreme, there are times when a client and a therapist who are working well together at the critical level will dip into intimacy (fifth level).

Some of the therapeutic steps which may aid in this work are the following:

- transferring responsibility for interview movement,
- making explicit the manifest-but-implicit,
- penetrating to the subjective,
- maintaining needed continuity.

In addition, a number of other dimensions of therapeutic artistry contribute to getting and maintaining depth. Among the most important of these are:

- attending to client affect (Chapter 6),
- shifting the level of abstraction (Chapter 7),
- exposing resistances (Chapter 10).

Transferring Responsibility for Interview Movement

Usual conversations outside the consulting room tend to be a form of verbal ping-pong. One person speaks and pauses; the other picks up and then stops; the first resumes, and so on. This is appropriate in such settings; it is, however, likely to be counterproductive in a psychotherapy which aims to foster the client's deepened inner awareness. In that enterprise—and particularly in its earlier phase—therapist verbal activity often needs to be kept to a minimum, so that the client can focus attention on his own subjective flow.

In an early therapeutic contact, it is usual to collect certain factual information—e.g., education, occupation, family status, medical problems, presenting problem, business arrangements. My own practice here is to use a simple form (see Figure 3.1[2]) to secure these data so that the question-and-answer routine will not get started. Follow-up can occur in a fashion which encourages the client to take greater responsibility for elaboration.

Once this necessary task is out of the way, it is helpful to make an explicit transfer of responsibility for conversational movement.

Figure 3.1.   Personal Data Summary, which collects relatively objective information and frees the therapist to give more attention to the subjective. (This is not copyrighted and therapists who wish to may copy it for their own use.)

PERSONAL DATA SUMMARY

Today's date: _____

TITLE: Ms./Mr./Mrs./Miss/Dr. Name: _____

RESIDENCE:
Address: _____ City: _____ State _____ Zip: _____

Phone: _____ Age: _____ Sex: _____ Birthplace: _____ Birthdate: _____.

EDUCATION:

School and location	Dates	Major	Minors	Degrees and honors

OTHER TRAINING:

Form and place	Dates	Main areas covered

PRESENT POSITION:

Title	Employer (name, address, phone)	Dates	Duties

How long employed here? _____ How long in the same field? _____

(*continued*)

PRIOR POSITIONS:
Titles   Employer (name, location,   Dates   Duties

_____   _____   _____   _____

_____   _____   _____   _____

_____   _____   _____   _____

_____   _____   _____   _____

MILITARY: Service: _____ Branch: _____ Rank: _____ Dates: _____

Overseas Service? Area: _____ Dates: _____ Combat? Y N Hospitalized? Y N

MARITAL STATUS:
S ( ), M ( ), W ( ), D ( ).
   If currently married, when? _____ If separated or divorced, when? _____
If married more than once, give dates of prior marriages,
   how terminated, number children: _____

_____

_____

				Living you you?
CHILDREN: Names	Sex	Age	School and level	
_____	____	____	_____	____
_____	____	____	_____	____
_____	____	____	_____	____
_____	____	____	_____	____

KEY PEOPLE in your life:

Name	Age	Educ.	Occupation	Comment (e.g., health)
Father _____	____	____	_____	_____
Mother _____	____	____	_____	_____
Sisters _____	____	____	_____	_____
_____	____	____	_____	_____

and _____ _____ _____ _____ _____

Brothers _____ _____ _____ _____ _____

_____ _____ _____ _____ _____

Spouse _____ _____ _____ _____ _____

Other _____ _____ _____ _____ _____

Important _____ _____ _____ _____ _____

People _____ _____ _____ _____ _____

In Your _____ _____ _____ _____ _____

Life _____ _____ _____ _____ _____

Place "N" beside the name of persons who live at the same place that you do now. Show date of death of any deceased.

CHILDHOOD:

Were your parents ever separated? _____ If so, for how long? _____

How old were you at the time? _____ With whom did you stay? _____

Did you ever live with anyone other
than your parents while a child? _____ With whom? _____ How old were you? _____

PHYSICIAN: _____ Address: _____ Zip: _____ Phone: _____

Date last consulted: _____ Last physical: _____ What current medication? _____

NEXT OF KIN: _____ City: _____ State: _____ Zip: _____

PREVIOUS COUNSELING OR PSYCHOTHERAPY:

Names:	Profession	City	Dates	Frequency	Indiv./Gr

What are the main concerns that bring you to us?

_____

_____

_____

(*continued*)

By whom were you referred? _____ Relation: _____

INSURANCE:

Will any part of your fees be paid by insurance or some other "third party?"
    Yes _____ No _____ Not sure yet _____

If you answered, "yes" or "not sure," please provide the following information:
    Group policy _____ Individual _____

Insurance company _____ Policy # _____

COMMENTS (Please provide any further information about yourself or your insurance which
may be helpful:

_____

_____

_____

_____

Segment 3.1
Client: Tom Freed; Therapist: Gwen Black

TH-1: Tom, we've had a couple of sessions to get to know each other and to
       handle some details. Now we're ready to move into the main body of
       our work together, and I want to propose a way of conducting this
       work. It's a way that may be unfamiliar but one that in the long run
       has usually proven to work well.

CL-1: Okay by me. What do we do?

TH-2: I'd like you to take on the job of telling me about yourself. Tell me
       more about the concerns that bring you to therapy, about what those
       concerns make you think of, about what your earlier life was like, and
       about how you want the future to go for you. That's not a list you have
       to follow; those are just examples. Basically tell me what concerns you,
       what matters to you, and everything you can think of or discover
       within yourself about what matters to you.

CL-2: Well, that's pretty much what I have been doing so far, isn't it?

TH-3: In a way, yes, but there's an important difference. Up to now you've
       mostly been telling me things you already knew and thought out be-

fore. Now I want you to try to discover in yourself much more about these concerns of yours. Another difference is that I'm not going to be talking back and forth with you as we're doing now and as people mostly do outside of this office. Instead, I want you to take the time to think, feel, and discover inside of yourself without my intruding much. Once in a while I'll have things to say—sometimes maybe a lot—but mostly you just keep describing what you find inside yourself without waiting for me to reply.

CL-3: Huh! I don't know whether I can do that. I mean, I think I've already told you most everything I know about what's bugging me. It would help a lot if you'd ask me some questions.

TH-4: Sure, I know it feels that way, Tom, but actually you'll find you have a lot more to say than you realize now. And I will throw in questions sometimes, but it's really important for you to try to keep going from inside of yourself. If I'm too active, I'm likely to get in your way when you look inside.

CL-4: Oh no, Doc, you wouldn't be in my way. You'd be helping me.

TH-5: I hear that that's the way it feels to you, and that's okay. Let's just try it out for a bit now and see how it goes.

CL-5: Yes, . . . well, I guess so. I don't have any idea where to start. Can you give me a starter?

TH-6: Sure. Why don't you just tell me in any way that comes to mind what your life's been like the past two, three months as this problem has gotten so intense?

CL-6: Yeah, well, like I said the other day, it's been pure hell. That's what it's been. I can't seem to get myself to . . . .

Tom, in the example, is a fairly typical of new clients who have difficulty catching on to the idea of this way of working. From time to time the therapist will need to give him a boost with a broad question or even by restructuring the way of working. However, the general structuring (TH-2 and TH-3) provides a reference point to which attention may frequently be returned until it gradually becomes a familiar way of using the therapeutic opportunity.

CL-11: It seems funny to have you just sit there and not be saying anything while I ramble on all the time.

TH-11: I know this is a different kind of conversation than you're used to, than most of us have outside of this office. Sure, that's one of the ways talking in therapy is different from outside talk. You'll remember I told you that it would be this way, and it takes some getting used to, but you're doing okay. Just hang in and see what comes next when you think of your life as it's going these days.

In cases in which this adaptation does not occur, therapist should realize that a significant resistance is being encountered. Then she needs to move to work with it in whatever manner she usually employs with such processes (see, for example, Chapter 10).

Making Explicit the Manifest-But-Implicit

It is a familiar phenomenon of psychotherapy, one which surprises every neophyte, that the client may be vividly expressing feelings nonverbally and yet be unaware of those very emotions. The old joke about the choleric man, red of face, fists clenched, voice loud and furious, shouting, "Who's excited? I'm damned well not!" expresses the layman's recognition of this pattern.

If well-timed and phrased, reflecting back in plain words what is so evident but has not yet been verbalized is a potent therapeutic tool.

Segment 3.2
CL-A: I've been trying and trying, but . . . . Oh, hell, it's just the same old story over and over, but I've got to keep at it; still . . .
TH-A: You're tired of the repetitiousness, but there's no way to get out of the situation.
CL-B: (With a big exhalation) You know it! (Pause) Damn but it's good to have someone finally really hear that.

Timing and phrasing are essential. They are most apt to be effective if closely matched to the ongoing flow of inner experiencing in the client. To say to the choleric man we spoke of above, "You're really angry," or "Yes, you are; you're really excited," will miss his experience and only result in an argument. Contrast the following sequence.

Segment 3.3
CL-A: Who's excited! (Furiously, face red, body tense) I'm damned well not!
TH-A: You want me to hear that you're not excited.
CL-B: (Heatedly) Of course, I do. It's no use . . .
TH-B: (Softly interrupting) And you're shouting it at me so that I won't think you are.
CL-C: (Startled) Huh! Yes, (pause) yes, I guess I was. Hmm, maybe I was more worked up than I realized.
TH-C: That happens to us sometimes.

The point is that what was manifest was not simply the excitement or anger but the unawareness. To make explicit only part of the client's experience (the excitement) often results in that person's feeling not understood and, perhaps, chided.

Another example occurred during an intake with a woman who had insisted on an emergency appointment because she felt desperate, having just learned of her husband's infidelity.

Segment 3.4[3]
Client: Jennifer Stoddert; Therapist: James Bugental
    (Jennifer was determined to provide factual, impersonal information for some time, but eventually I interrupted this process.):
TH-1: Why don't you just let it come out the way you find it inside of your thoughts, and then we can get more details as we go along?
CL-1: Very well. (Pause, catches her breath, getting set) All right then . . . (pause). I think I am going to kill my husband. (Sits back breathlessly)
TH-2: (Calmly, softly) Since you're here telling me about it, you must have some other thoughts about it too.
CL-2: Yes. But if I don't kill him, then I must divorce him. And if I do that, I'll kill myself.
TH-3: Those are hard choices. Take it slowly now, and just tell me about it. (Voice trails off.)
CL-3: Well, I'll try. . . . It would help if you'd ask me questions so I can more efficiently give you the information you need.
TH-4: When you say "the information I need," what do you have in mind? What do you want me to do?
CL-4: Why to help me, of course.
TH-5: To help you what?
CL-5: So that I won't kill my husband! Oh! (Cries in quick convulsive sobs)
TH-6: You seem surprised to find out how much you don't want to kill him.

Taking this sequence as a whole, one can see how it makes explicit what has been only implicit to this point. Doing so serves to forward the therapeutic work generally; in this case it is also a means for developing the client's readiness to make a "nonviolence contract." Therapist uses an early response (TH-2) which prepares the way by pointing toward the unrecognized motivation to not kill her husband. Still, it is evident that the client does not yet fully recognize this part of her feelings (CL-2). It is necessary to help the client to move deeper into those feelings (TH-3) and then test her readiness (TH-4). Her reply (CL-4) is still ambiguous, but since she hasn't taken flight, the therapist (TH-5) sets up her self-disclosure (CL-5) and then (TH-6) confirms the recognition.

Penetrating To The Subjective

The responses just reviewed are good examples of how penetration to the subjective can be fostered. Whenever we deal with the implicit in this fashion, we are bringing to the surface some of the inner life of the client. There are other ways in which this is accomplished, of course. Here are four responses to the same client statement; note the contrasting influences they have on what client will say next:

Segment 3.5
CL-1: They are always making nasty remarks about me, and I get so mad I could just tell them to their faces what I think of them (pause, face changes). But I'm afraid of what would happen if I did.
TH-A1: What do they say about you?
TH-B1: You got mad at them, huh?
TH-C1: What would you like to say to them?
TH-D1: You feel fearful when you think of telling them off.

The first (TH-A1) stays on the surface of the experience about which the client is concerned. It deals only with the (supposedly) objective report of what the other people say. Superficially, the second response (TH-B1) is more subjective, since it speaks of feelings, but note that in fact it is also objective because the feelings with which it deals are in the past. Even though they were there a minute ago and might be reawakened, other feelings are present in the subjective now. The moment for the question about client's impulse to respond (TH-C1) has similarly passed. Only the last therapist reflection (TH-D1) directly seeks contact with the immediate subjective.

The *true* subjective nearly always has the following qualities implied or explicit:

- first person,
- present tense,
- feelingful aspects,
- intentionality, directionality,
- congruence between content and immediate experience,
- fewer qualifications regarding feelings and perceptions,
- less abstract, more concrete.

If some of these qualities are absent from the client's responses, it may indicate that the client is objectifying himself and very likely needs help in becoming more centered and moving to a deeper level. That help may well take the form of highlighting the quality lacking in the client's responses. To illustrate, let's follow this same conversation further, assuming that therapist replied with TH-D1. We begin with the original client response so that we can get the feel of the development.

Segment 3.5 (continued)

CL-1: They are always making nasty remarks about me, and I get so mad I could just tell them to their faces what I think of them (pause, face changes). But I'm afraid of what would happen if I did.

TH-D1: You feel fearful when you think of telling them off.

CL-D2: Of course, wouldn't you be?

TH-D2: It's how *you* feel that we need to focus on.

CL-D3: Well, yes, I do feel sort of hesitant. I mean, you never know what some people will do.

TH-D3: "Sort of" sounds like you're not very sure.

CL-D4: Uh, well, I guess so. I mean, I feel hesitant all right, but I don't know what I ought to do.

TH-D4: I hear that hesitation right here as you think about this and keep using words like "sort of" and "I guess." What's that like inside of you right now?

CL-D5: When you keep pushing at me that way, I can feel the scaredness coming up right now, and I don't want to feel that.

Let's see how the absence of subjectivity is reflected in the client's talk: He switches to the second person (CL-D2), suggesting a defensive need. This flight is made even more marked (CL-D3) as he becomes abstracted from the lived situation ("some people") and introduces qualifiers ("sort of" and "I mean") that reveal hesitation to fully engage the issue. The therapist is working closely with the client's resistance here, picking up and feeding back the cues to his subjective experience (TH-D2 and -D3). She makes the confrontation more immediate (TH-D4) after the client gets in touch with his feeling of helplessness (CL-D4)—even though he needs an additional qualifier as he does so. This results in the client's finding the fearful feelings occurring here and now (CL-D5) and recognizing his resistance to facing his fear. The suggestion of annoyance toward the therapist is a good sign that the client is more fully in the moment and may offer a place for further work now or later.

Maintaining Continuity

Experienced therapists come to recognize how important it is to stay with a theme or experiential dimension rather than allowing the conversation and its process dimensions to wander. Usually it is worthwhile to allow an initial settling-in period (ranging from less than a minute to ten or fifteen minutes with most clients), after which a dominant theme may be noted.[4] This needs to be followed for some time. Such a theme may be the concern of which client is most aware in the moment, an emotional cluster that needs expression and working through, an issue that has been the recurring center of attention for several sessions, or some resistance pattern which the therapist judges is ready to be analyzed further.

Examples of such themes from some of my clients may make this clearer:

> Recently a client[5] has recognized her need to be pleasing to everyone; today I am reflecting and magnifying this trait whenever it shows up in relation to others or to me.

> I repeatedly show one client[6] his continual use of many qualifiers and vague generalities, which makes it difficult to get a sense of his actual inner experience.

> A client is annoyed with me for my plan to take time away from the office; she only hints at these feelings; I frequently point out her evasions.

> A client announced at the end of the last session that he needed to cut his schedule to once a week. Today I open the hour by questioning this decision and by alluding to his waiting until the end of the hour to announce it. He tries to quickly explain it all away and go on to other matters; I refuse to be diverted.

Let's see how this last instance goes:

Segment 3.6
Client: Dave Snyder; Therapist: James Bugental
TH-1: It's obvious you're uncomfortable with your wish to drop to once a week.
CL-1: Oh sure, I don't like doing it. It's just that I have no choice. Can't afford to spend so much time coming here.
TH-2: You have no choice?
CL-2: Not really. Just so much work piled up, and the boss doesn't like my being away so much. Anyway, I want to talk to you about this fight that Janis and I got into again last night.
TH-3: Again you're moving away from what's happening to your commitment to your therapy and to your life.
CL-3: Oh, come on. It's not that way. I'd be here every day if I could afford it and if . . .

TH-4: Dave, you're very determined to treat this as a minor matter and one that you don't want to really look at. I don't buy it. I think there's something more going on.

CL-4: I meant to tell you about the schedule change sooner, but we just got started on something else, and I never got around to it.

TH-5: You sound as though you're caught in something wrong and need to make excuses.

CL-5: Oh, no. Anyway, that's not what I want to talk about now.

TH-6: Wow! You really are going to push this whole thing away if you can, aren't you?

CL-6: No, no. (Light tone) It's okay if you want to say something more about it.

TH-7: Dave, it sounds as though it's my therapy, not yours, or my life, not yours.

CL-7: Oh sure, it's important, but I can't change the facts. (Casually) Just one of the breaks, you know.

TH-8: No, I don't know.

CL-8: What's the big deal? (Edge of irritation) I just need to cut down for a while, and . . .

TH-9: First you were sounding so far away, so casual. Now some other feelings are beginning to come in.

CL-9: (Challenging) Okay, okay. How do I get there, back to where we need to be?

TH-10: Now you're trying to pass the buck to me. Do you really want to be here?

CL-10: Sure, I just don't know how.

TH-11: I don't buy that. I think you're not only trying to cut down how often you're here, but you're also trying to get away from really being here emotionally even today when you're here physically.

Note that I don't simply accept a statement or two and allow the subject to be changed. More importantly, I don't allow the excuse to keep me from pressing the more fundamental point of how he is evading therapeutic involvement. This sort of close tracking and frequent confrontation is best used with basically committed clients who are used to working at the critical occasions level and who are pulling back to lighter involvement.

THERAPIST'S OWN CONVERSATIONAL LEVEL

To this point we have spoken chiefly about the client's presence, but it should be apparent that this is not entirely independent of the therapist's own accessibility and expressiveness. Recalling our earlier description (pages 27–29) of the seven veils in which we wrap ourselves, Figure 3.2 schematically shows therapist and client as both present to a very shallow extent (i.e., at the contact maintenance level). As pointed out above, this is not a truly therapeutic engagement. Figure 3.3, on the other hand, illustrates a more intense interaction, with both participants working on the critical occasions plane. The is a genuine therapeutic alliance.[7]

Of course, client and therapist don't always neatly attain the same level, but in general it is desirable that they be as nearly so as possible. In contrast, Figure 3.4 portrays a situation favored by some therapists, but which in my experience is appropriate chiefly to short-term and manipulative approaches. Clients who work toward major life changes over many months and even years usually want and need genuineness in their partners in the enterprise. This does not mean similar content but it does mean authentic accessibility and appropriate expressiveness on the therapist's part.

Developing Therapist Sensitivity to Trend

At times therapists find questions pushing for attention as they listen to their clients:

> If our talk continues pretty much as it is now will client become more deeply immersed or less so? Will he, of his own accord, move to a level at which we can deal more effectively with his issues, or must I intervene in the flow in some way to encourage that movement? In the way he's responding now is there a hint of his being threatened? Do I need to change the way I'm taking part to reduce the possibility that he may withdraw from our involvement?

Seldom as conscious, explicit, or numerous as these examples, still implicitly these questions depict the attempt to keep alert to the direction in which the conversational partner is trending. Trend is a subtle matter but one that is clearly important to effective guidance of the conversation. When the therapist is repeatedly taken by surprise by developments in her partner's participation, she is not likely to be effective in furthering their work.

One learns to sense conversational trends from participating in many, many conversations, participating with senses attuned to what is going on and to the subtle and chiefly nonverbal hints of what is just over the horizon. When it is otherwise appropriate, it can be useful to the therapist's developing intuition to check her impressions. This can be a helpful form of intervention as well:

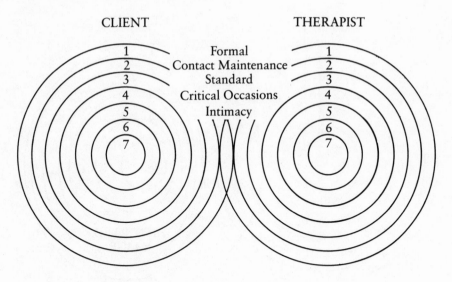

Figure 3.2.   Shallow Immersion in the Conversation.

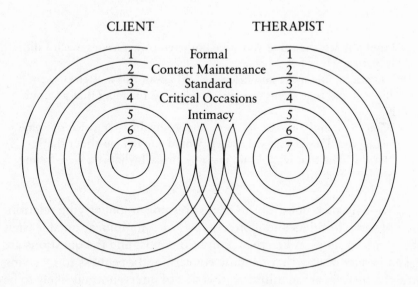

Figure 3.3.   An Effective Working Therapeutic Relation in Which Client and Therapist are Both Immersed.

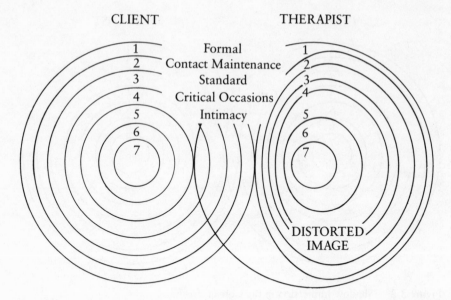

Figure 3.4.   One-sided Engagement in Which Therapist Withholds from Full Immersion.

- I thought just then that you were bothered by my saying what I did. Is that right?
- You are finding more and more feelings about this matter as we talk about it and that seems to surprise you. Am I reading that accurately?
- When you spoke just then there was a hint in your voice of some feeling that I hadn't sensed earlier. Would you tell me about that?
- I have a sense that what I said just now missed what you were feeling inside; is that so?

Obviously such questions as these presume an underlying relationship of some firmness and a present level of communication at least at the standard stage. When these conditions exist and the questions are asked in such a way that genuine concern and openness to receiving straight answers are manifested, this sort of intervention is likely to be received with appreciation and responded to with candor. It may, in itself, help to move the conversation to a deeper level. But the openness needs to be truly genuine so that the therapist is actually set to hear and consider (inwardly at least) that she has misread the client.

A PSYCHOTHERAPIST'S JOURNEY

My first true experience as a psychotherapist came during World War II when I was a non-com psychologist in an army hospital. I was assigned to "talk with" a young soldier newly evacuated home from Tarawa, the scene of a terrible battle in the Pacific. He was suffering, the chart said, from "combat fatigue." He was nervous, irritable, restless, miserable, and he wanted to talk to someone. I brought him from his open ward to my small office and encouraged him to let me be that someone.

For three and a half hours he took me into horror: "The noise never stopped . . . blood everywhere . . . shit my pants before I knew it . . . saw his leg just disappear . . . could walk across the fuckin' island on the bodies . . . shot the sonovabitch just as he looked up . . . my buddy had a big hole in his belly . . . blood all over me . . . goddam big boom . . . the motherfuckin' Japs wouldn't quit, damn them . . . piece of meat was all it was . . . always the noise . . ."

He poured out anguish, fright, self-hatred, fury at the army and the world, despair, terror that he might be sent back, and bits and pieces of his prewar life. At the end of that time we were both drained, or so I thought, judging from my own condition. My client was tearfully grateful to me, and I felt quite pleased with my new therapeutic skill.

Thirty minutes after my client returned to his bed, the psychiatrist in charge of that ward called me. His voice was indignant, "What the hell did you do to Jones, Sergeant? For the first time since he got here I've had to put him in restraints!"

So I learned the power and dangers of unmodulated catharsis and got a dramatic first view of the depths of the subjective.

In the more than four decades since those days, I've been on a search for understanding of that mysterious realm. I didn't know this was my quest for a long time, but it is increasingly evident that it is so. I have more words for that which I pursue, but I do not know its full name yet. I doubt I ever shall. *Subjectivity, the unconscious, our deepest center* are some of the words. They do not all point in the same direction, but there is enough commonality that I feel I'm making some progress.

As a psychotherapist, I have been drawn to work which is long-term, concerned with the inner lives of my clients. Such work seeks to explore the nature of our being, and it has the possibility of rousing the sleeping potentials within us. It can, at times, bring about major life changes. This is work which is set in that realm that I have been seeking and exploring, the subjective.

Over the years I have acquired and discarded various aids to the search. I gave up the various tests—standardized and projective—some time ago because, though they offered valuable and intriguing perceptions of the people with whom I worked, they ultimately made those persons objects of study rather than partners in the enterprise. I have come to believe that only with a truly subjectively centered and highly motivated companion can my quest go forward fully.

This book is describing some of the ways I've found that help in the process of aiding my clients to contact their own inner resources and that facilitate my being with them when they are in their truest being, their subjective sovereignty. One of the foremost of those ways is that of helping my client to be fully and concernedly present in his own life and in his own therapy.

CHAPTER 4

Interpersonal

Press

Whenever we talk with someone we intend, consciously or not, to change something—in ourselves (e.g., our understanding of that person, our feeling of uncertainty about what we need to do next in the conversation) or in the other person (e.g., her view of her opportunities, her tendency to become confused when in conflict with someone). The change we seek may be in feelings, in ideas, in words, or in acts. To bring about these changes, human beings have developed an immense array of influencing agents. Here we will, of course, restrict our attention to those employed in therapeutic conversations.

Seeking to encourage our patients to inquire into their own subjective living, we are alert to many cues and bring into play many aspects of ourselves. The most apparent is the manner in which we select the words we say and how we say them. This range of patterns for inducing changes I term interpersonal press.

This chapter describes and illustrates the use of interpersonal press. It uses the image of a keyboard to suggest the many ways and intensities of press, and it proposes we think of four modes of press: listening, guiding, instructing, and requiring.

INTERPERSONAL PRESS HAS to do with how strongly the therapist attempts to influence what the patient will think, feel, say, or do as a result of the conversation. Such influencing may have any conceivable purpose. The therapist may want to understand more about the patient's early life, to bring the patient to greater awareness of suppressed emotions, to help the therapist himself feel more confident about an intended interpretation, to encourage the patient to make a deeper commitment to the work, to bring the interview to a close, or any of an infinitude of other changes in himself or his patient. The changes sought may be for the benefit of either of them or both.

Is Press Manipulation?

The use of interpersonal press is *not* necessarily or desirably a matter of manipulating or objectifying the patient. Of course, it can be used manipulatively, but that is a product of the intent of the person using it, not an inherent quality of interpersonal press as such.

Fully understood, press is a universal characteristic of human interactions of all kinds. Sometimes we imagine that any effort to influence another person is a kind of intrusion or offense to that person's autonomy. Nothing could be further from the truth. When we value others and our relations with them we care about their actions and experiences, and that caring issues into the ways we attempt to help them. Thus the press we use with someone is a demonstration that that person matters to us; only with those to whom we are indifferent do we have no intention to affect them in any way.

Press has many forms and degrees of intensity. For example, here are four possible therapist responses to the same patient statement. They differ in how much press they bring to bear:

Segment 4.1
Patient: Joy Lindsey; Therapist: Joe Bridgeman
PT-1: So I told him that I was getting sick and tired of his always complaining about the way I am and that if he didn't stop, I was going to move out, and . . . (She trails off, looks uncomfortable.) Well, anyway, I think that it's time I took a stand and . . . (Again she seems to lose momentum and sits restlessly.)
TH-1A: You look pretty miserable right now, Joy. What's going on in you?
TH-1B: Um-hmm. (Waits expectantly)
TH-1C: If you stop yourself every time you get to something uncomfortable, you're going to keep therapy from being of any help to you.
TH-1D: Would you like to tell me what it's like inside of you when you run out of gas that way?

So which is the right answer?

Of course, the right answer is any of these or none of them. It depends on a number of other matters. For example, if this is in the first few minutes of Joy's first interview with a therapist, patience (TH-1B) probably is indicated. If this is the 37th interview with Joy, and Joy continually stops herself from expressing any emotion that comes up, a candid confrontation (TH-1C) may be closer to the mark. In between there are clearly places in which directing attention to Joy's feelings (TH-1A) or inviting her to disclose her inner experience (TH-1D) would be most useful.

What this demonstrates is that there is a scale here which ranges from letting Joy continue pretty much as she chooses to making a strong effort to change what Joy will say next. This scale, *interpersonal press*, describes how much we "press" on the person with whom we're talking, how much we try to affect what that person will feel, think, say, or do so that it will be different from what it would have been had we said nothing at all.

Viewed in terms of the scale of interpersonal press, TH-1B is putting on the least press, TH-1D is next, then TH-1A, and finally TH-1C is pushing hardest. Right here at the start, let's be very clear about one thing: In no way is this a scale of good/bad responses. There are occasions in psychotherapy for all degrees of interpersonal press. The artistry lies in knowing how much to employ and when and how to do so.

THE KEYBOARD OF INTERPERSONAL PRESS

Imagine a keyboard on which various therapist responses are "keys," as in Figure 4.1.[1] To carry out the metaphor, we may think of the total range of interpersonal press as divisible into four octaves. Just as on the musical keyboard, the eighth note of one octave is the same as the first note of the next. This emphasizes that there are no

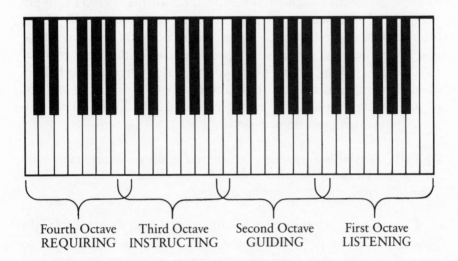

| Fourth Octave | Third Octave | Second Octave | First Octave |
| REQUIRING | INSTRUCTING | GUIDING | LISTENING |

Figure 4.1. The Keyboard of Interpersonal Press and The Four Main Octaves (modes) of Press Intensity.

sharp lines of division between these segments of the total scale. Similarly, we need to remember that there are infinite possible gradations and variations. The black notes on the keyboard represent some of these.

Each octave consists of responses which exert roughly the same general amount of influencing effort. Thus we speak of the first quarter of the keyboard as being that in which therapist is chiefly *listening*. The second clusters around *guiding* efforts, the third involves *instructing*, and the strongest press is that in which therapist is *requiring* some change from patient. These terms are representative rather than limiting; thus, not every response in a particular octave will fit those characterizations.

The Verbal and the Nonverbal

As the first chapter recognized, most of my suggestions deal with the verbal facets of therapy. These lend themselves best to written communication in a book. But there must be a clear understanding: Nonverbal communication is crucially intrinsic in actual conversations. Alert therapists know that their own body language — facial expressions, gestures, posture, speech patterns — speak to their patients forcibly, and they keenly observe the communications of their patients on these same channels.

These observations about the importance of the nonverbal apply with special significance when we come to talk conceptually about usual degrees of press of various therapist responses. In actual clinical usage any particular response may be expressed with such a manner that it might belong at any point on the scale. Often nonverbal accompaniments of the words spoken bring about shifts in the amount of press being exerted. For example, silence, the lowest "key," can convey very high press on occasion:

PT-A: Doc, I'm feeling desperate. I mean, you've just got to help me. I can't go on. Please tell me what to do right now. Please!
TH-A: (Silence; impassive manner)

While this rarely would be a suitable response to such a distraught patient, the point illustrated is that the silence, i.e., the refusal to respond overtly, may itself be a response of strong interpersonal press.

TABLE 4.1
Summary of the Scale of Interpersonal Press

First Octave: Listening
- Functions: Drawing out patient, encouraging patient to keep talking; getting patient's story without contamination by therapist.
- Examples: Getting details of patient's experience, listening to emotional catharsis, learning patient's view of her own life or her projected objectives.

Second Octave: Guiding
- Functions: Giving direction and support to patient's talk, keeping it on track, bringing out other aspects.
- Examples: Exploring patient's understanding of a situation, relation or problem; developing readiness to learn new aspects or get feedback.

Third Octave: Instructing
- Functions: Transmitting information or directions having rational and/or objective support.
- Examples: Assignments, advising, coaching, describing a scenario of changed living.

Fourth Octave: Requiring
- Functions: Bringing therapist's personal and emotional resources to bear to cause patient to change some way.
- Example: Subjective feedback, praising, punishing, rewarding, strong selling of therapist's views.

The main features of the interpersonal press scale are summarized in Table 4.1. Below we now examine each of the octaves to illustrate possible responses and their uses. Within each octave, the sample responses are in a sequence of increasing amounts of press.

FIRST OCTAVE: LISTENING

The most fundamental skill of the psychotherapist is productive listening. Everything else the therapist does needs to be founded on his developed ability to hear on many levels simultaneously. Such listening is much more than passive recording; it is a dynamic alertness which involves many sense modalities plus intuition, reflection, and cultivated empathy.

This octave of interpersonal press is typified by response forms in which literal content is secondary to a strong message to the patient to use the therapeutic opportunity to say what needs to be said and to say it as fully as possible.

General Characteristics of This Octave

Therapist's implicit message: "I am interested in what you have to say. I am trying to understand it fully. I accept your saying it without necessarily agreeing or disagreeing at this time. Just say it in your own way."

Quantity of talk: The patient is encouraged to talk much more than the therapist. The latter chiefly seeks to support full self-expression and seldom brings his own thoughts or views into the conversation.

Subjectivity: The patient largely determines how much to get into the subjective, although the therapist may selectively respond to such elements when they do appear (see Part III, Subject Matter Guidance).

Overt persuasion: The therapist avoids any such efforts, making it a point to demonstrate the patient's freedom to proceed as she chooses.

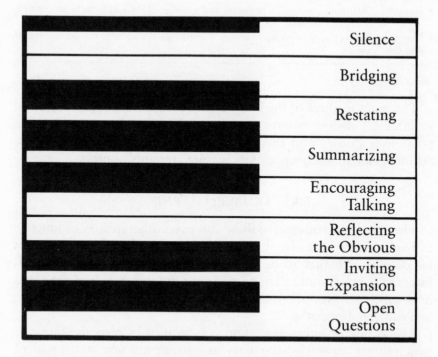

Figure 4.2.   Examples of Response Forms Typical of the First or *Listening* Octave of Interpersonal Press.

Therapist's role: The therapist's tasks are to encourage the patient's self-expression, to attend as fully as possible, to demonstrate genuine acceptance of the patient's right to her own views, and to receive such impressions and information as may be useful at other points in the work.

Examples of Typical Response Forms

Silence: The therapist doesn't speak, but by his manner seeks to convey acceptance and understanding which will aid the patient's self-expression.

Bridging: These are the sounds which we all make when attentively listening and which subtly transmit support to a speaker: "Uh-huh." "Ummmm." "I see." "Yes" (not as an answer to a question).

Restating: The therapist says back to the patient some of what the latter has just said. Often this is accomplished by using synonyms for some of the patient's words, although this is by no means always necessary. This form of response is especially helpful when the patient is caught up in strong emotions, but it can be counterproductive when parrot-like, routine, and mechanical.

> *In this section the examples have a continuity in persons and content to aid reader's grasp of context. This must not be read as suggesting such continuity is or is not desirable in the use of these response levels in actual practice.*

Here is an example of the appropriate use of restatement:

Segment 4.2
PT-3: I've tried. God knows, I've tried as well as I could, but nothing seems to work (sighs, shakes her head).
TH-3: (Understanding tone) Nothing seems to work.
PT-4: That's right. Honestly, sometimes I get so discouraged and feel as though it's all hopeless.

Summarizing: Therapist draws together some related thoughts from patient's presentation and feeds them back to demonstrate understanding.

TH-5: You've tried repeatedly, Joy, and it seems as though you can't reach

him. You think of moving out; you think of just giving up. Sometimes
you feel really desperate.

PT-5: Yeah, that's it. That's just the way it is.

Therapists sometimes try to teach or interpret to patients through
summarizing comments. While this is certainly an appropriate step at
times, it needs to be recognized that doing so moves out of the listening mode. It brings more press to bear (thus changing to the instructing mode, third octave).

Encouraging talking: The therapist offers general supporting comments which do not point in a particular direction but encourage the
patient to continue her account: "You're doing fine; keep
going. . . ." "I'm getting it; you're coming through loud and clear."

Reflecting the obvious: Therapist puts into explicit words patient
feelings or attitudes which have been manifest but implicit to this
point. This is particularly helpful with patients who have difficulty in
recognizing their own emotions or perspectives. Again it needs to be
recognized that it is a departure from the listening mode to use this
form to try to disclose unconscious material. In this octave the experience being named needs to be so manifest that the patient will readily
recognize it.

PT-6: I talked to him again last night, and he just won't budge. He doesn't
really hear me even (sighs heavily). Yet I hate to give up because
. . . well, sometimes we . . .

TH-6: As disappointed as you are now, you still think of how it's been at
other times.

Inviting expansion: The therapist points to something the patient
has introduced into the conversation and encourages the patient to
say more on that topic or feeling. If the therapist seeks to stay in the
listening mode, care needs to be taken to stay within what the patient
has already expressed rather than introducing some new matter.

TH-7: You said you sometimes felt "desperate," Joy. Would you say some
more about that?

Open Questions: These are questions in which there are few explicit or implicit limits on what the patient can reply: "What do you
see as important for me to understand about you?" "Tell me about

what you've been thinking since we talked last time" (an invitation that is not in formal question form but is actually a question in intent).

Summary

The listening mode is one in which the main thrust of the conversation is left to the patient, while the therapist confines his efforts to encouraging, accepting, and observing (to himself). Since its merit is that it offers a less contaminated view of the patient's way of presenting herself and viewing her world, this approach is useful at many points in depth therapeutic work, three of the most usual being: (a) when the therapist seeks information about the patient's background, concerns, emotional life, and similar matters; (b) when the therapist is reflecting on what has been done to this point, watching for the effects of some intervention, or trying to select a course of action; and (c) when the patient has learned to carry on her inward exploration without need of frequent therapist interventions.

SECOND OCTAVE: GUIDING

Many of the values of the listening mode are present as well in this octave. However, it offers the therapist a tradeoff: some increase in ability to follow up at the expense of some loss in patient spontaneity of self-presentation. The scale here is a flexible one, however, and skillful therapists can modulate this cost/benefit issue to their own and their patients' interests.

In general, conversational guidance that is unobtrusive, fostering of increased immersion, and sensitive to patient's needs in the moment is desirable. There are frequent occasions in which the therapist will need to steer toward important but neglected topics or feelings, and there are other times when the guiding mode will be employed chiefly to aid the patient in maintaining sufficient continuity to open up fresh perspectives on familiar issues.

General Characteristics of This Octave

Therapist's implicit message: "I want you to talk to me about matters which concern you and which you want me to know about. You take the lead in our talk, but I'll make suggestions from time to time about how we should proceed."

Quantity of talk: While the patient usually talks more, the therapist is active to a degree which may range from seldom to frequently. It needs to be recognized, however, that frequency of intervention tends to increase the amount of press, no matter what the form of the intervention.

Subjectivity: The therapist is restrained in self-disclosure but may encourage the patient toward opening up her inner experiencing. This is not one-sided manipulation but an effort to give priority to the patient's needs and experience. Guiding is a mode often used to aid patients in moving from detached accounts of themselves to more personal and affective disclosures.

Overt persuasion: Therapist efforts to influence are relatively mild and clearly linked with what the patient is already presenting. If one stays in this mode, there is no departure from that boundary to bring in new influencing material.

Therapist's role: The therapist conveys genuine interest in what the patient has to say and uses guiding comments to deepen and expand

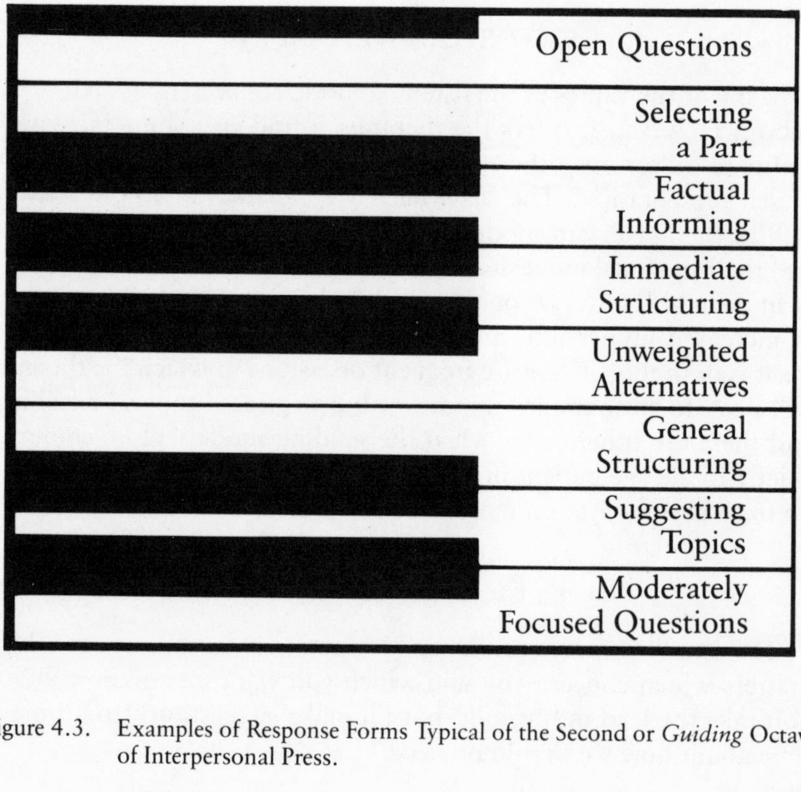

Figure 4.3.   Examples of Response Forms Typical of the Second or *Guiding* Octave of Interpersonal Press.

that account. The therapist clearly has some general orientation about what needs attention and seeks to foster that direction.

Examples of Typical Response Forms

Open questions: This is the same form discussed at the end of the listening octave. Typical questions at this level are: "Give me a general picture of what led you to seek therapy." "What are your thoughts about what has brought about the way things are for you these days?"

Selecting a part: Some aspect of what the patient is saying is chosen by the therapist as needing further elaboration. This is similar to "inviting expansion" in the listening mode; the difference is that in the guiding mode the therapist selects an aspect not directly being addressed by patient.

PT-8: I've urged him to see someone for years, literally for years. I know he needs help, and I can't do it for him.
TH-8: What first made you think he ought to get help?

Factual informing: The therapist gives information pertinent to what the patient is talking about but without implying what the patient should do with that information.

TH-9: Sometimes people need to try everything they can think of before they're willing to seek help.

Immediate structuring: Structuring responses are those in which the therapist proposes a way of using the conversation itself. Immediate structuring has to do with what is going on at the point at which the suggestion is being made.

PT-10: It's always the same. We start off okay, and then . . . well, like last night. . . . Oh, what's the use?
TH-10: Just tell me about last night now, Joy; save the worrying about other things till later.

Unweighted alternatives: The therapist points out choices open to the patient without urging one over the others. This is a genuine open invitation, not a subtle attempt to persuade her to adopt a course the therapist believes best.

TH-11: As I see it, you can either stay with him while you're working things out here or you can move out for a while and see if that relieves some of the tension. Which seems more realistic to you?

General structuring: This form of structuring sets a more general pattern for the therapeutic work — for a whole session or even a longer phase of the work.

TH-12: We've reached a place in our work now in which that work will probably go best if you will take on more responsibility for telling me about the thoughts you're having these days as you try to decide what to do. Meantime, I'll be listening and occasionally throwing in a thought or suggestion, but I won't be talking as much as I have been up to now. In this way you can explore more deeply within yourself to be sure your decision is as sound as possible. Does that sound okay to you?

Suggesting topics: The therapist proposes subject matter which the patient may want to discuss. There is an implication that what is suggested can be useful, but it is clear that the patient may disagree or take some other tack if she chooses.

TH-13: What may be helpful now, Joy, is for you to pick some one of all these matters you've said are bugging you and explore it as fully as possible. You've mentioned a trial separation, going for a trip together, seeing a marriage counselor, and several other possibilities. Which seems most to need your examination now?

Notice that therapist gives a range of possible topics.

Moderately focused questions: Some limitations are put on what would be an appropriate response. These may be explicit or implicit in the context from which the question arises. "What were your sisters like when you were young?" "What are your thoughts about the source of this recurring sense of anxiety?" Contrast these responses with the open questions of the listening octave or the more limiting ones from the high end of the third octave, "How did you and your sister Helen get along?"

Summary

In comparison with the listening mode, guiding has the therapist taking a more overtly active role, although the main responsibility for the flow of the conversation is still kept with the patient. In this octave, the therapist is selecting from what the patient presents those aspects which he judges will be most fruitful if followed up. A great deal of control of the conversation can be exercised without intruding disruptively into the patient's immersion. The artistry of gently but firmly guiding to bring the patient to greater self-awareness is a mark of the true virtuoso therapist.

THIRD OCTAVE: INSTRUCTING

In everyday talking, the word *instructing* is used in two related but contrasting ways: We speak of "instructing the students," meaning to teach them, but we also speak of "instructing the workman," that is, speaking with authority to give orders to be carried out. Both meanings are pertinent in thinking of this mode of interpersonal press, so long as in both instances the therapist is instructing on objective or rational bases. The influencing effects of this octave are explicitly cast in objective (and to that extent, impersonal) terms. More personal and subjective influencing agencies are mobilized in the fourth octave.

General Characteristics of This Octave

Therapist's implicit message: "I want you to consider some objective and important points which bear on what we've been talking about. They have implications which you need to consider." (Note the word *objective*.

Quantity of talk: This varies widely in the instructing octave, with some tendency for therapist participation to be in clusters intermixed with periods of relatively low amounts of input (perhaps dropping into the first or second octaves). Personal styles and theoretical orientations are the source of much of the variance among professionals in the use of instructing.

Subjectivity: In his own interventions the therapist relies chiefly on the objective, but in what he seeks to elicit from the patient he is often concerned with that person's subjectivity.

TH-14: Joy, you have seen already that when you try to work out of your depression by reasoning with yourself it doesn't help much. Now you're sliding back into using that way again. Wouldn't it be more to the point to let yourself get into your feelings this time?

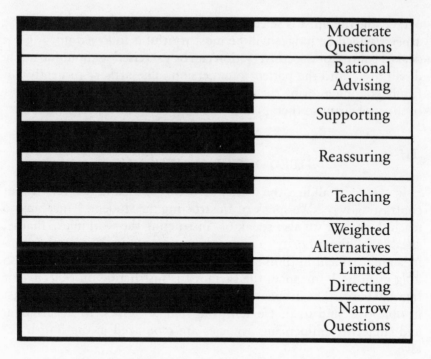

Figure 4.4.   Examples of Response Forms Typical of the Third or *Instructing* Octave of Interpersonal Press.

Overt persuasion: The therapist's efforts (as just illustrated) are manifest in what he says and how he says it. The force of reason and the support of objective information may be brought to bear to move the patient toward feelings and thoughts or words and actions that might not otherwise come about.

Therapist's role: When operating in this mode, the therapist is teaching, directing, and using the authority of knowledge and position. There is a seeking for the patient's understanding and cooperation which goes beyond simply that of person to person and often at least implicitly involves the therapist's professional role.

Examples of Typical Response Forms

Moderate questions: This coincides with the high end of the guiding octave, of course: "What kind of sex education did your parents give you?" "Take some time now and fill me in on your decision to get a divorce."

Rational advising: The therapist invokes common sense, professional information, or special knowledge of the patient to put power into some suggestion or directive.

TH-15: I know you're angry and want to do something to strike back, Joy, but I need to remind you that every time you've done that you've regretted it later. Knowing you, as we both do, you better cool off some before acting.

TH-16: The statistics are pretty overwhelming: Teenage marriages have an extremely high rate of failures. I think you need to tell your daughter that in a way that she can hear and understand. Can you do that?

Supporting: The therapist, leaving the relatively neutral stand typical of the listening and guiding modes, clearly indicates his judgment on some issue. That support, however, is objective and rational, not personal or emotional.

TH-17: You've had a tough time facing this issue, Joy, but now you seem to be making real progress in doing so. Already you're seeing that really bringing your emotions into the picture gives you a better basis for deciding what you want to do.

Reassuring: Therapists vary in the degree to which they feel it is appropriate to reassure a patient. It is unwise to offer a flat rule in this regard. When the patient is truly ready to receive it, reassurance based on objective or rational grounds may be quite useful. This is particularly so (as in the following example) when the support is based on the patient's demonstrated strengths and is not encouraging dependency on the therapist. Of course, if offered prematurely reassurance can be patronizing or even distracting.

PT-18: I've tried so damned hard, and I don't seem to get anywhere. For a while things seem better, and then it all goes to hell, and I'm right back where I started from.

TH-18: I know it's hard to keep trying when things go so badly, but you need to recognize you're not really back where you started. Remember last month, after trying without success most of the year, you were able to work out that whole problem on the house. Now this month it looks as though you're making some headway on the financial agreement. There've been setbacks, but if you look at the whole picture, you're still making progress.

Teaching: The therapist seeks to help the patient learn information, skills, new perspectives, or other material that is judged useful to the latter. This may be a straightforward imparting of the material, or it may take the form of indirect coaching. Teaching is another form in which therapeutic doctrine varies from almost complete avoidance of teaching by some to the view held by others that this is one of the central tasks of therapy.

TH-19: One thing that's making it hard for you right now is that you don't know what is required to get into that program. As long as you're just guessing and unsure, it's not surprising you feel gloomy. None of us likes to be in the dark on things that really matter to us.

TH-20: From what I know, you need three things in order to qualify for that place: You must have the right degree, which you have. You must have at least three years of qualifying experience; you and I don't know about that one. And you must have the endorsement of an experienced member of the organization, which you say you can get. So it looks to me that you better bear down on that second one.

Weighted alternatives: While recognizing that several possibilities exist for patient, this form makes evident that the therapist favors one in particular. The therapist can modulate the pressure he puts on a favored alternative from slight to nearly crushing. (If, however, he brings personal values or urgency into the effort, the response belongs in the fourth or requiring octave.)

TH-21: Helen, you know how to get confused or anxious and put off facing things. As we've seen together, you've used anxiety and confusion many times, but now you also know how to take hold of the problem and really grapple with it. You, and only you, are going to decide which way to take it now, but you will have to choose one way or the other soon.

Limited directing: The therapist gives the patient directions, assignments, or information which call for some action. When therapist is a physician, instructing may take the form of giving a prescription. Other therapists with appropriate training may administer some form of physical treatment. In all of these the authority of the therapist's role and professional position support the instruction.

TH-22: What we need now is for you to collect the views of everyone concerned with this whole matter. Go to each one, tell them what you're doing, and ask what they have to say. When you have this information, bring it back here and we'll think about next steps.

Narrow questions: The therapist closely defines the realm within which an answer will be appropriate. "Will you be taking part in that event?" "Your face just changed expression markedly; what happened just now?" To an agitated patient near the end of the hour: "Where are you going when you leave here? What will you need to do there?" As the last two examples illustrate, narrow, factual questions can be used to help ground a person and to help her plan how to handle emotional distress.

Summary

The instructing mode is one of great diversity and the scene of strong conflicts of views within the therapeutic community.[2] It has the potential for exercising a strong influence on patients. In my opinion, if it is used with sensitivity and skill it can materially contribute to patients' progress, but if it is used clumsily or excessively it can just as surely obstruct the depth and durability of the therapeutic impact.

FOURTH OCTAVE: REQUIRING

Although there are a few therapists who are known for (and pride themselves on?) their dramatic use of strong press, probably for many psychotherapists this is the least used, least valued, and least understood octave in the entire interpersonal press scale. This comes about in part because therapists generally value highly humane, mutually respectful interactions with their patients, and so they see bringing emotional force to bear as dictatorial, unhumanistic, or egotistical. This attitude can also mask fear of provoking anger or rejection from patients. (I have certainly had that apprehension.) A common misunderstanding of the use of high interpersonal press links it with punitive or hostile reproaches. It can be used that way, of course, but it is by no means limited to that vein, as our examples below will illustrate.

What all this means is that both the value judgment and the fear are ill-founded. Most patients want and respect strength of conviction and of participation in their therapists. Moreover, when they receive that within a context of reciprocal respect and manifest concern for their growth and well-being, they are powerfully reassured and supported in finding their own strength.

Therapy which relies heavily on the requiring mode is no therapy at all, in my view, but therapy which never risks that mode can easily become flaccid and ineffectual. The virtuoso therapist needs to be able to run the entire interpersonal press keyboard with sensitivity to patients' needs, to timing, to formulation, and above all with adherence to his own dignity and commitment.

General Characteristics of This Level

Therapist's implicit message: "I intend to persuade you—or, if necessary and possible, force you—to change in some way that I believe is important. To do this, I will bring to bear whatever forces I can muster. I hope you will know that I do this in what I believe are your best interests, but whatever you believe I am determined to make the effort." (The suggestion of force would be appropriate only at the high end of this octave.)

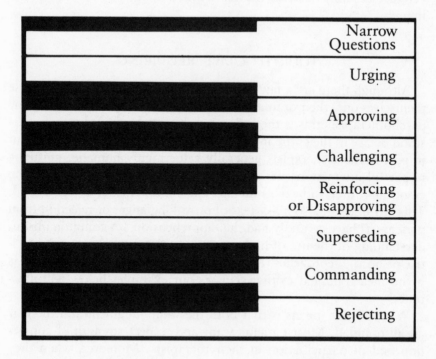

Figure 4.5.   Examples of Response Forms Typical of the Fourth or *Requiring* Octave of Interpersonal Press.

Quantity of talk: This varies widely, with instances in which the therapist preempts almost the whole of an interview and others in which he makes only occasional (but highly charged) interventions.

Subjectivity: The therapist openly but selectively brings to bear his own feelings, emotions, values, and judgments. He is ready to take responsibility for doing so, and employs these resources in meaningful ways. Indeed, the essence of this mode is just exactly this mobilization of therapist subjectivity. In extreme instances, this may well mean some submerging of the patient's feelings and outlook.

Overt persuasion: Obviously that's the name of the game in this octave. Note the word "overt"; betrayal of the patient can occur if the therapist uses his own values, emotions, or judgments but pretends they are objectively based. Use of this mode calls for the therapist to be willing to accept the responsibility for bringing his own subjectivity into the action.

Therapist's role: Exercising authority, giving explicit directives, setting limits, insisting on outcomes, and allowing his own emotions to be manifested—these are tools to bring about ends the therapist judges highly important.

Examples of Typical Response Forms

Narrow questions: Questions which allow relatively little latitude for what would be an appropriate response have an obvious requiring impact. This is heightened when the question is abrupt and not in context; it is lessened when it grows meaningfully out of what the patient is saying. "So what did you decide in that case?" "When are you going to pay the amount that you owe me?" 'Seeing how much pain that gave you, I wonder whether you've thought of leaving the situation?"

Urging: Emotional and personal appeals are used to bring the patient to do as the therapist directs. These convey a subjective urgency and may be supplemented by objective and rational materials typical of the instructing mode.

TH-23: You know how important it is for you to get some medical attention for that condition, Joy, and I personally hope you won't put it off any longer.

Approving: The therapist commends the patient's statements or actions. The key element here is the therapist's personal note.

TH-24: Well, I must say I'm relieved to hear that it's nothing more serious. I'm glad you found out.

TH-25: It's good to hear you take some responsibility in this thing instead of just being the poor victim again.

Challenging: The therapist confronts the patient with contrasting or refuting perspectives. Sometimes the challenging material is what the patient has herself said previously; sometimes it is from an external source.

TH-26: I'm tired of listening to you go over and over the same old shit! Why the hell aren't you tired of it too?

PT-27: I just stood there when she did that. What else could I do? I was helpless.
TH-27: You'd rather be helpless than face the conflict which was right there in front of you.

TH-28: You've told me again and again that you wanted an opportunity to make things different with her, but somehow you pulled out on yourself again.

Reinforcing or disapproving: The therapist employs authority, value judgments, or other strong support for or in opposition to the patient's views, actions, perspectives, or similar material.

PT-29: I've told you all I can think of about it. There is nothing more to tell; I've said it all.
TH-29: Helen, there just isn't any end to what you can say; there's only an end to how much you'll commit yourself to getting fully into this. I don't believe there's no more in you.

TH-30: You've really done well in exploring this whole thing, and now it's no wonder you're kind of empty. We both know there's more you need to get to, but not today. Just take it easy for a few minutes now.

Superseding: The therapist uses authority to take over responsibility generally or in some particular way. This may be as total as having the patient committed to a mental hospital to protect her or others or as limited as telling the patient not to persist in a futile or punishing line of inquiry or action.

PT-31: I went back again today, and all I got was the runaround again. They keep stalling me, and I'm getting kind of desperate.

TH-31: Let me see what I can do. I know the manager down there, and I'll give him a ring and see whether we can get some action right away.

Commanding: The therapist gives orders unilaterally affecting patient. There is no indication of the possibility of appeal or discussion.

TH-32: You keep making these suicidal threats and refusing to reconsider them; so I'm telling you very seriously that you are not going to leave this office except with a police officer. Your only alternative is to work out a clear contract with me so that I can be assured you will take no action against yourself before we talk again.

Rejecting: The therapist unilaterally dismisses the patient in such a way that the negation clearly extends to the patient as a person.

This is not a therapeutic form.[3] It is included here only to complete the scale. In the few instances in which I have seen this happen after some degree of therapeutic alliance has been established, the resulting trauma to the patient and to the patient's ability to enter into a trusting relation with another therapist has been quite serious. Still it must be recognized that it is sometimes necessary to terminate a therapeutic relation that has begun. If the bond is very new and not deeply welded, this can be done at the instructing level of press. If, on the other hand, a well developed relation has been established but a premature termination is necessitated for some reason (e.g., therapist illness or moving some distance away), then much work must be done at other press levels to prevent the patient's experiencing the termination as a personal rejection.

Summary

This octave constitutes an important part of the therapist's armamentarium. Too seldom are new therapists given help in learning to use it with facility, comfort, and effectiveness. There are, in most long-term and life-changing therapeutic courses, times when the strength and values of the therapist need to be brought into play; to be too mild at such points is to be countertherapeutic and to lose an opportunity to deepen the work.

USING INTERPERSONAL PRESS IN
THERAPEUTIC PRACTICE

Using All Octaves of the Scale

It should be evident that effective therapy calls for therapists to be able to use all levels of interpersonal press as the work of the moment may necessitate. It is wise to operate in one mode for a time rather than randomly moving up and down the keyboard. A typical session early in the therapeutic course might have a pattern something like this:

Opening. . . . . .Listening.

Transition. . . . . .Brief guiding.

First work phase . . . . .Listening chiefly, some guiding.

Transition . . . . .Very brief instructing.

Second work phase . . . . .Listening, slightly more guiding.

Transition . . . . .Brief instructing.

Closing . . . . .Guiding.

Now, of course, in one way that outline is nonsense; no interview can be so plotted in advance. But what the outline demonstrates is that the therapist seldom conducts an entire interview in one mode. Moreover, during any single phase, the therapist will be unlikely to make every response in the dominant mode of that phase; more typically most responses will be in that mode, but there will be sprinkling of responses from other octaves.

Patient Use of Press

Every time one person speaks to another she uses interpersonal press; it is not just an esoteric phenomenon of the therapist's consulting room. Thus it is a valuable lens through which to observe conversations in other settings, and the tyro therapist does well to use it so. Recognizing this means recognizing also that it is wise to pay attention to the ways in which patients use press. Some estimates of patients' ways of relating to others, of how much power they feel themselves to have, and of their likely social effectiveness may be had from taking note of interpersonal press patterns.

What follow are thumbnail characterizations of some of the most familiar ways in which patients employ interpersonal press to try to influence their therapists. By no means do these provide an exhaustive catalog, but they are suggestive of the general tenor of such efforts.

Patient Listening Responses: These are apt to be limited to bridging ("Uh-huh," "I see," "Yes") and restatements of what the therapist has said in all but the most didactic of therapies.

Patient Guiding Responses: The patient asks for advice, encouragement, or reassurance, proposes topics to be dealt with but waits for confirmation, or asks the therapist to clarify or amplify what he has said.

Patient Instructing Responses: The patient provides information, presents data or informed opinion in support of her views. She tells the therapist of her needs or desires from him in such a way as to convey these are her right as the patient. There is an emphasis on the reasonableness or general acceptability of what the patient advances.

Patient Requiring Responses: These are distinguished by the heavy emphasis given to the patient's emotions and needs. Thus they tend to be more personal and urgent. Typical would be the following:

PT-33: I'm so miserable these days. Can't you do something to help me feel better? (Weeps) I just don't think I can take any more if someone doesn't help me.

PT-34: Damn it, you just sit there and collect my money, but you don't do a single thing to earn it. Will you, for God's sake, get off your damned throne and tell me what to do?

PT-35: What you said last time made such a great difference in the way I see things. I can't tell you how much it meant to me. You have such a wonderful way of seeing things and helping me see them that I feel very lucky to have your help. I'm not just buttering you up; I really mean it. And I wish you'd do the same thing today about this whole situation with my mother. I've just got to get a fresh idea of what to do there, and I know you can help me get it.

A Word of Caution

Having said how important it is for therapists to learn to sense patient use of press, I need to recommend reserving these kinds of observations until therapists have achieved a fair degree of mastery in observing and using the press scale for their own work. Before this point, the attempt to observe press while conducting therapy can only lead to confusion and loss of authentic therapist presence.

A PSYCHOTHERAPIST'S JOURNEY

The experience with my first therapy patient occurred about the same time that I discovered a book which opened a new world for me, Carl Rogers' *Counseling and Psychotherapy*.[4] The book and the experience combined to bring me some early awareness of a realm of human experience largely unknown to me before. I had no name for it, but I sensed it had to do with things in people which weren't usually seen or talked about and which had the potential to produce unexpected effects, such as Pfc. Jones's heightened agitation following our supposedly helpful and friendly talk (see Chapter 3).

Rogers' first espousal of the *nondirective* approach in therapy was quite polemic, suggesting that other therapists were directive, i.e., dictatorial. Since this came during our war against dictatorships, the thrust soon received counterthrusts from some who felt attacked. After a time, Rogers abandoned that adversarial name and called his perspective by an only somewhat less provocative title, "client-centered." Of course, this still suggested that those who were not of his persuasion were "counselor- (or therapist-) centered," but enthusiasm for the battle waned, and this latter name has continued.

Stone was one of the first to suggest that there was a continuum of directiveness with Rogers at one end and his loudest opponents at the other. As my experience in working with people grew, Stone's view came to be the one that best accorded with my own observations.

Although I retained (and retain today) adherence to the Rogerian valuing of human dignity and autonomy and although I continue to use patient-centered responsiveness, my clinical practice has taught me that some patients require other therapeutic vehicles. As my range of patients became wider (especially as it included noncollegiate, less cognitively oriented people), I found that the essentially reflective, Rogerian posture did not have a significant impact on some people. I noted also that even the most loyal patient-centered therapists were adding other dimensions to their work. (I am convinced there is no such thing as an old Rogerian. To his credit, Rogers himself continually outgrows his own earlier formulations.)

Out of these experiences, I have come to believe that I can aid some people to get deeper into their subjectivity by being more forthcoming in our conversations. Still, just what form that forthcomingness takes is a highly significant and constantly evolving matter.

At first, as I see it now, it took the form of becoming paternal and overly involved in taking care of my patients. Putting limits on time, payment, and availability seemed inhumane, and permissiveness ruled the day. Sad experience demonstrated this course was not truly therapeutic and often engendered great dependence and increasingly impossible demands. It was a costly lesson—in time, money, high hopes—but a valuable one. I have come to recognize that limits are important, therapeutic, humanistic, and essential to my own survival as a therapist. Along with limits comes the need to be more than an excellent, mirroring listener. The recognition of a range of responses from the most receptive to the most demanding has been the product of thousands of hours in the consulting room.

When I was teaching at UCLA I received several grants to study interviewing skills. One of the first skills which my research assistant[5] and I examined was this scale of *interpersonal press* (which we then called "leading"). We found that we could fairly reliably identify 57 varieties of press, and for a while we thought of it as the "Heinz" scale.

Daily in the consulting room and in teaching and supervising new therapists I recognize the great value of artistic use of this scale, how it can aid patients in confronting their lives and in entering more fully into their inner experiencing.

When I first was working with this scale, "inner experiencing" chiefly meant reporting conscious thoughts and feelings. Only later, as the further dimensions of this realm opened to me, did the further values of the Heinz scale become evident.

Subject Matter
Guidance

CHAPTER 5

Topical
Paralleling

If we are to refine our sensitivities and skills we need language to identify points and processes significant to our work. The terms proposed in this book are useful pointers, not discoveries of natural laws. One such helpful reference concept is what I call paralleling.

Topical paralleling directs attention to a simple comparison of the degree to which one speaker—therapist or patient—deals with essentially the same subject matter as did the immediately preceding speaker. As subsequent chapters will demonstrate, paralleling is a much broader concept than simple attention to the manifest content of what is discussed, but that is an important and potent starting point for understanding and developing this perspective.

This chapter proposes four levels of topical paralleling: staying with the same topic, developing the topic to the next logical step, diverging from the main thrust of the preceding response although not totally abandoning it, and definitely changing the subject.

THE MOST FREQUENT ERROR of inexperienced psychotherapists is becoming overly involved with the content of what is being said and missing the real core of what is going on. The most frequent error of those who with some therapeutic experience recognize the first error is that they become so disenchanted with content that they let it go unattended and thus miss much of what is going on. Seems like you can't win? Sure does.

But, fortunately, we're not in this work to win. An art is not a contest; it's a continual growing. Whenever the artist thinks she's mastered the craft, she's stopped growing and so has stopped being an artist. True art is only to be found on the edge of what is known— a dangerous place to be, an exciting place to work, a continually unsettling place to live subjectively.

In this and the next three chapters, I offer a perspective which will aid therapists artistically to balance attention to content with recognition of the processes which support it.

THE CONCEPT OF "PARALLELING"

Paralleling is a way of thinking about the content being dealt with in the therapeutic conversation. It provides a perspective for understanding that content more fully and for using its development through the interview to form hunches about the patient's intentions, the health of the relationship between patient and therapist, and the likely course of the talk.

How Much Attention To Give the Implicit

When we talk about subject matter guidance, we give primary, but not exclusive, attention to that which is openly and explicitly said by the two speakers. My intent here is not legalistic, not to narrowly define what should or should not be considered when thinking about paralleling. When implicit elements of patient experiencing are quite manifest, they are to be taken into account, of course. What experience demonstrates is that there is value in having ways of observing at several levels on the range from dictionary-explicit to subtle inference. Paralleling is most helpful when we work at the more overt end of the scale. Other dimensions (e.g., objectivity-to-subjectivity in Chapter 9) are more productive when greater attention is given to the implicit.

Unspoken meanings may be implied or inferred and may indeed be important to the therapeutic task; however, this section deals with them only when they are most apparent — as when the patient weeps, laughs, rages, or otherwise quite overtly displays inner experience (but, perhaps, does not explicitly name it). Later chapters deal with more subtle dimensions. Somewhat paradoxically, this limitation on what we will observe through the window of paralleling aids us in examining how the phrasing of responses may affect the more subtle elements in the patient-therapist interchange.

As we talk about the evolution of the subject matter, we use the organizing concept introduced above having to do with the similarities or differences between the two participants: how well they "parallel" each other. Here is a segment of a therapeutic conversation which we can use to illustrate this process:

Segment 5.1

Patient: Harry Fordyce; Therapist: Dorothy Taylor

PT-1: I've known Bill for 15 years, and we've had our ups and downs, but I know he's one guy who's solidly there for me.

TH-1: Bill is a guy you know you can count on, eh?

PT-2: Right! I mean, I've had a lot of friends, and some of them are damn good drinking buddies, if you know what I mean. But Bill is something more or different some way.

TH-2: He's not just a good friend; he's special for you in some way.

PT-3: Yes, he is. I wish I had more friends like him. Like maybe some of the people on the job. I mean, they're okay, and some of them are real friendly and all, but they just seem kind of. . . . Oh, I don't know, just not my kind of people.

TH-3: Although the people at work are generally okay, you just don't find they're the kind you can really warm up to, eh?

PT-4: Yeah, that's right. I can't think of one of them that I'd really want to go hunting and camping with. (Pause) Except maybe that new secretary (laughs), but I guess her husband would object.

TH-4: (Smiling) Yeah, he probably would. How would your wife react to that idea?

PT-5: (Laughing) Oh, she'd have my neck, for sure. But don't get me wrong, I'm not the kind of guy who plays around. My lady is woman enough for me.

TH-5: Sure, I understand. But back to thinking of the people at work: You haven't said anything about your supervisors. How are they?

PT-6: Oh, they're okay. Bud Spencer—he's the guy I mostly report to—is a good man, knows his work and really tries to be fair to everyone.

TH-6: Spencer's okay, you say; yet some way I don't feel you're very enthusiastic about him.

PT-7: Yeah, that's right. I'm not. Nothing really wrong with him, understand, but he's just not the kind of person I can really get close to, you know.

TH-7: Why do you think that is?

PT-8: Well, to tell you the truth, I'm not sure. I just can't imagine the two of us raising a little hell together. Some way he's too uptight for my taste.

TH-8: You like someone you can cut loose with some times, and he doesn't look like the type, huh?

PT-9: That's right. Don't think I make any big trouble or anything. Just like to let down after the week's work and tie a small one on; you know what I mean?

TH-9: Not sure whether I do. Better tell me.

PT-10: Oh, you know, go down to the local pub and have a few brews with a buddy. Maybe play a little cards or talk about our cars or something like that. Just low key, you know.

TH-10: You're making the point that you're not into any big blowout, is that it?

Figure 5.1 diagrams this conversation in terms of how the partici-pants do and do not parallel each other. As we look at the lines connecting one patient response to the next and one therapist re-sponse to the next, we can see that they remain side by side through

Supervisors   Coworkers   Friends   Family Recreation

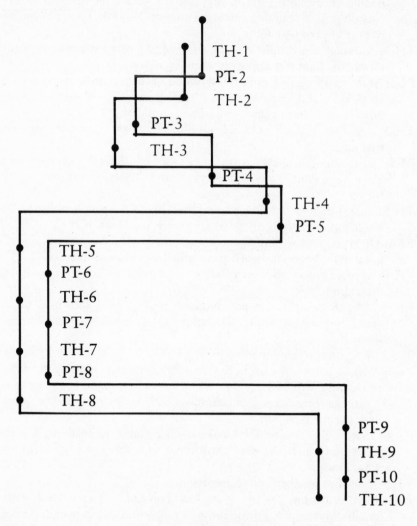

Figure 5.1.   Illustrating the Concept of Paralleling.

the first two responses of both. They are *in parallel* that far. Then the patient changes the subject from "friends" to "coworkers" (PT-3). The therapist follows to the new topic (TH-3), and so we say that she parallels the patient. Next (PT-4) the patient brings the subject back to "friends," but this time the therapist, while briefly acknowledging this, moves the focus to the patient's wife ("family," TH-4). Now the patient parallels the therapist (PT-5), but then the therapist switches attention to "supervisors" (TH-5), and they stay parallel on this topic for three responses each. Finally the patient gets onto the kind of "recreation" he likes (PT-9), and the therapist follows into this topic.

Now it is obvious that the term *paralleling* is being used to describe a range of response patterns in which only some are geometrically parallel. Just as when we speak of a vehicle's "speed" we may mean anything from crawling along at less than one mile per hour to the supersonic rates of jets, or when we say that patient presents a "trust issue" we may actually be thinking of a lack of trust, so with *paralleling* the name literally applies to only one end of the continuum but is being used for the whole of it.

Was that dialogue good therapy? I don't know, because I don't know why the patient is here, whether this is the first or the 15th or the 115th session, or a lot of other things one would need to know to make a responsible judgment. If this is the first interview with a new patient, relatively naive about therapy and anxious about being here, then it seems to be going all right, although therapist is moving in rather strongly at the end of the segment (TH-10). If this is the 15th session with a similar patient, I would note with some dismay that we are still at a contact maintenance level (see Chapter 2). In that case, my style is to not go along with the joking about the secretary and patient's wife (PT-4 and -5) in order to encourage his move into at least the standard level of engagement.

More on the Meaning of "Paralleling"

I am using the term "paralleling" to refer to how much or how little one speaker—therapist or patient—phrases the content of what he says in the same general way as has the previous speaker in the conversation. When they are talking about the same things in about the same way, we may say they are "in parallel" or "paralleling each other." When they are not so in phase, we can speak of the conversation as showing little paralleling.

As we noted above, paralleling is not a generally desirable or undesirable attribute of therapeutic interviews; it is simply a dimension which may be examined to deepen appreciation of the way the two participants are carrying out their work. At some points, it may be useful for the therapist chiefly to keep in parallel—for example, early in the work when she seeks to intrude as little as possible on the patient's own way of seeing and presenting his concerns. At other points, the therapist may want to depart markedly from being in parallel—as when the patient is caught in ruminative and resistive circling and needs help to break out.

Clearly, different conversational purposes call for different degrees of similarity, but equally clearly, it is important for the therapist to know how much she and her partner are together and how well that degree of paralleling is serving their purposes.

Patient paralleling therapist. Alert therapists may use the paralleling dimensions in two ways: (a) They modulate their own imput, as has just been illustrated, to fit the needs of the work. (b) At the same time they monitor patient participation to keep aware of increases or decreases in verbal congruence with therapist patterns. With practice both of these helpful activities can be largely delegated to one's preconscious, only entering focal awareness when a significant change is occurring or is called for.

Uses of attention to paralleling. Awareness of paralleling patterns frequently aids in sensing turning points in the conversation before they would otherwise be apparent. These early cues to the trend of the patient's participation may facilitate therapist intuition and provide hints of what may not be explicit but needs sensitive attention. For example, advance warning of patient impulses to withdraw or resist may be signaled by his reducing the parallelism of his participation. Conversely, reductions in opposition are often foreshadowed when resistant patients begin bringing their talk into greater accord with the therapist's.

Sensitive use of paralleling aids therapists in keeping a low profile while guiding the conversation in desirable directions. This is especially helpful with a deeply immersed person (at the "critical occasions" level), when one does not want to disrupt the internal focus. At such times, gentle modulation of the paralleling dimensions can give the therapeutic process greater impact while preserving patient involvement.

TOPICAL PARALLELING

The Steering Wheel of the Conversation

To the inexperienced, the explicit content of a conversation is the only element of importance. As we mature we recognize that, while content is never unimportant, it is by no means the sole aspect of significance. Meaning is the ultimate currency of communication generally and of psychotherapy particularly. Meaning calls for content, process, and purpose to be skillfully and sensitively blended to preserve the essential message.

In a rough analogy, topical paralleling in therapeutic interviews is similar to the steering wheel of an automobile: Each is a direct method of guiding where the vehicle will go. Neither the steering wheel nor the conversational content is a source of energy to take us where we want to go; both require other agencies. When we become more expert in driving we use some of these other elements—speed, brakes, the banking of the road—to increase our ability to guide effectively and smoothly. When we become more experienced as therapists we similarly use other dimensions (such as are described in this book) to effectively and smoothly guide the therapeutic enterprise. Recognizing all this, we need also to recognize the central value of the steering wheel and of topical paralleling.

This steering function can be illustrated by returning to the patient we saw at the beginning of this chapter (Segment 5.1). That segment is typical of an early phase of therapy; now we look in on the work some months later.

Segment 5.2
Patient: Harry Fordyce; Therapist: Dorothy Taylor
   (The session has been going on 20 minutes, and Harry is now deep into his recurrent feelings of anger, frustration, and desperation about his 16-year-old daughter.)
PT-11: Dorothy, I think she's going to drive me right up the goddam wall! She's so ready to trust anybody who sweet talks her. But not me. Whenever I try to talk to her, try to be reasonable, she just shuts off. I want to woodshed her, but my wife say she'll report me for child abuse if I do. Christ! What am I supposed to do? Just stand by and see her ruin her life with pot and God knows what else?

   (Now here are four possible therapist replies:)
TH-11A: You're worried terribly that she might get into real trouble or be hurt because she's so trusting, huh?

TH-11B: What else have you thought of doing? Besides whipping her, I mean.

TH-11C: In the past has she actually had bad experiences from being too trusting?

TH-11D: Have you had any trouble with your other children?

It is apparent that these four possible therapist responses are on a scale from directly paralleling (TH-11A) to radically changing the subject (TH-11D). Figure 5.2 diagrams this and shows probable effects on the conversation's direction.

Table 5.1 identifies these four levels and provides other examples from the interview excerpt at the start of the chapter (Segment 5.1).

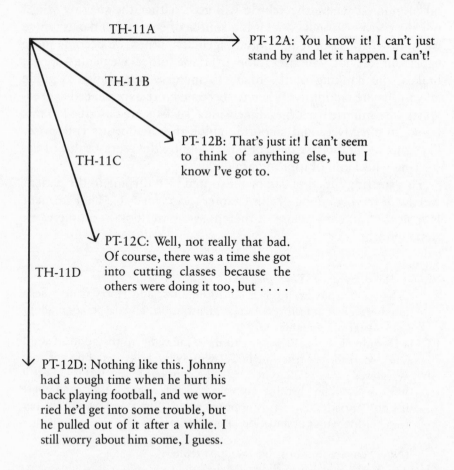

Figure 5.2.   Illustrating Four Levels of Topical Paralleling and Contrasting Possible Patient Responses to Four Different Therapist Interventions.

TABLE 5.1
Four Levels of Topical Concurrence
(Numbers refer to responses in Segment 5.1)

In parallel: TH-11A. The speaker stays in the same general topical area as that on which the previous speaker centered.
Other examples: PT (none). TH-1, -2, -3, -8, -10.

Developing: TH-11B. While the speaker stays with the general topic on which the previous speaker centered, she brings in a new element which is the logical next step in developing that topic.
Other examples: PT-2, -5, -6, -7, -8, -10. TH-6, -7, -9.

Diverging: TH-11C. Some attention is given to the topic on which the previous speaker centered, but a material change in focus or emphasis is made by the speaker. This change is likely to move the conversation to aspects not previously considered.
Other examples: PT-3, -4, -9. TH-4, 5.

Changing: TH-11D. The speaker largely ignores — or gives only perfunctory attention to — the topic on which the previous speaker centered. A significant shift in subject matter is advanced.
Other examples: None.

A caution: It is important to recognize that reading these responses with varying intonations and phrasing might change the level of any of them. Undoubtedly, the reader will see other possible placements. Indeed, it is quite arbitrary — although convenient — to recognize only four levels where there is, of course, an infinity of possibilities. These ratings are crude pointers, valuable to help us refine our sensitivity but not to be used as though they were precise or objective measurements.

Topical paralleling and the conversational levels. The patient is obviously very immersed ("critical occasions" level; PT-11), and equally obviously the four therapist responses are scaled in terms of the extent to which they would be likely to disrupt that immersion, as Figure 5.2 illustrates. In general — but certainly with significant exceptions — patient immersion is fostered by maintaining parallelism. Nevertheless, there are important — even crucial — junctures in depth psychotherapy when the therapist's responsibility is to break out of paralleling. We will discuss these matters further in later pages.

APPLICATION TO THERAPEUTIC
INTERVIEWING

The protocol which follows is a reconstruction of a typical therapeutic interview. It has been abridged to make it possible to demonstrate within a reasonable space a number of issues and procedures in
therapy. It is not ideal therapeutic work since the therapist is more
active than desirable. It does, however, provide material to which we
can refer to our further discussion of paralleling.

Segment 5.3
Patient: Darrell Benedict; Therapist: Jean Marshall
PT-1: Well, it happened again. Same damned thing.
TH-1: Mm-hmm.   [parallel]
PT-2: You remember that new woman I met that I told you about? You know
    the blonde at the library.   [developing]
TH-2: I remember.   [parallel]
PT-3: So I got up my nerve. I went up to her, made some conversation,
    finally asked her to go for coffee.   [developing]
TH-4: Uh-huh.   [parallel]
PT-4: She said okay, and we went down to the snack bar. Coffee, cake,
    cigarettes, and talk, you know. All very cozy and going well. Right?
    No, not right! Why the hell did she go with me at all? Why? Just to
    tease me along, make herself feel good, I'll bet.   [diverging]
TH-4: You're mad at her or at something or someone.   [diverging]
PT-5: Hell, yes, I'm mad. Mad at . . . well, not really at her. At myself, I
    guess. Why do I try? Why do I get my hopes up? Stupid ass dumb,
    that's why. I'm stupid ass dumb.   [changing]
TH-5: You get your hopes up, and you get hurt.   [parallel]
PT-6: That's right. That's the same old story. Over and over. I'm tired of
    hoping, tired of trying, tired of wanting a good relationship with
    someone. To hell with it all.   [diverging]
TH-6: You'd like to just give the whole thing up.   [developing]
PT-7: Yes, I would. Well, no, I really wouldn't, but I wish it would be
    different. Just once. Just once, I wish I'd find someone who
    would. . . .   [diverging]
TH-7: Someone who would. . . .   [parallel]
PT-8: (Energy drained, downcast.) I don't know. Anyway what's the use
    thinking about it? It's not going to happen. It's never going to change.
                                                           [changing]
TH-8: Feels as though it's just going to keep on the way it's been.

                                                           [changing]
PT-9: It's been three months now that I've been coming in here, and as far as
    I can see nothing's different. Don't you think we should be getting

someplace by now? [diverging]

TH-9: It feels like we're not moving, does it? [parallel]

PT-10: Yeah, sure. Why? Do you see anything changing? [diverging]

TH-10: It's your life; so it's the way you see it that matters. [diverging]

PT-11: Yeah, I know, and I don't see anything happening. [developing]

TH-11: Uh-huh. [parallel]

PT-12: Well (impatiently), anyway, what do you see? [diverging]

TH-12: I see how much you want things to start changing, and I hear how you don't think they are. [developing]

PT-13: Well, are they? (Challengingly) [developing]

TH-13: Darrell, I think when you're here in therapy you're more able to get into what matters to you. That's not having an immediate effect on the outside, so far as you can see, but it's an important step. [diverging]

PT-14: Okay, so I can get more into what matters to me, but what matters to me is that things begin changing on the outside, not just in here. [developing]

TH-14: You want *things* to change, you keep saying. What *things*? [diverging]

PT-15: Oh, you know what I mean. [changing]

TH-15: That's a cop-out, Darrell. What *do* you mean? (Forcefully) What do *you* want to change? [changing]

PT-16: Well, the way I can't seem to make any relation with a woman that lasts, the way they all like me at first and then pretty soon are too busy to see me. Like the feeling that I must have bad breath or come from Mars or some damn thing because nobody stays interested in me . . . (pause) unless . . . unless like you . . . I pay them to. [developing]

TH-16: You even have to pay me to stay with you. [parallel]

PT-17: Yeah. You know that. (Mildly resentful tone) You wouldn't see me if I didn't pay you. [parallel]

TH-17: So? [parallel]

PT-18: Well, would you? [parallel]

TH-18: I frankly don't know. That's not the situation in which we really are. If we were in a different situation, I'd have to see how I felt then. [developing]

PT-19: That's a cop-out too. [diverging]

TH-19: Yes it is, in a way. But it's also trying to get you to look at what's going on in you instead of focusing on "things" out there or on what I might or might not do. [diverging]

PT-20: You always explain away everything I say about you. [diverging]

TH-20: I know it seems that way, Darrell, but it's hard for you to look into yourself. You need again and again to focus outside of yourself, and that contributes to your feeling so powerless in your relations with others. [diverging]

PT-21: (Disgustedly) Yeah, I know. [parallel]

TH-21: Today you're feeling annoyed with me, wanting me to make things different for you, and wanting more from me than you think I'm giving you; yet it's hard for you to come out directly with those feelings.

[developing]

PT-22: Well, I'm not really mad at you.   [developing]

TH-22: Do you have to be "really mad" to feel justified in having your feelings?   [diverging]

PT-23: It seems like that's the only way I have a right to do it.   [parallel]

TH-23: That means you have to either submit to the other person or be ready to end the relation. That's a lousy pair of choices, I'd say.

[diverging]

PT-24: (Reflectively) Yeah, it sure is.   [parallel]

Therapist's Use of Topical Paralleling

In the three months in which these two people have worked together, the patient has been encouraged to take responsibility for beginning sessions promptly, without socializing, and with the expression of what is subjectively and emotionally most pressing at the moment. In today's interview, he does so with a burst of feelings which the therapist receives in a low-key, highly parallel (TH-4 and -5) manner. The therapist notes that Darrell moves quickly through what he has to say, often changing the subject, although following the same basic theme. This suggests that the content expressed so far is not the patient's true concern.

Meantime the therapist is trying to get a sense of how present and truly in touch with his concerns Darrell is. This phase actually would go on longer in most instances, although the therapist would want to protect sufficient time before the hour ends to work with the material thus brought forward in this session.

What is manifest at this point is the patient's angry, even petulant, protests, which put the locus of power in his relations outside, in other persons (especially PT-4). It is significant that he doesn't really even say what happened with the woman he met in the library. One possibility is that this omission suggests that that woman is not the one with whom the patient is most concerned (PT-5), as the therapist hints (TH-4).

Next there is a brief flurry of self-blame (PT-5 and -6) which is Darrell's substitute for actually taking responsibility for himself. This might have been worth exploring, but it is so brief that it is likely the patient is not really involved yet in examining his own part in his unhappy experiences. Note how impersonal and external is the source of the patient's distress as he tells it (PT-7 and following keep referring to "it"). The therapist chooses, by keeping in parallel (TH-5 through -8), simply to help the patient bring out his story. It is important that the patient have a sense of having been really heard before the therapist takes a more active role.

In time the patient is probably getting to the real focus of his emotional energy in this session (PT-9). It is moot whether he is conscious of wanting to reproach the therapist or whether this emerges into awareness as the interview progresses. Significantly, as this protest becomes the subject matter, he begins to be more parallel in topic. Probably the therapist is the woman about whom he wants to complain.

The therapist takes a more active role in the final portion of this segment. She uses a number of diverging responses (TH-10, -13, -14, -19, -20, -22, -23) to bring Darrell back to attention to his own feelings. These make one think of a sheepdog circling the pack to force strays back into the fold. Their effect is evident in the fact that of his 23 responses, Darrell is never in parallel until the 17th, and then four of his next seven responses are parallel. In contrast, 8 of Jean's first 11 responses parallel the patient's, but only 2 of the next 11, a clear demonstration of her greater effort to steer the conversation in ways she felt it needed to go.

Summary on Topical Paralleling

The extent to which the therapist stays with the same subject matter as that addressed by the patient and to which the patient stays with the therapist's content areas provides a useful dimension for monitoring and influencing the course of the psychotherapeutic interview. Subject matter is often the site of the conscious concern of the patient, and it must always be given therapist attention for that reason. However, additionally, the topics dealt with provide avenues for appreciating other more implicit aspects of patient subjectivity and for having an impact on those aspects.

A PSYCHOTHERAPIST'S JOURNEY

After my disappointing first course in psychology, I was fortunate in my graduate education (at George Peabody College and Ohio State University). It was chiefly offered by humane and dedicated teachers.

They cared about their students, and they were caring about human beings. Still, with few exceptions, they saw our field as concerned with objectifying that which it studied, whether white rats, college sophomores, or people. This was the way of science, the path of truth, and the vision of knowledge.

One of my first graduate courses was in statistics, that *via dolorosa* reputed to be the royal road to reality. The first lecture began with the words, "Whatever exists, exists in some number." And nobody cried out that with this dictum most of what matters in life is banished to non-existence. This was typical of the time; happily today it is increasingly being recognized as the warped fossil it truly is.

My education as a psychologist was typical of the time (1940–48). It emphasized basic psychological processes such as development, thinking, perception, learning, and memory. It included social and abnormal psychology, research methods (with an emphasis on statistics, of course), and psychological testing (only standardized measures; in the army hospital I added the new projectives—*Rorschach*, *Thematic Apperception Test*, and *Bender-Gestalt*).

A little mention of counseling occurred in the child psychology course, but I doubt if the word *psychotherapy* was ever mentioned. If so, it was something mysterious that European psychoanalysts did. Counseling was largely rational advising, directed toward aiding adjustment to life circumstances, and deliberately quite objective.

Looking back at that period, nearly a half-century ago, I find it surprising that neither I nor my teachers ever took note of the one-eyed view of ourselves which was our vision. Allusions to the inner world of experiencing certainly occurred occasionally. One professor with whom I occasionally ate in the school cafeteria once enjoined me, "Bugental, I think you should do your dissertation on how people select things in a cafeteria. It's my observation that we begin with one thing that we don't really want very much—say, a salad that, on examination, proves worn out. Then we choose the next thing to complement the salad, and that turns out to be a meat we'd usually bypass. From there it goes downhill as we keep matching new choices we don't particularly like to the tray's accumulation of things we'd rather not have." He was joking; just the idea of studying such internal choice processes was a part of the joke. How could you objectify it? Wouldn't it be hopelessly . . . (well, come on, say the terrible word) . . . subjective? What could you count? How could you compute a standard error?

Nineteenth century scientistic thinking was regnant. Objectivity was the only salvation from the sin of subjectivity, and subjectivity was a hopeless morass in which sentimentality and fantasy would destroy any hope of true knowledge being attained. A handy but quite arbitrary convention, the "Law of Parsimony" (known also as "Occam's Razor" and "Lloyd Morgan's Canon") was elevated to the status of divine edict, and that in the face of a nature profligate with variety and complexity! (Why do we need so many varieties of flowers?) The horrors of anthropomorphism — of thinking about our subjects as though they were human — were a favorite sermon topic of senior psychologists addressing neophytes.

It is understandable, of course, that the vision of science which had accomplished such wonders within the lifetimes of our teachers should seem revealed truth to them. It still has its hold on me at times. Within my own life, I have seen so many world-changing manifestations of the power of that kind of science: the general use of automobiles, radio, telephone, electric lights, television, aircraft, electric refrigeration, sound and sight recording, and space exploration. The discovery of DNA, the splitting of the atom, the conquering of infantile paralysis (polio), the general use of computers, and the development of the hologram are only some of the more apparent products of this potent influence.

My doctoral dissertation[1] involved examining several thousand thought-units in verbatim psychotherapy protocols to determine the attitudes explicitly directed toward the self and the not-self and their interrelations. Later I published two further papers extending this "explicit analysis" method, which I proposed as a way of objectively exploring the inner experience of those whose protocols I analyzed. All three investigations were replete with statistical embellishments. Looking back now on these studies, I am aware of how much I was trying to use the prevailing notion of science to get at that "something more" and how naively I assumed the explicit could sufficiently plumb those depths.

Topical parallelIng, as this chapter has presented it, is a direct descendent of those explicit analysis efforts. It is indeed a helpful tool, but it only leads us to the threshold of the subjective. Other vehicles and our irreplaceable intuition are the means for venturing more deeply.

CHAPTER 6

Feeling
Paralleling

Talking together we seek to attend to and convey what is mean-
ingful. It is not sufficient to know only the topics dealt with; we
need and have a variety of resources on which we can draw to
distinguish the significant, to express attitudes, to clarify impli-
cations, and to do all the other needed tasks of therapeutic inter-
viewing. One such resource, particularly important in therapy,
centers on the amount of attention given to the client's feelings
and emotions.

Listening to the client, the therapist must make a rapid deci-
sion as to how to reply. He chooses how much to deal with the
same subject matter and whether to emphasize what is already
on the table about the client feelings—these being but two of
many considerations to be instantly assessed. This quick and
largely intuitive (and preconscious) process is aided by his having
developed a subliminal capacity to note what has been happen-
ing up to this point in terms of the degree to which he and his
partner are following parallel patterns in these important dimen-
sions. While by no means is it always desirable to do so, by all
means it is desirable to be aware of what has been occurring and
what options are available at this point.

In this chapter, I describe the values in giving the same, more,
or less emphasis to client feelings than she herself has given to
them.

WE START WITH A CLIENT'S self-description, which occurs about
midway through an initial interview. Then we will imagine a carica-
ture of how the therapist might respond to her.

Segment 6.1
CL-1: I've been so lucky—in my job right now, at least—in finding a job in
which I can do just about whatever I want. The man I work for now
and I see things the same way, and I do really enjoy that. I've worked
for other people before, and there aren't very many like this man. . . .

110

TH-1: (Interrupting) What's the name of the company you're working for?

CL-2: Huh? Oh, uh, Jones & Bloom Engineering. But I work for Don Davis. He's old Mr. Bloom's son-in-law, and he's very smart. He doesn't have to be related to the owner to hold the job. Why, it's gotten so customers call up and ask for Don instead of one of the senior partners. Isn't that something?

TH-2: Yeah. How long have you worked for them?

CL-3: Oh, about 2 1/2 years. Let's see, I started the fall after I graduated so . . .

What's wrong with this scene? Well, a lot of things. First of all, why have a clinician there at all? A clerk or a paper-and-pen question-naire could do everything that this supposed therapist is doing and could do it a lot cheaper. If this question-asker wants to find out anything but simple facts about this client, he had better start listen-ing more and giving more response. In other words, there is a need for attention to feeling paralleling—both in terms of observing the client and in terms of drawing her out. (The excuse that the clinician is testing out the client's motivation not only is founded on a nonsen-sical notion of how to understand a human being but is blind to the damage being done to the development of a true therapeutic alli-ance.)

THE PLACE OF EMOTIONS

The Interplay of Feelings and Ideas

In something of an oversimplification, we can recognize that what-ever a person says has both feelingful (affective) and ideational (cog-nitive) aspects. The relative amount of each will vary widely, of course, but neither will ever be totally absent. Figure 6.1 illustrates this conception.

The effort to be totally without affect usually reduces us to dry facts, "Today is the eighth of March." Even for this cryptic announce-ment, intonations, gestures, and facial expressions may suggest the apparently missing feelings: "Oh, good lord, look how much of the year is gone already!" or "Thank heavens, I've still got two weeks before the deadline." Similarly, it is difficult to conceive a purely feelingful statement. "Ouch!" conveys little beyond the message that the speaker is having some painful surprise. Still that's quite different from "Yippie!"

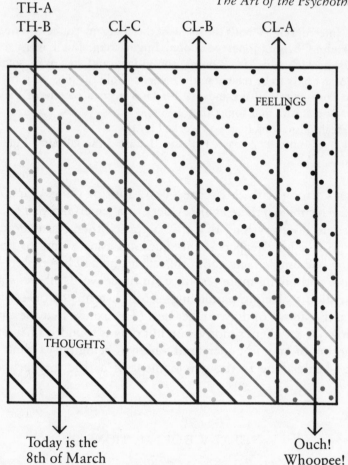

Figure 6.1.   Thoughts and Feelings Are Both Present in Each Thing a Person Says.

Values in Feeling Paralleling

Being in parallel in feelings means that one speaker gives about as much attention to the *client's* affect as did the preceding speaker. Two things are important about this definition: It is the client's feelings with which this dimension is concerned, and the comparison is always — as it is for all paralleling forms — with the immediately previous response.

A clinician proceeding as in our caricatured interview above seems not to know that a first step to understanding or influencing someone is to show responsiveness to that person's affectivity. The top of Figure 6.1 shows how therapist emphasis on the factual-ideational (TH-A and -B above) can cause the client to reduce expressiveness (and often to become more self-conscious). The three client responses (CL-A, -B, -C) move from being strongly expressive of the client's subjectivity (at the right) to cool impersonality (at the left).

When I am talking with someone and trying to understand her genuinely, I tune my awareness to take note of what affects her emotionally—either as she reports it or as it is demonstrated in our immediate interaction. I watch how she adapts to our talking: Is she restless, engrossed, observing me intently, unaware of me, seeking approval, defiant? I listen when she tells of her experiences and her thoughts: What turns her on or off, what does she hope for, what dread? What sorts of people has she drawn into her life and how do they accord with her conscious values?

In all of this, I attend to what she says, of course, but also to how she says it. Words pointing to feelings—"lot of fun," "really hated that," "the damn situation was a loser," "dream of a guy"—provide a dimension to be set beside facial expressions, gestures, body language, tears and laughter, incomplete thoughts, and the many other subtle and obvious clues to that mysterious and important inner world of the client's experiencing.

Emotions and Psychotherapy

Emotions in psychotherapy are similar to blood in surgery: Both are inevitable as the work goes forward: both importantly serve a cleansing function and foster healing; both must be respected and dealt with by the professional, and *neither is the point of the procedure.*[1]

Our American, middle-class culture—especially the men in it—has an ambivalent relation with its emotional dimension. Suspect as in some way feminine or "soft," emotions are often avoided, curtailed, or denied. Other people, often in an inverted reaction to the first group (their parents?), have celebrated and intensified feeling states, even seeking chemical amplifiers. Currently a swing back toward restraint is apparently occurring (among the children of the children?).

Psychotherapists are by no means exempt from the swings of fashion. We know emotions are important—indeed, the question "What do you feel?" has become so stereotypic that it is embarrassing and losing its value.[2] Yet we often fail to relate emotions to other parts of our efforts. We try to elicit emotions as though that were a good thing in itself, but then we go on to try to "solve the problem," seeking some cognitive formulation of the history of client's concern and expecting that that formulation will in some way relieve the symptoms which are presented.

With most people it is relatively easy to elicit emotions. Most, if not all, adults have at least some stored up feelings of pain, disappointment, loneliness, self-blame, and existential anxiety which can be tapped into with a modicum of kindness and persistence. The question that is too seldom asked is: When those emotions are brought forward, what is then to be done?

I said above that emotions are importantly part of the process but are not its purpose. That purpose is, I believe, to increase living awareness — in plain words, the consciousness of one's own being, one's own powers and choices, and one's own limits.[3] In the pursuit of that increase we must help our clients become aware of how they are constricting their lives and their awareness and of the possibilities that are latent for them. That process of becoming aware is inevitably guided and accompanied by strong feelings of fear, pain, guilt, remorse, hope, apprehension, and fulfillment.

Monitoring a client's feelingful attitudes toward her own life and toward the therapeutic process will yield clear indications of areas needing inquiry, perceptual structures supporting or impeding growth, and motivational resources that can be tapped in time of stress. Therapist use of more or less attention to client affectivity does much to modulate the emotional flow, keeping it optimally motivating, and helping the client avoid becoming lost in emotion for its own sake.

Using Attention to Feelings

People vary in how readily they talk about and show their emotions. Some stick to the idea dimensions and avoid any "emotional display." Others seem always to swim in their feelings. The therapist's job is to help his partner to express genuine feelings as they are pertinent to the life concerns which motivate therapy.

In developing the therapeutic enterprise, it is well to start a new relation by giving about as much attention to a client's feelings as she does. In this way, the therapist gains an appreciation for the subjective style of the client and how able she is to express genuine concerns fully. Depending on how the therapist then assesses the client's readiness, he may introduce more reference to emotions into his own comments and pick up more directly on any feelingful elements in the client's talk. These steps will often help the other person to bring more of the subjective and feelingful into the work. Sometimes it is desirable to give chief — or even sole — attention to whatever affect is presented. The following sample dialogue illustrates these points.

Segment 6.2
Client: Cindy Blue; Therapist: Bob Maxwell

CL-1: I've been thinking maybe I'd be better off in a different line of work. But, you know, the job market today doesn't make it too smart to go jumping around much.

TH-1: You'd really like to be happier in your work, but . . .

[feeling emphasis]

(Therapist is putting chief emphasis on the feeling and giving the other elements — changing type of work, job market — no explicit attention. By leaving the sentence unfinished, he strengthens the pull on the client to carry the matter forward. The client is likely to respond with more emotional content.)

CL-2: Yes, I would. I mean, my job's okay and all, but it just doesn't satisfy me. After four months I knew all there was to it, and now it's just the same old grind every day.   [parallel]

TH-2: It's okay in some ways, but in others it's dull, repetitious.   [parallel]

CL-3: That's it. Ugh! I get restless and bored a lot these days. I'd like to find something else that had a little more life in it. I mean, sometimes I think I'll just give it all up there.   [feeling emphasis]

(By choosing not to parallel the client's balancing of ideas and feelings (CL-2) but to put a clear lead toward the emotional side, the therapist helps bring out how truly fed up Cindy is becoming. This can be the opening to deeper issues of impulse control or alienated self-perceptions. In any case, therapist and client are solidifying their alliance and getting ready to work more effectively.)

Emotional Extremes

Some clients present a different kind of problem: They seem to flood the scene with their emotions, and the therapist may have difficulty discerning the sources and significances of these outpourings. As a general guide, it is well to distinguish which of three possible patterns is being presented in such instances.

Situational explosions derive from some current incident which has provoked the emotional discharge. Betty comes in complaining about being bawled out by her boss. She's mad; she needs to blow off some of her anger, and then she'll be able to settle down and think about the incident and its possible relation to other issues being worked on in therapy.

A *lifestyle* of continual emotional display is sometimes encountered. Roy needs little provocation to launch into affective fireworks. Today it's the thoughtlessness of his office mate, the high prices in restaurants, and the traffic that held him up coming here. At his last session it was the draftiness of his apartment, the staleness of his lunch sandwich, and the smog. The biggest task with Roy is to get beneath this crust of affective sludge and to find what really matters to him. Roy doesn't know, and indeed his continual emotionality is probably unconsciously designed to keep himself and his therapist from finding out.

Deeper psychopathology may lie behind a third form of emotional flooding. With these clients, it soon becomes evident that the emotions are not so much situation-linked as derived from inner promptings and probable autistic associations. Poor ego boundaries and unworked-through dependency seekings combine with deep feelings of unworthiness and isolation to elicit moods and emotions which ill accord with external circumstances.

Client Paralleling Therapist

Our attention thus far has been on how the therapist chooses to remain in parallel or depart from it in responding to his partner. It is also important to be aware similarly of the extent to which the client parallels the therapist in dealing with her own feelings. Here are three different responses to the same therapist reflection. Note how they vary in their feeling paralleling.

Segment 6.2 (continued)
TH-5: As you talk about your dissatisfaction in your work, I hear a kind of angry note as well as your boredom.
CL-5A: (Heatedly) You're right! I'm damned angry. I've told the boss I didn't like what he was assigning me. I said it in his office, and I've said it when we all get together for a meeting. And what's happened? Not a single thing. Not one lousy thing.   [feeling emphasis]
CL-5B: Yeah, I suppose so. I'm mostly just fed up, but I guess there's some anger too when I think of how long I've been trying to get a change, and nothing's different.   [parallel]
CL-5C: (Plaintively) Well, is it wrong to feel sad—or even angry—when

you're in a bad situation and you've done what you can to get it
changed and nothing works? I mean what else can I do?

[idea emphasis]

The second response (CL-5B) parallels therapist's in giving some
attention to client feelings but also bringing in reasons with equal
emphasis. Notice that the first response (CL-5A) also brought in
reasons but they were accorded much less energy. In contrast, the last
response (CL-5C) acknowledges feelings but gives more effort to jus-
tification than to expression.

Patterns such as these, occurring repeatedly, are the stuff from
which hypotheses may be formed about the client's ways of being in
her life and about what is important to her. It is manifestly foolhardy
to hypothesize from a single response; accumulating information,
however, prepares for the emergence of dependable estimates.

Values in attending to client paralleling. To illustrate the value of
attending to client paralleling, contrast CL-5A and CL-5C: In the first
it is evident that she only needs the implicit "permission" of the
therapist's response to burst out with what she feels is justified indig-
nation. Very differently, CL-5C suggests someone who feels she must
prove her right to her feelings and is building a case. The latter
individual may well prove to be a blame-preoccupied person who
hesitates to assert her inner experience directly and self-responsibly.
(In illustrating these hunches that might emerge from oft-repeated
patterns, I've just violated my own rule about waiting before hypothe-
sizing!)

Reflection

Our feelings about our feelings are often cues to important matters
about our lives: how well we fit into our lives, how we experience
ourselves, and how we relate with others. Emotions and all their
attendant expressions — moods, desires, anxieties, hopes, fears, affec-
tions, antagonisms — color our outlooks on life. They derive from our
experiences, assuredly, but equally they determine our experiences.
The expectations which so influence our perceptions are themselves
strongly colored by our emotional histories and anticipations. And
ultimately, our emotions contain us beyond escape, a point often
overlooked by those who seek to be unemotional and rational about
all matters. This intention to be without feelings paradoxically re-

veals how such people *feel* they will *feel* better and how powerful that *feeling* is!

A PSYCHOTHERAPIST'S JOURNEY

In earlier years, I moved from trying to maintain "objectivity" in my life and in professional conversations to prizing feelingful discharges by those with whom I worked — and even, at times, on my own part. I've come now to believe that neither extreme is to be valued for itself. In private life and professional life, purpose and meaning are the criteria which alone can identify what sorts of conversational activity are desirable. It is easy to enforce a deadpan unemotionality (on the outside), and it is not much harder — with most conversational partners — to evoke feelingful discharge. The challenge for all of us is to gain such a footing within ourselves (and to aid our conversational partners to it) so that we can get in touch with and usefully express the kinds and amounts of emotion most likely to further our own and our partners' reasons for talking.

An interesting subject for a doctoral dissertation — if it hasn't already been done — would be a history of humankind's attitudes toward our human feelings and emotions. I'm not sure whether that thesis belongs in mysticism, psychology, sociology, anthropology, biology, ethics, sexology, or perhaps chemistry or sorcery. Certainly within psychology there has been a wide range of viewpoints, from an introductory psychology textbook that captioned one chapter, "Emotions: Disorganized Responses" (!) to the academic version of the motto of the '60s: "If it feels good, do it."

From the vantage point of my years, my own course in regard to the affective dimension of life has been notably erratic. When quite young, I — as did so many of my peers — took my models from the movies. One actor whom I much admired is now scarcely ever recalled, Clive Brook. A splendid English gentleman, he was totally unflappable. The butler might come to tell him, "Sir, your wife has run away with the greengrocer; the mortgage on your estate has been foreclosed; the major powers have just started a nuclear exchange; and the dressing gown you're wearing has just caught fire." To all of this Brook would turn a slightly bored face, and while he meticulously placed the fingertips of his left hand against the fingertips of the right hand, he would say, "Very good, Jarvis. Please bring me *The Times*."

It was only some years later when I was making my first visits to mental hospitals that I actually saw people who were as unflappable as those Clive Brook portrayed. They were called "schizophrenic."

As I began to do counseling and move toward psychotherapy, I found a sense of power and a conviction of having a means for healing when I helped my clients get into their feelings. Despite my misadventure with Pfc. Jones and as have so many, I became converted to the belief that catharsis was the key to emotional and mental health. The therapeutic task, it seemed obvious, was to get to the suppressed emotions and to encourage their discharge. Pfc. Jones certainly did have some effect and doubtlessly began the process of my disillusionment. Still, when the '60s and early '70s brought in the heyday of encounter groups, it was easy to slide back into a modified form of the catharsis mode: It is not just that emotional release is desirable; it is important that that release occur in the presence of a number of others who warmly welcome it and who, in their turns, go through similar experiences.

Well, there is a limited truth to all of this, but how limited it is took another decade to fully appreciate. I wonder how accurately I see it now. It is likely that I'm only at another way station on the long road to eternal evolution.

As I now see it, emotions constitute an obvious and accessible route to subjectivity. Our feelings so clearly arise from depths not readily plumbed by rationality, objective measures, or deliberate intent. They evidence churnings and strivings which we can only incompletely verbalize or explain, even to ourselves. So the familiar, the stereotypic therapist question, "What do you feel?" is certainly on the right track. The difficulties are that it has been overused and that those who use it have sometimes mistaken the gateway for the whole realm which lies behind it.

What is that realm? In these pages I've tried in various ways to name it, to identify it, to point to it. It's as though I am forced to point, not with my index finger's precision, but with the blunt vagueness of my left elbow—or even of my right buttock.

Subjectivity, the unconscious, our deepest center—these are some of the word pointers, but what they stretch toward far eludes them. ("The finger pointing at the moon is not the moon."[4]) Still, there is enough commonality among these and other terms and concepts that I feel I'm getting a better fix on what it is I seek.

As a psychotherapist, I have been drawn to work which is long-term, which is concerned with the inner lives of my clients, which seeks to explore the nature of our being as humans, which has the potential for arousing the sleeping possibilities we all — one and all — sense within us, and which can, at times, bring about truly major life changes. This the work which has to do with that realm toward which I seek.

Over the years I have acquired many aids to that search. And I have left beside the road many of those I acquired. Standardized tests, projective techniques, hypnosis, empty chair enactments, role-playing, guided fantasies, psychoactive substances — all useful, some occasionally used by me still, all limiting even as they were facilitating. They offered, each in its own way, intriguing, even valuable, glimpses of the people with whom I worked. Ultimately though, they made those persons into objects — objects of my study, objects of investigation, objects of the techniques themselves.

I have come to believe that all of these aids to the quest for the true subjectivity are as still photographs of wild animals — or at their best, like seeing those animals in a zoo. They show the quarry but without the animating spirit, the action which is its most central, most meaningful characteristic.

I have come to believe that only with a truly subjectively centered and highly motivated companion can my quest go forward validly and as fully as I am capable of at this time.

CHAPTER 7

Frame
Paralleling

Familiar expressions in everyday and in therapeutic conversations: "Let's get down to brass tacks," and "What's the big picture?" We all know the importance of the dimension which I'm here calling "frame paralleling." It is a frequent practice of therapists to call on their clients to be more concrete, and almost as often—but more implicitly—they encourage those same clients to generalize from their experiences.

We frame our thoughts and words in many ways, but one that has particular significance for life-change work is in terms of our ability to move from the immediate to the general, from the abstract to applications. Clients describe repetitive experiences and somehow never seem to draw the line under them to see what they add up to . Other clients present such broad brush descriptions that their therapists are left unsure just what it all means in living terms.

Frame paralleling is a way of reminding ourselves of the importance of monitoring this dimension. We will demonstrate its obvious merits, speak of some of its implications, and then show how it may be used when the therapist suspects that the client is consciously or unconsciously deceptive.

IMAGINE YOURSELF in this scene:

It's a fine fall afternoon. The Saturday morning chores are finished—as much as they're going to be. Far away your favorite team is playing its archrival in the big game of the year, and TV is offering to take you there. You have laid in supplies of peanuts and beer/soda so that now you can climb into your favorite easy chair, tell nonparticipating members of the family the dark disaster that awaits anyone intruding, adjust the cushion, and. . . . Ahhh, good!

Turn on the set. You're just in time; the last commercial for at least two-and-a-half minutes is fading, and there's a good view of the stadium from high up on the shady side. You see the opposite stands, and the whole field spread out below with little figures busy with pregame preparations. Excitement, anticipation, in the stadium in your living-room.

Now the teams get set. Your team is kicking: a long line of little figures with one separate, obviously the kicker. The other little figures scattered to receive. Then your little figures go into action and the others respond. The two clusters of little figures begin to merge, and . . . !

"Little figures?!" You realize the screen is still showing the same nice big shot of the opposite stands and the full field. To be sure, those miniatures down on the field are squirming around and doing things, but it's hard to tell what—even though the announcer is trying to do so.

And so it goes. Or so it goes for 10 minutes or so before—beer flat, peanuts too salty—you turn it off in disgust. No change in the frame on the tube—always the big picture. Pfuii!

Well, then try this on for size:

Same day, same big game, same getting ready—chair, drinks, pea-nuts, anticipation. Same TV set tuned in just at starting time. But there's a difference: As the picture comes in you have a tight closeup of a football. Suddenly a boot swoops through, and you follow the ball as it twists in the air—the stands a blur in back. Abruptly two hands grab the ball and pull it close to a sweaty jersey. It jolts up and down briefly and then is lost in a welter of arms, legs, and other bits of anatomy.

Thus it continues—all tight, telephoto closeups. Ten minutes is probably too long for you to hold out before you shut this fiasco down.

So what's amiss? Quite simply, two efforts to bring you the game failed as communications of what was going on. And they failed because they did not vary the frame within which the action was being transmitted, so you could not follow that action *meaningfully*. That's the point: Faithful relaying of objective actions, gross or min-ute, is not sufficient to evoke meaning.

What is needed to bring the game to you satisfyingly is a zoom lens used with sensitivity for meaning. Then there would be an early, wide-angle shot of the stands and field, followed by a medium frame on the ball and the kicker, backing off to show the movement down the field, coming in close for the catch, backing a bit to reveal the tacklers moving in, close up again for the tackle, and so on. The game would be brought to you—or you to it—in an involving, satisfy-ing, meaning-filled fashion. Indeed, your chair in your livingroom a thousand miles from the stadium would have a better view of the action than would a box seat on the 50-yard line.

FRAME PARALLELING, THE ZOOM LENS

The process of attending to the frame within which something is said provides conversations with a zoom lens. Just as the TV communication of a football game is made more effective through use of that optical device, so our talking together gains immeasurably from skillful modulation of the generality or specificity with which a topic is addressed. Some therapists are too little aware of this powerful aid to their work. Old conversational habits cause them to overdepend on wide-angle generalities or on detail-preoccupied telephoto approaches. Of course, many therapists operate chiefly in the intermediate ranges, a practice which has the merit of giving some balance, but they are likely to miss the perspectives that a well-selected broad view can provide or the power that close-in details can offer.

Putting the Zoom Lens to Work

Virtuoso psychotherapists know the frame paralleling dimension as a facile instrument to their purposes. Some examples of familiar clinical situations in which its use is particularly indicated:

- Amplifying understanding of a client's "complaint" by calling for its setting and background or by pressing for concrete instances.
- Fostering greater emotional involvement by encouraging the client to relate in great detail experiences which are emotionally charged but which he is keeping abstract.
- Exploring blockings or resistances by encouraging the client to get more familiar with the stoppage rather than trying to push past it.
- Examining a significant life event to learn more about its personal and less conscious significance.
- Making certain that suggestions or instructions to the client for use either in the hour or on the outside are truly understood and that there is motivation to follow through.
- Inquiring into matters about which the client may, consciously or not, have impulses to conceal or distort information

In each of these instances, the therapist is well advised to frame the content at several levels of generality or specificity, not being content with any single frame. In each also, the assumption is implicit that there is latent in the client more information or other subjective material (e.g., attitude, emotions, unconscious associations) than will be presented in any single response. The zoom lens effect of shifting frames will aid the client in accessing that material and bringing it out.

Segment 7.1
Client: Darrell Benedict; Therapist: Jean Marshall
CL-31: I've been having these worries for months now, and I've just got to find some relief. It's really getting too much for me to take.
TH-31: You're feeling just too burdened with the worries that go on and on, eh? [parallel]
CL-32: Yeah, they just seem to be running me down, never giving me any peace. [parallel]
TH-32A: Tell me more about these thoughts that won't let you alone. [narrowing]
CL-33A: Just sort of anxious, worrying thoughts. I feel as though something bad's going to happen to me . . . or maybe already has. [narrowing]
TH-33A: What sort of thing? [narrowing]
CL-34A: Oh, like, uh (pause), . . . like maybe I've got cancer of some awful disease—like AIDS or something—or maybe I'll lose my job or get in a wreck or something. [narrowing]
(Note: These few exchanges would very likely be part of a series at least ten times as long in an actual session. They are pulled out here to illustrate the skeleton of the development of this complaint.)

As is often useful, the therapist begins by remaining parallel with the client (TH-31A). Then gently (TH-32A), she draws the frame in a bit to encourage a reduction from the vague, general level of CL-31. In the next response (TH-33A), she narrows the frame even more markedly, seeking more on the troubling thoughts. A product of this is the reference to "AIDS," suggesting another possible line for inquiry.

Enlarging the frame. Sometimes the task is aided by opening the frame so that a wider picture displays connections that might otherwise not be seen. We can illustrate this by using the same first few responses but then having the therapist broaden (at TH-32B).

Segment 7.1B
CL-31: I've been having these worries for months now, and I've just got to find some relief. It's really getting too much for me to take.

TH-31: You're feeling just too burdened with the worries that go on and on, eh? [parallel]

CL-32: Yes, they just seem to be running me down, never giving me any peace. [parallel]

TH-32B: What have you thought about this situation, about these thoughts and worries and all that's plaguing you now? [broadening]

CL-33B: Oh, I don't know. (Considers) I think they started around last Thanksgiving, but I'm not sure. [narrowing]

TH-33B: Can you recall what else what going on in your life at about that time? [broadening]

CL-34B: Nothing unusual that I can think of. No, I don't think so. [parallel]

TH-34B: Not so fast, Darrell. Give yourself a little more time. How were things for you last fall and into the winter? How was your Thanksgiving? What can you recall in any way? [broadening]

CL-35B: (After a brief pause) No, nothing, nothing special. We spent Thanksgiving with my wife's parents, and it was all very nice, . . . I suppose. And then at Christmas, we had company, my brother and his family, and. . . . No, it was all pretty routine. [narrowing]

Once again therapist begins with a period of parallelling (TH-31), but then moves to open the frame by asking about the client's thoughts in a very general way (TH-32B). The reply (CL-33B) is vague, but operating on the hunch that whatever the client offers at a point such as this is apt to have unconscious roots that make it worth exploring, the theraist again provides a broad frame (TH-33B). The client's response (CL:34B) is manifestly a deadend. Wisely, the therapist notes the lack of motivated inner inquiry and encourages the client to take another look (TH-34B). That yields more detail and several leads which may be worth following (possible in-law tensions—note that "I suppose").

In any conversation directed toward deepening understanding of a person's experience, the framing dimension provides a powerful and evocative tool. This tool serves not only therapist but client as well, often aiding him to come to richer understanding of his own internal meanings.

(A reminder: *Due to the condensation of many exchanges into three or four responses from each partner, our examples above have the difficulty of seeming to suggest that therapists are looking for clues in the manner of a detective in a whodunit. In my opinion that is not the best mode for psychotherapy; instead I believe we should be fostering client self-exploration and discovery.*

Example of Using Framing to Foster Inner Searching

Segment 7.2[1]
Client: Hal Steinman; Therapist: James Bugental

> (The following excerpt portrays a session occurring after some months of work to help a client become more aware of his resistance to inner exploration. This is not the culminating point of this effort, but it is a milestone. The client is a research psychologist who values objectivity greatly and finds it difficult to follow the therapist's guidance toward greater introspection. He comes to therapy because of repeated episodes of losing his temper with his teenaged son.)

TH-1: What are you thinking just now?

CL-1: Oh, I . . . I was just wondering if you were going to say something to me.   [narrowing]

TH-2: No, I'd just like to know what your concerns within yourself are.
                                                                    [parallel]

CL-2: Well, I worry a lot about Alice. She's dating this new guy a lot now, and I have a hunch she's not a virgin anymore. I mean, I'm not a prudish father and all that, but I hope she knows how to take care of herself. I feel like I ought to do something, but I don't know what. She just seems to go her own way. I asked June if she'd given Alice all the information, you know, and June said Alice probably could teach her things. I guess there's not much you can do when a girl is nearly 19, and yet you kind of feel you ought to. . . .   [narrowing]

TH-3: Hal, you're talking about a "you" who would worry. Is it hard to say these things in the first person? (Some way I suspect that Hal has come prepared with this "concern about Alice," and thus it sounds impersonal and distant.)   [parallel]

CL-3: Oh, yeah. No, it's not hard to say in the first person. I worry a lot about Alice. She's a really good kid, and I wouldn't want her hurt. See? First person.   [narrowing]

TH-4: Right. Tell me about how you worry, Hal. Can you just sort of do it out loud and let me listen in?   [broadening]

CL-4: Okay. Well, I just think she's such a good girl, and really she is so young, you know. And I'd hate for her to get hurt in any way. And uh . . . she's got a good figure; I imagine all the guys are wanting to get to her. I guess that's about it. That's what I think inside. [parallel]

TH-5: Hal, it sounds like you are beginning to get more in touch with what's going on inside, but I imagine there's a great deal more. For example, I wonder if you had any thoughts about how you had raised her, what you'd taught her about sex, how free she might feel to talk to you if she were concerned, what she might be like as a sexual woman, what you might do to someone who did hurt her, and so on and on.   [broadening]

CL-5: Oh, yeah, sure all those things. I do think about all those things. I really think she knows she can talk to us anytime about anything. And of course, I would really want to get anybody who hurt her.

[narrowing]

TH-6: Hal, we're still missing something, although I think we're getting closer. Each of those ideas I suggested might lead you into a whole chapter of thoughts and feelings. Those were like the chapter headings. Each has a whole lot of ideas and feelings that belong with it. Just now you picked up two of them like they were questions and gave them quick answers. That's only the beginning, not the end, of exploring your concerns.

[broadening]

CL-6: Jim, I know you're trying to help me, but I just don't think I'm the introspective type. I mean, you analytic guys go squirreling around in all that kind of stuff, and I suppose with some people it does a lot of good. But I don't know; for me I'm not sure it's the thing. I need to deal with the problem more straight on.

[narrowing]

TH-7: What problem are you thinking of when you say that? [narrowing]

CL-7: Well, just any one. [broadening]

TH-8: No, pick one. What problem is it that you want to deal with more straight on? (Insistently. I'm challenged; face it.) [narrowing]

CL-8: Oh, like how I still can't really keep cool when I talk with Tim. I know it's been a little better lately, but I expect it'll blow wide open any day now. Nothing's really changed. [parallel]

TH-9: Okay, so say what the problem is there. [narrowing]

CL-9: Uh, well. I can see where you're headed. The problem is me, and you know it damn well. And so do I. Why can't I keep my cool? [narrowing]

TH-10: Okay, so what's your answer? Why can't you keep your cool when you talk with Tim? [parallel]

CL-10: Oh, shit, Jim, I don't know. [parallel]

TH-11: What's the head-on way of tackling that problem? (Rubbing it in.)

[narrowing]

CL-11: Finding out the reason I keep blowing my stack and changing it.

[parallel]

TH-12: How do you do that? [narrowing]

CL-12: Try to figure it out. Try to apply reason. [parallel]

TH-13: Okay, let's do it. Figure it out, apply reason right now. Let me listen in. [narrowing]

CL-13: Oh, you know it won't work, and so do I. I've tried a thousand times. I just don't get anywhere. (Chuckle) I sure teed you off though. [broadening]

TH-14: Yes, you did. I think it's another example of how you avoid recognizing something you don't do well and yet need to do and do now. [narrowing]

CL-14: Hey! You know? I can kind of get a sense of that. I mean I know I really wanted to get away from that feeling of being up a blind alley.

[parallel]

This passage is marked by my persistence in holding the client to confront the failure of his former overdependence on rationality. This was accomplished by setting the task in TH-4, -5, and -6. These three uses of a broad frame (and the rationalistic challenge implied in them) then became a reference point for a long series of narrowing responses (seven of the next eight). Again we see the "sheep-dogging" function. Notably, a part of this protocol is the continual forward thrust of the work, evidenced by 12 of the client's 14 responses and 8 of the therapist's 13 being at the "developing" level in the topical paralleling. That level often portrays a good working relationship (in contrast to protocols in which there is a great deal of diverging and changing).

Inquiry Into Withheld Material

Generally therapy clients are consciously motivated to disclose whatever information about themselves is called for. However, there are always some exceptions, whether the client is aware of them or not. These withheld materials usually have to do with topics about which the client is uncomfortable, embarrassed, or ashamed — anger and hostility, sexual impulses and actions, financial details, religious and spiritual convictions, difficulties with the law. Almost always, such client discomfort signals a realm of emotional and subjective importance.

Deal With the Resistance, Not the Impulse

Here is a point at which the experienced therapist is clearly distinguishable from her less practiced colleague: Put most succinctly, the lesson is this: Concentrate on the resistance to full disclosure, not on that which it holds back.

The need to withhold marks an area of content which often intrigues the neophyte therapist and which may be attacked by Draconian methods (e.g., hypnosis). Much that might be learned about the client's psychological makeup is lost in such efforts. It is almost always wiser to deal with the need to withhold than to try to circumvent it to get at the material behind it.

When the need to withhold has been well investigated, the material which was hidden often comes forward readily (and often proves disappointing to the therapist's voyeurism). More importantly, when this roadblock has been resolved, other areas which might never have been noted (because they were held back less consciously by the client) emerge into consciousness and can be brought into the therapeutic arena.

Thus, there is good reason to bring the process of withholding forward into consciousness. The frame paralleling dimension is helpful in this. Therapist may approach the loaded area with a series of steps moving from the very general to more specific, meantime keeping alert to cues of a nonverbal nature. Here is an abridged illustration of this process:

Segment 7.3
Patient: Harry Fordyce; Therapist: Dorothy Taylor
TH-31: You've had quite a number of different jobs since you left school.
CL-31: Yeah, had a bunch of bad breaks. Couldn't find something that suited me.   [parallel]
TH-32: What sort of "bad breaks"?   [narrowing]
CL-32: Oh, you know, the usual thing. Just some places that were not my type.   [broadening]
TH-33: I'm not sure I understand how you mean, "not your type"?[parallel]
CL-33: Well, the kinds of people or the kinds of work just didn't fit me very well. You know how that is.   [narrowing]
TH-34: That's still not very clear. Can you give me an example?[narrowing]
CL-34: Oh, sure, like the job I had last year at the fairgrounds. I really thought that would be a good one, but the boss was a wino who didn't really know what he was doing and who always was cussing everybody out for not doing the right things or enough work or something. Damn, he was a loss, believe me!   [narrowing]
TH-35: How did you leave there?   [narrowing]
CL-35: What do you mean? I just had had enough and got out of that situation. Believe me, it was bad news.   [broadening]
TH-36: Harry, level with me, have you ever been fired from a job?
                                                               [narrowing]
CL-36: I've never had to leave a job I wanted to keep.   [broadening]
TH-37: You still aren't saying you've never been fired.   [narrowing]
CL-37: I'm saying that a lot of different things go into whether or not a particular job is satisfying to me and whether I'm the man the boss wants. I have my own ideas of what kind of place I want to work in.   [broadening]
TH-38: I can understand that, but it doesn't answer the question I asked. It must be hard for you to give me a straight answer about whether you've been fired from any job.   [narrowing]
CL-38: No, it's not hard. I just don't see the point of it. (Pause) So okay, yeah, I've been fired twice from lousy jobs that I didn't really want anyway.   [parallel]

The therapist kept control of this conversation by feeding back to Harry his evasions (TH-33, -34, -36, -37, -38), by a nonpunitive but firm continuity,by repeatedly narrowing the frame so that Harry had to confront his own uneasiness (TH-32, -34, -35, -36, -37, -38), and by not shrinking from the confrontation when the stage was properly set (TH-38). Harry used the framing dimension at both of its extremes in his efforts to escape revealing himself: At one point (CL-34) he is specific about a particular position (albeit describing it in a very loaded fashion), while at another (CL-36 and 37) he becomes quite abstract and overly general.

Reflection

Because we each have our own comfortable, familiar level of framing and because we like to feel we understand others readily and are as quickly understood, we may easily mistake agreeableness for understanding. The example just given is one form of this potential misunderstanding, but it often occurs without the intent of either party to conceal or deceive. With experience—some of it dismaying—the therapist comes to be sensitive to the difference between the same meaning being conveyed at two different levels of abstraction and genuine differences in meanings obscured by being at two different levels. It is sound practice to rephrase any important material at several levels in order to double and triple check that genuine understanding is occurring.

This is a process which truly calls for all the artistry one may have. There can be no predetermined list of questions to be asked or observations to be made. The possibilities are truly infinite, and it is only in the living moment that one can judge which tack to take. This dependence on individual sensitivity and skill is even greater when we consider how what is observed must then be apprehended, collated, interpreted, and put to use.

The general rule is this: *Information understood only at one level of generality/concreteness is information misunderstood.*

A PSYCHOTHERAPIST'S JOURNEY

I received my Master of Arts degree in the summer of 1941, just before Pearl Harbor. At that time a master's degree was less frequent than a doctorate is today, and it opened many doors to me. One of my first professional jobs was for the U.S. Farm Security Administration, which was making a study of the Tennessee hill people (some of the original "hillbillies").

Young psychologists, medical interns, nursing students, social work graduate students, and administrators descended on the small town of Jackson, Tennessee, there to exercise our various skills in examining people who were brought in from the rural areas. Some of those we saw had not been out of the hills in many years; some never. Jackson (population 10,000, as I recall) was "the city" to them.

We psychologists gave a battery of tests, selected by I don't know who. They included many a museum piece (even then): the Porteus Mazes, the Knox Cubes, the Ferguson Formboards, and the 1916 Stanford-Binet vocabulary are the ones I recall now.

Those hill people were so patient with us and our strange requests: "Put your pencil point here and without lifting it or crossing any line, find your way out of this box as quickly as you can." "Watch the way I tap these blocks, and then you take your block and do it just the same way." "See whether you can fit these pieces together to fit neatly into these slots." "What does the word Mars, M-A-R-S, mean?"

The formboards, a set of jigsaw-puzzle-like tasks, seemed most to interest our subjects. The vocabulary answers were the most interesting to us. To the question quoted above, the modal answer by far was, "You mean like where the cow mahrs (mires) down in the pasture." The rules said that was wrong, but in their culture, it was right. We followed the rules, of course. It wouldn't have been objective if we hadn't.

Sadly, we who were supposed to be knowledgeable about people tended to regard them objectively in many ways, to see them as quaint or odd. None of us really tried to see the world from their perspective. They were objects to be studied. And we who studied them used only the telephoto lens of the objective tests. This reducing of the person to the explicit answers or overt movements prevented us from really meeting or learning about or knowing these people. This is the hard lesson those who seek to be objective need to learn but seldom do: Reduction is destruction.

CHAPTER 8

Locus

Paralleling

As the therapist develops sensitivity to the fluctuations of the various forms of paralleling in the patient's responses and skill in modulating his own paralleling, other possible uses for this revealing and empowering perspective become evident. This chapter introduces just such an extension of this therapeutic tool, locus of attention paralleling.

That the main site of therapeutic work needs to be in the patient's subjectivity has been repeatedly demonstrated in these pages. In this chapter I describe one helpful way of estimating the extent to which that attempt is successful. It is also, of course, a mode which encourages the patient to enter further into her own innerness.

Attention to the locus of the patient's inner perceptual field is the key to accomplishing these purposes. What is the focus of the patient's concern as she speaks? Who are the persons she is consciously describing? Of the many possible loci for patient attention, we identify four and consider their roles: focus on the patient's inner living, focus on the relation between the patient and the therapist, focus on the patient's relationships with others, and focus on the therapist.

DEPTH PSYCHOTHERAPY CALLS for therapist and patient to give priority attention to the inner living of the latter. In doing so, it is advantageous to the therapist to try to get and maintain some sense of the phenomenal (perceptual) field of patient (i.e., the inner stream of awareness and the perceptual structures which are abiding features of it). The awareness stream will at various times center on different objects — for examples, the world at large, other people important to the patient, the patient's main activities, the therapist, or the patient's reflexive awareness of herself and her way of being.

The virtuoso therapist is the one who has a continuing intuition about that inner stream of patient awareness and who is able to use that intuition to facilitate the patient's inner explorations and to time and phrase his own interventions for optimum effect.[1] One of the prime dimensions of the stream of awareness is that which has to do with the persons in focal position at any given time.

THE CONCEPT OF LOCI OF ATTENTION

Everything that therapist and patient say directs attention to one or the other of them or their relationships with each other or with the outer world. We use the term *locus* to designate that object of attention. Segment 8.1 offers four different therapist responses to the same patient statement, illustrating the four loci which are our concern in this chapter. These examples will clarify the meaning of the term *locus* and begin to demonstrate its importance.

Segment 8.1
Patient: Belle Canyon; Therapist: Charles Snyder
PT-1: I get very self-conscious when I try to tell you about my spiritual life. It's important to me, but I feel reluctant to talk about it.
[patient/therapist]
TH-1A: Is there something about me that makes it hard for you? [therapist]
TH-1B: Don't push yourself too fast, but it will be helpful to our work when you can share this important area of your life with me.
[patient/therapist]
TH-1C: Do you have this difficulty when you talk with other people also?
[patient/other]
TH-1D: As much as you want to deal with this important area, you still find yourself holding back. [patient]

These four possible therapist responses are clearly distinguishable by where they direct the patient's attention: The first (TH-1A) asks the patient to think about the therapist himself and his impact on her; the second (TH-1B) also points toward the relation between the patient and the therapist, but now there is a different emphasis—the first encourages thinking about the therapist's characteristics while the second directs attention to the patient's own inner experiencing. The third (TH-1C) moves to the patient's relations with other people, and the last (TH-1D) asks the patient to be aware of her intrapsychic conflict.

CHOOSING AN APPROPRIATE LOCUS OF ATTENTION

Although there are many ways of identifying possible loci for attention, at this point we are considering only these four. Obviously no one of these is the only "right" placement; nevertheless, there is merit in knowing which each speaker is selecting for the bulk of her attention at any given point. Similarly, it is usually desirable to attempt some concentration in one for a time. To say the latter point differently: The therapeutic impact of a conversation is apt to be greater when the locus of attention remains relatively constant for some period rather than being casually switched among the possible placements.

In actual practice, one need not look on the subjects being discussed in terms of the neat categories we are here employing. These are helpful to sensitize and train our awareness, but when with patient we need to let this formal organization drop into the subconscious while we find the unique patterns of this particular individual's perceptual space.

Placement on the Interpersonal: Patient/Others

This area includes all persons other than patient and therapist, as well as objects with which the patient concerns herself in the therapeutic work. Obviously this is a tremendous range, with an extensive scope of possible feelings and attitudes potentially available. While our discussion here will not attempt to work out all the possible subdivisions of that immensity, it is apparent that the therapist will note and work with distinctions between persons close to the patient and those more distant, between persons and things, between present and past or future objects, and such other contrasts as are meaningful.

Unsophisticated patients often gravitate to the interpersonal patient/others locus initially. To them it seems the least threatening because it most easily lends itself to relatively objective handling; it avoids direct content-engagement with therapist, and it can permit the patient to be the sole source of data.

For these very reasons, I am inclined to move the locus away from this area as promptly as the patient can tolerate. This policy grows not out of my covert sadism, but out of my observation that there is an economic (time and energy) gain for our work to be had from giving priority to the intrapsychic locus. When the patient can tolerate work in this area, the gain arises from working out understanding of the patient's patterns of directing her inner life first and then being able to readily see those patterns reenacted in other loci subsequently.

As an example, Belle (Segment 8.1) came to the recognition that while her spiritual life was indeed important to her, it was permeated by great anxiety. She was regular in spiritual practices, but within herself she avoided confronting disturbing questions which were at the periphery of her awareness. Once this avoidance pattern was clear from work in her intrapsychic area, it was relatively easy for her to see that her hesitation to talk with the therapist about the spiritual realm was a reenactment of the same pattern; talking with him would very likely lead to those same dreaded issues.

It can be objected that one could start with the interpersonal patient/others locus and discover that avoidance pattern and then later see its repetition in the intrapsychic. Certainly that is possible, but often that route requires several excursions—e.g., seeing how the patient avoids threatening discussions with friends or with clergy, how she pulls away from certain books and movies, and so on—before the more central generalization is recognized.

Three occasions are ordinarily most suitable for guiding patient's focus toward the interpersonal patient/others locus:

- As a preparatory or transition zone for work in other areas which may be more threatening to the patient. New patients often need a period of adjusting to the work, of solidifying their alliance with the therapist, and of accepting the routine and responsibility of self-exploration.
- As a testing ground or arena for trying out and extending self-learnings gained in other areas. Once significant and pervasive patterns of how the patient structures her own identity and her world outlook have been disclosed and at least partially worked through to consciousness, there is value in seeking out how those patterns are reproduced in the patient's relations with others in her life.
- As a zone of less threat which can be used as a rest or cooling off time when the work has been excessively stressful. Segment 8.2 shows how this can be done.

Segment 8.2
Patient: Beatrice Broyles; Therapist: Herbert Drake
PT-1: (Weeping, breathing heavily) Oh, I don't know what I'm going to do. I just can't go on with things the way they are, and I can't risk trying to change them. I feel as though I'm at a dead end.   [patient]
TH-1: You're feeling really caught right now, and that scares you.   [patient]
PT-2: Yes, yes. (Cries) I can't stand it. I just can't! What can I do?   [patient]
TH-2: I know it's hard to see your way out of this place, but that's what we're working on together. Tell me, have you had these kinds of desperate feelings before?   [patient/therapist]
PT-3: Oh, no, never! (Pause) I mean, not just like this. Why?   [patient]

TH-3: Who was with you when you had feelings something like these?
                                                              [patient/others]
PT-4: I don't remember. I think it was something like this when the baby
      died; it's hard to remember for sure now, but I think so. My husband
      wasn't much help; he was so upset himself, but we sort of helped each
      other. And his mother was just a rock to lean on. I never appreciated
      her so much before.   [patient/others]

In this abridged passage, the therapist is helping the patient feel
heard and understood (TH-2) while gradually fostering her movement out of her intrapsychic agony by bringing in awareness of therapist. When patient begins to reflect (PT-3) on her current distress in
the perspective of other times and circumstances, there is already
some movement. Other personal experiences are apt to be more
cognitively and objectively regarded than the highly subjective perceptions of the present stress (PT-1). This step carries this transition
along (in TH-3) and brings in other people, which has the effect of
reducing the isolation which gripped patient earlier (PT-4).

Placement in the Interpersonal:
Patient/Therapist

Patients vary widely in the comfort with which they can talk about
their relation with the therapist. Some find this familiar and readily
express themselves; others, quite to the contrary, are hesitant and
threatened. Moreover, some patients address or refer to the therapists
explicitly without engaging him genuinely. The reality of the fact of
transference is difficult to question, although, to be sure, some experienced therapists seem to find no use for the term.

Obviously the tone of the talk about the relation between therapist
and patient is critical to whether this locus is apt to threaten the
patient. One time we may intend support and understanding, but
another we may need to expose and explore mistrust, conflict, dis-
cord, anger, or, contrastingly, sensual or sexual feellings, seekings for
extratherapy relations, or intimacy. There is much variation in how
readily patients can work in this zone. For some there is comfort or
reassurance in dealing with the alliance directly; for a large number
of patients (particularly for those less sophisticated) the reverse is the
case — there is high threat in talking about an immediate relation.

Intimacy or conflict. Those who experience this threat generally
do so because in their pasts the only times when two people engaged

in direct and explicit talk about their relation have been times of intimacy or of conflict, both possibly threatening occasions. Indeed, for some segments of the population it is a serious breach of good manners to talk about one's perceptions of and feelings about a conversational partner.

There are some patients who handle the threat by coming on strongly at/toward the therapist. They may be injustice collectors complaining about fees, schedule, or supposed therapist coldness, misunderstanding, or some other sin. They may be those who depend on assertion and taking charge; to them the dependence on the therapist poses an almost intolerable threat. They may be overly dependent and want constant guidance, reassurance, or decisions from the therapist. In other words, the gamut of lifestyles can — and eventually needs to be — played out in the relationship with the therapist. The key to effective use of this locus is timing.

Preparing for intrapsychic work. As I indicated in our discussion of the interpersonal patient/others locus, there is much to be gained from working rather thoroughly in the patient's intrapsychic zone as early as possible. That maxim, however, is seldom applicable when the patient is someone whose main mode of operating is, as in the examples in the previous paragraph, one that plays off of the other person. In such instances, it is almost always necessary to work in the interpersonal patient/therapist locus for some time before any truly meaningful work can be accomplished in the intrapsychic. Segment 8.3 illustrates this work.

Segment 8.3²
Patient: Frank Connelly; Therapist: James Bugental
> (Frank is a bellman in a cheap hotel. He is a semi-hippie, bearded, infrequently bathed, and angry at the world.
> Early in this segment, Frank is directing all of his attention outward, disavowing any personal connection to what he reports. This emphasis is shown in some of the notations by *other* being italicized. Later some of the responses that are noted as "*patient*/others" and "*patient*/therapist" rather clearly are moving toward greater emphasis on Frank's inner experiencing. These are marked by *patient* being in italics.)

PT-1: I was at the library and this character comes up to me and says, "Why don't you take a bath, you bum?" So I told him to go fuck off, and he gets all red in the face and says he'll have me arrested. Christ! What creeps there are everywhere.   [patient/*others*]

TH-1: So what do you think about the incident, Frank?   [patient/*others*]

PT-2: So what's to think about it? (Angry sounding) They ought to lock some of these square nuts up. He shouldn't be running around loose
[patient/ *others*]

TH-2: Yeah, I know. But what about it for you?   [patient/others]

PT-3: What do you mean, what about it for me? I told you. I think the guy's off his rocker.   [patient/ *others*]

TH-3: So he's off his rocker. So what?   [patient/others]

PT-4: So he's a menace.   [patient/ *others*]

TH-4: Okay, he's a menace. So what? Who cares?   [patient/others]

PT-5: I sure as hell don't.   [patient]

TH-5: You sure as hell must. You've just spent nearly 15 minutes telling me all about this guy you say you don't care about.   [patient/others]

PT-6: I'm just doing what you told me to do.   [patient/therapist]

TH-6: What's that?   [patient/therapist]

PT-7: Tell you whatever comes into my mind. You said that's what I was supposed to do and now when I do it, you bawl me out. Honestly, I . . .   [patient/therapist]

TH-7: Frank! I did not tell you to tell me whatever comes into your mind. There's far too much, . . . tell me what concerns you, what really matters to you in your life, and while you're doing so, throw in anything that comes along.   [patient/therapist]

PT-8: First time you ever said that.   [therapist]

TH-8: Okay, Okay. Now it's said. What do you feel concerned about in your life right now?   [patient]

PT-9: Well, why do you always sound so much like you're just able to put up with me?   [patient/therapist]

TH-9: Frank, you've got me. It's a combination of things, some in you and some in me. The odd part is, I really like and enjoy you, but somehow I do come off at you in a continually chiding, exasperated way.
[patient/therapist]

PT-10: I don't know why you say I do something to make you do that.
[patient/therapist]

TH-10: Frank, you're not that stupid. You know, at least at some level, very well what I mean. You're just making points off me right now because I let my guard down for a minute.   [patient/therapist]

PT-11: Now why should I want to do that?   [patient]

TH-11: Because you don't know what to do except gripe and attack.
[patient]

PT-12: Where do you get off telling me I gripe and attack? Almost everything I say you find fault with.   [patient/therapist]

TH-12: That's true, I'm afraid. But you really ask for it, Frank.
[patient/therapist]

PT-13: Now how the hell do I ask for it? Why would I do that?   [patient]

TH-13: Something in you keeps needing to provoke other people. I see you doing it right here with me, and I'm sure you do it with others.

[patient/therapist]

PT-14: It's always something I'm doing. Well, if you had to eat as much crap everyday as I do, you'd. . . . [patient]

TH-14: Frank, you'd rather bellyache about life than do something about it. [patient]

PT-15: I really feel bad when you say that. I thought I was supposed to tell you what I was feeling, and it's so lousy for me that . . . [patient]

TH-15: Yes, I know. I know because you've told me over and over again. I know because you tell me with so much satisfaction. And now you feel I've treated you unfairly because you've just been doing what I tell you to do. [patient/therapist]

PT-16: I suppose I just never have much of interest to tell you. It's all pretty much the same, and I wake up every morning with this blue, crappy sense of foreboding, and then I bring it all in here and dump it on you. . . . [*patient*/therapist]

TH-16: You have become so invested in telling your story of how badly life treats you that you do it routinely and with a griping manner that turns people off or makes them angry. You don't like to look at that, but it's so, and I think some part of you knows it. [patient]

PT-17: I don't like being unhappy. It isn't any fun seeing other people having all the jollies while I'm all alone and just going around the same shitty treadmill all the time. [*patient*/others]

TH-17: Did you ever consider what it would be like not to feel miserable?

[patient]

PT-18: It would be a great relief (flatly). [patient]

TH-18: No, Frank, you're just talking from the top of your head. Let yourself feel into it: How would it be if you didn't feel unhappy, if you had no sad, lonely feeling? [patient]

PT-19: (Silent for a minute, really letting himself consider the idea. Then face suddenly intense, voice angry.) If I ever gave up my misery, I'd never be happy again. [patient]

We can smile at the paradox of Frank's insight, but the ironic truth of his outburst is his recognition that he depends on his angry stance to provide him a place in the world, to let him feel he has some power in a life in which there are many frustrations and disappointments.

In this greatly abridged segment, it is still apparent how the extensive work in the patient/others area led toward Frank's being able to begin looking at his way of being with the therapist, which in turn opened up the way for the breakthrough into his intrapsychic discovery.

Placement in the Intrapsychic

It is manifest by now that it is my conviction that some of the most fundamental and lasting psychotherapeutic work comes from careful exploration of the intrapsychic realm. In no sense is this to deny the powerful significance of the interpersonal in both of its aspects. Indeed, a case can be made that the ultimate source and testing ground of psychological difficulties (psychopathology) resides in that realm. Nevertheless, those difficulties get built into perceptual constructions in the inner life of patient, and these require therapeutic attention.

To speak of working in the intrapsychic locus is not to say that such work includes no references to persons or objects outside of the patient herself. Such references are frequent, but the chief intent of what is inquired into, described, and reflected on is how the patient has structured her own identity and the nature of the world in which she lives (the "self-and-world" concept or construct system).

The significance of this perspective is that often the therapist especially watches for the internal aspects of what is said. Here are examples:

PT-A: I've been so sad since mother passed away. She was such a comfort to me in all my troubles.   [patient/others]
TH-A: You feel alone in facing things now.   [patient]

PT-B: They don't seem to understand what I'm trying to tell them. Instead they are always telling me what I should do instead.   [patient/others]
TH-B: Somehow you can't find the way to make yourself really understood, huh?   [patient]

PT-C: I don't see why you can't tell me what to do. You have so much more experience in these things than I have.   [patient/therapist]
TH-C: You feel too inexperienced to make these decisions for yourself, is that the way it is?   [patient]

Of course, none of these responses stands alone. As the work with Frank (Segment 8.3) illustrates, it is only with repeated exchanges and consistent confrontation with one's own way of being that recognition can come of the hidden but pervasive ways in which we may be self-defeating.

Placement on Therapist

While references to the therapist may be frequent, they often are not reflective of a genuine focusing of the patient's perceptual field on the professional. Rather they may be passing allusions, tangential inclusions, or intended courtesies. These are not what is meant by this locus. We are concerned here with the frame of reference of the patient as she talks, with what are the foreground figures of her concern. After the first settling-in period of therapy, for many patients the therapist drops into the background.

A rash generalization: There are, for the most part, only four circumstances under which the locus is appropriately on therapist alone:

- When the patient's way of being in the world causes her to be preoccupied with the therapist's views, judgments, needs, and responses so that she cannot risk relinquishing that focus to attend to her own processes.
- When therapy has run its course and the patient has gained a significant degree of self-understanding and self-direction and needs to work through residual expectations and concerns about the therapist as a person (including transferential elements).
- When therapist and patient are caught in a collusion which is producing an impasse for therapy and the therapist is prepared to disclose his part in this as a way of breaking up the blockage.
- When the therapist's own needs are such that he must bring them forward in order to maintain the alliance or to deal with some aspect from his own life that intrudes or may intrude on the therapy. Examples: the therapist is seriously ill or must have major surgery; the therapist is going to move to another city or retire from practice; the therapist is going through a personal crisis about which the patient may hear or which may intrude on the work (divorce, being widowed).

Preoccupation with the therapist. In the first of these, the patient's psychodynamics push to put the focus on the therapist. Often such instances resolve into resistances to going forward with the self-inquiry that is the appropriate main business of therapy. Nevertheless, especially in the earlier stages of the work, patient preoccupation with the therapist may need to be dealt with in a direct manner.

When doing so, the therapist takes note of implicit and explicit references to himself, evaluating whether to encourage further attention to how he is seen and reacted to. Th-1A (in Segment 8.1, page 133) is a direct effort to do this and would be appropriate when the alliance is solid and the patient has some experience in explicit discussion of their relation. It would be less suitable with a newer and less sophisticated patient who might find her self-consciousness increased by this question. For such a person, the approach to bringing out the basis of her hesitation might require a number of steps, as in Segment 8.4.

Segment 8.4
Patient: Belle Canyon; Therapist: Charles Snyder
PT-1: I get very self-conscious when I try to tell you about my spiritual life. It's important to me, but I feel reluctant to talk about it.

[patient/therapist]

TH-1: Your spiritual life is important to you, but still . . .   [patient]
PT-2: Yes, it is. (pause) I know it would be good if I could talk about it, but . . . but it's as though my throat gets tight when I try to. [patient]
TH-2: You want to talk about your spiritual life, but you find yourself blocking when you try to.   [patient]
PT-3: I can't see why I . . . why I . . . I guess I'm afraid you'll . . .

[patient/therapist]

TH-3: Some way your fears about me get in the way of your talking about it.   [patient/therapist]
PT-4: I know that's not the way I should feel, but it does seem that way. I mean, I keep wondering what you would think.   [patient/therapist]
TH-4: What I might think is a big block to what you want to do here, huh?   [patient/therapist]
PT-5: I guess so. I wonder, for example, do you have a spiritual life too?   [therapist]
TH-5: I will be glad to answer that some other time, Belle, but right now it's more important for us to look at what you're feeling about me. Is there something about me that makes it hard for you?   [therapist]

This has been, as is usual in our examples, a condensed version of therapeutic work that might take many times more exchanges and might, indeed, stretch over several sessions. The intent is to demonstrate to the patient that her hesitation is acceptable to the therapist and that it is in itself an appropriate subject for therapeutic investigation. Concurrently, the therapist has been doing several things to foster increased motivation to deal with this blocking: Leaving a response incomplete (TH-1) subtly pulls on the patient to complete it, at least subvocally. Then two responses (TH-2 and -3) are designed to help the patient become aware of her intrapsychic conflict, with the hope that this will reduce possible anxiety about being at odds with the therapist. Next (TH-4) the therapist brings attention to himself but in such a way as to link it with the patient's inner conflict and to suggest that talking with the therapist is tied to a desired reduction of that conflict.

Note that the key question (last sentence of TH-5) is the same as in the earlier example (TH-1A in Segment 8.1), but now the ground has been prepared by encouraging the patient to move the focus of her attention from general self-consciousness to the specific relation to the therapist (narrowing the frame paralleling). The patient's readiness for this step has been signaled by her own focusing on the therapist (PT-5).

Other occasions for focus on therapist. Each of the other three circumstances may well devolve into a situation in which the therapist chooses to make some kind and amount of self-disclosure. A full treatment of all that is involved in such a step is beyond the scope of this book. Here, however, are summary suggestions or guidelines.

First and foremost: Strict honesty is required. This means that there should be no distortion in the information given patients. Our patients rely on us to aid them in their reality testing. If we are inauthentic in this regard, we are fundamentally betraying them. Honesty does not mean that we must say everything on whatever subject is of concern. Indeed, it is often responsible not to do so, but then honesty requires that we be candid about the withholding:

> I can tell you something about this matter in which you are interested, but I will not tell you all I know about it because to do so would be to violate a confidence (or would be to say more than I feel comfortable saying at this time or in these circumstances).

If said quietly and firmly, this will often be respected. If the patient needs to argue, wheedle, or try to overcome the limit, that should be taken as an appropriate matter for therapeutic investigation (and perhaps treated as a resistance; see Chapter 10).

Second, disclosure of one's immediately pertinent reactions having to do with the work is more appropriate than getting into matters falling outside of therapy with this particular patient. Therapists have a right to their own privacy, and the fact that they ask their patients to be fully self-disclosing imposes no similar obligation on therapists themselves.

Third, disclosure of process responses—feelings and thoughts about the work and the way it is going—is usually more suitable (and more what patients validly seek) than is disclosure of details of one's personal, extratherapy life. This is, of course, less valid when the extratherapy life is intruding into the therapeutic work.

Fourth, disclosure of hostile, resentful, punitive, erotic, seductive, and competitive feelings in relation to the patient must be undertaken only when there has been careful preparation of the patient and when the therapist has taken time apart from the patient to examine as fully as possible his own needs, motives, and intentions. When such feelings are quite strong, the therapist will do well to secure supervisory or collegial consultation before getting into such matters in any depth.

Summary

As the therapist listens to the patient and selects when and how he will respond, he is likely to be attending to many aspects in addition to the explicit content: amount and kind of emotion, quality and direction of reasoning, self-portrayal, attitudes and values generally, how the therapist himself is perceived, and so on and on. Experienced and effective therapists operate on many perceptual and intuitive levels at once. Obviously there is much more that needs the therapist's attention than can ever be detailed in full or analyzed completely in explicit fashion. In this chapter we have identified four constellations of such focal awareness which we have called "loci of attention": on patient's relations with others, on patient's relations with therapist, on the therapist, and on patient's inner world of subjectivity.

A PSYCHOTHERAPIST'S JOURNEY

I have heard that in the traditional Hopi language there was no first person singular pronoun, no "me," no "my," no "mine," no "I." Only "we," "us," and "our." Erich Fromm[3] points out that individuality is a relatively new human evolution. For millenia it was the sole prerogative of the privileged few. Probably even they knew it as something that set them apart, and that knowing made it something not quite human, something that always carried with it the scent of danger.

And if individuality is a new evolutionary attainment of human beings, what then is the personal subjectivity? We must not make the false equation of feelings and emotions with the personal subjectivity as that error was described in Chapter 6. Humans have had emotions throughout their history. Indeed, human history can be viewed as the history of emotional vicissitudes played out on the nations, the cultures, and the lives of multitudes. Emotion, much more than reason, has dictated the course of humanity's story, as Barbara Tuchman[4] so relentlessly documents. Nascent subjectivity has always been ours, of course. It is manifested in dreams, legends and myths, the great archetypes, artistic productions of all kinds, creativity in science and affairs, and the humble excellence that loving hearts and hands can bring to small things such as preparing a meal, arranging a room, talking with a friend, comforting a stranger.

Yet these excursions of subjectivity have been outward and usually the emphasis has been on their products — as my list just now demonstrates. The end result has been valued as though it were the sum of its source, when in fact it is more likely that it often was simply a byproduct. It hardly seems likely that the great creative spirits exhausted their potentials in what they brought forth.

The point is that once again we have mistaken the pointing finger for the moon. The products of subjectivity are not the subjectivity.[5]

What then is our subjectivity?

Here we can speculate, propound dogma, wax poetic or philosophic, but we cannot specify. Of course not. To specify is to objectify; to objectify subjectivity is to destroy its very nature.

Perhaps once again ontology recapitulates phylogeny; once again the evolution in the individual retraces the path of the species.

The individual patient is likely to want to talk about external events, forces, people, and circumstances. She will seek to explain herself as caused by those influences. She resists the imputation that she chose the course that now leads to her misery and dissatisfaction with her life.

How strange! Why does she not eagerly seek that affirmation of her power? Why does she continually insist she is victim rather than author? How is it that it seems preferable to her to seek, to demand, to entreat rescue than to open her own cell door and walk out?

The culture has taught determinism, has insisted on objectifying us, has held the scales in terms of guilt and blame, right and wrong. She wants to be right, guilt-free, and help-able, and she will pay with her freedom, her choicefulness, and her subjecthood to get what she wants.

In this chapter we have shown how the ultimate scene of depth psychotherapeutic work must be the intrapsychic locus, the confrontation with oneself, one's own identity, and the world one has created. But we have seen also how patients direct our attention outward, to their relations with others, to their relations with us, their therapists, and sometimes to us, but how they resist coming into their own centers, their own inwardness, their own subjectivity.

That resistance is not just cultural conditioning. It is their dim sensing that once they take up residence in their own centers, they may never find the familiar world familiar again. It may be their intuition that assuming the throne of subjective autonomy means bearing the unrelenting burden of choice, carrying the inexorable load of guilt for having failed their own potentials, and living always before a vista of uncertainty, ambiguity, and incompleteness.[6]

So confronted, who would not flee from the prospect? It is scarcely an offer that can't be refused — as literal millions refuse it daily. Yet is it such a partial, such a distorted and distorting presentation.

When we come closer to our own centers, we find we have long lived under a burdensome and limiting image of who and what we are. We have allowed ourselves to be misled by the envelope of the skin. We have thought the envelope of our conscious awareness was who we are. We have assumed that the manifest objective fences around us — fences called time, place, circumstance — truly contained us.

That is fanciful language but perhaps as adequate as any generalization can be. What it means is that our truer identity is much larger than we have believed. It includes much more than our self-imposed limits have permitted. When we think about some issue, we too often stop before we have begun to explore all that our unfettered consciousness could bring to bear on the matter. When we relate with another person, we have let language and body set the terms and missed the further engagement that occasionally we briefly sense.

Getting Greater Depth

CHAPTER 9

Objectification-Subjectivity Ratio[1]

Paralleling (Section III) fosters sensitive attention and skillful intervention, but it is not enough, in itself, to bring patients to greater depth of participation. In this chapter, I suggest ways to further meet that need.

In much of what the patient does in intensive psychotherapy he intends to try to describe and understand some problem, complaint, concern, or issue. (I will use concern *to cover all such matters.) How the patient engages in that effort is revealing of the extent to which he has truly incorporated responsibility for his own life and has learned to use the power of his own subjectivity. There are many forms through which patients present and explore their life issues. This chapter describes four clusters of these forms: largely objectifying, tending toward objectifying, tending toward subjectivity, and largely subjective.[2]*

An important task in therapy is aiding patients in becoming more immediate and centered in their grappling with the life issues which bring them to treatment. Commonly patients distance themselves from those very issues and thus lose the sense of authorship and the power to bring about the changes they want so dearly. The dimension of objectifying-to-subjectivity is concerned with this frequent patient pattern and with how we can aid those who consult us in better taking hold of what troubles them.

As the therapist becomes familiar with this scale, she will discover it has several values: Observing how the patient "takes hold of" his concern provides a rough estimate of his investment in therapy, and it offers steps to increase that involvement.

AMONG SEVERAL THOUSAND other tasks, the therapist needs to keep aware of what issue is implicitly the focus of the patient's work at any given point. With some sense of that in mind, she must next take note of how the patient is working with it. This chapter describes some typical ways in which patients carry out this activity — not a complete catalog, but some of the most frequent modes. Four clusters are distributed on a continuum from largely objectifying through two intermediate patterns in which both objectifying and subjectivity are present and ending with highly subjective and individual forms.

These clusters and representative modes are shown in Table 9.1. The therapist needs to get the general sense of this dimension rather than mechanically seeking to match patient activity to the modes listed in the table. Our patients have not studied these matters in a systematic way; thus they continually and thoughtlessly produce additional patterns which do not easily fit into our schema.

TABLE 9.1

Patient Patterns for Presenting Concerns

Patterns Objectifying the Concern
- Naming
- Describing
- Valuing

Patterns Tending Toward Objectification
- Associating Functionally
- Associating Causally or Analytically
- Detailing History or Life Events

Patterns Tending Toward Subjectivity
- Bodily Awareness and Associating
- Describing Dreams and Fantasies
- Emotional Associating
- Recognition in Process

Largely Subjective Patterns
- Spontaneous Fantasy
- Free Association
- Concern-Guided Searching

We begin with an initial interview which provides an opportunity to examine the various ways patients describe their concerns.

Segment 9.1
Patient: Andy Campbell; Therapist: Blanche Nathan
'Scei (Scene: Dr. Nathan's office. Time: First interview; therapist and patient have just met, exchanged names and pleasantries, and then Dr. Nathan asks:)
TH-1: What brings you to me at this time?
PT-1: Well, I've thought for some time I ought to get some help, but I kept putting it off, and. . . .
TH-2: Mm-hmmm?

PT-2: It just never seemed the right time, I guess. I thought several times that. . . . I asked my girl friend what she thought, and she said she thought I ought to do it. So I talked to my doctor, and he said sometimes therapists are helpful and sometimes not; so I didn't know for sure, but . . .

TH-3: It was difficult to know what you should do, eh?

PT-3: Yes. I mean, it seemed as though I . . . I didn't want to make a big deal out of something that wasn't that important, but on the other hand, it is a continual problem to me too.

TH-4: I'm unclear what it is that is the problem to you.

PT-4: Oh, sure. I'm sorry. It's my hesitation. I mean my problem is my hesitation. I seem to be always so uncertain about things. I know everybody has that. . . . I probably shouldn't think I'm different, but. . . .

TH-5: I see (expectantly).

PT-5: Yes. It's this habit I have of being unsure about things. I mean, I don't want to go off half-cocked, you might say. I don't want to just . . . but then, I don't really think I would anyway. I don't know, though.

TH-6: Tell me more about this hesitation and how it's a problem for you.

PT-6: Well, I just have trouble whenever I have to make a decision about anything. It seems as though I just go back and forth inside myself, and I never know what the right thing is. It's been that way for a long time. I would like to be more sure of myself, but I'm not. In fact, I think maybe it's getting worse.

TH-7: It may be getting worse. You may be more hesitant now than you used to be?

PT-7: Well, probably, . . . but I'm not sure, you know. Sometimes it seems like it's getting better, but then pretty soon I have to make some decision, and there I am back in that confusion again.

TH-8: Sometimes it's better; other times it's worse?

PT-8: That's right. Yes, I think that's the way it is. Oh, it makes me so damned mad. I just hate it. It makes me feel so indecisive, such a wimp! But there it is: That just seems to happen to me over and over.

Andy Campbell is presenting his problem at two levels: He talks about it, and he enacts it. Apparently (but not surely) he is unaware of the latter, and Blanche Nathan is choosing not to call his attention to this yet. It will be useful, however, to examine how he is verbally presenting his complaint.

At first (PT-4 and -5) he simply *names* it, "my hesitation." Beyond accepting ownership of it by the pronoun, "my," Andy seems to treat his complaint as an independent force. He might be describing a disease he's contracted ("my tuberculosis is a problem to me"), in other words, "an alien thing is troubling me."

It is only after several accepting and encouraging responses from Dr. Nathan that Andy (PT-6) provides some *description* of how this problem affects him. Now he gives a generalized restatement of the matter, a quick glance at its history, and an estimate that it's worsening.

A third step comes when Andy reacts in a *valuing* way and expresses his anger with this pattern of hesitation (PT-8). The annoyance had been implicit to this point, but now it comes out more clearly, and as it does so, we see a reduction in the implicit acting out of the concern (PT-8 shows less indecision than any previous response).

PATTERNS OF OBJECTIFYING THE CONCERN

The subjectivity of a person is the seat of his uniqueness, his individuality. When the patient makes himself but an interchangeable observer of his own condition, it is evident that he is objectifying himself and that condition. To objectify oneself in this fashion means to render oneself impotent to do anything about the concern. We have seen Andy Campbell use three different ways of taking hold of his concern. All three were objectifying of the matter and of Andy himself. Now I will review these and suggest some of their further implications.

Naming

Imagine that while you are blindfolded an unfamiliar object is put into your hand. You feel it, turn it, press it with your fingers, perhaps smell it or rub it against your cheek. It is interesting, and its identity briefly eludes you; then suddenly you recognize it: "It's a rock." Abruptly, you are apt to realize, the thing in your hand is *nothing but* a rock. What was interesting and personal when unknown is transformed into the commonplace by being categorized in this manner. You set it aside without further interest in it.

In the same way, a patient's problem may be assigned a categorical name—hesitation, impotence, shyness, loneliness, depression, whatever. The process of naming has the effect of making a thing of the issue, of putting it at a distance. Implicit, often, is the notion that anybody afflicted by this same malady would be similarly troubled; the sufferer is not seen as unique.

When using the example of the rock in one's hand, we suggested a significant phenomenon that can also be observed when a person comes to therapy but with only vague complaints—i.e., when no name or categorization has been found to cover the condition. At this point, the patient is often caught up in trying to articulate what troubles him and, indeed, may seem to have an attachment to his distress. Then, if someone provides a name (diagnosis) which is accepted, the relation of patient and complaint is likely to change. There is a reduction of emotional involvement, and the condition seems to "move away" from the sufferer and to take on an independent existence (and now becomes the concern of therapist).

Here is a further demonstration of this significant process: Figure 9.1 presents three puzzle images. There is no relation among the

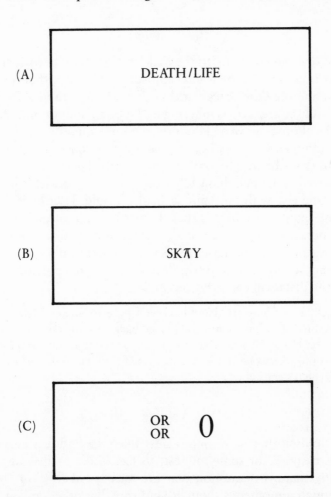

Figure 9.1.   Three Puzzles to Illustrate Effects of Objectification.

three, but each separately represents a familiar phrase. The first (A) is "life after death." Now look at the other two and decide what they represent. DO THIS BEFORE READING FURTHER.

The second (B) puzzle's answer is "Pie (pi) in the sky." If you didn't get it sooner, you may find you have an minor emotional reaction to my giving the answer in this offhand way. Many find it disappointing or frustrating; they would prefer to work the puzzle out themselves. Moreover, whether the answer is given in this way or is arrived at by the reader, one loses interest in the puzzle once the solution is known. This is the effect of objectification.

The answer to the third puzzle (C) is given in the Notes and Comments section at the back of the book.[3]

Describing

If you once again attend to the rock that you have been examining, you may note that it is heavier than usual for its size, that one end is rounded and the other irregular. In other words, you note *its* characteristics. These are seen as inhering in the rock, and it is manifest that any rational observer would discover the same qualities.

When the patient goes beyond naming his concern, a usual next step is to describe it. The problem is described as though it were an object having inherent characteristics, as does the rock. It is implied that anyone else with the same difficulty would describe it the same way. The significance here is that there is little, if any, sense of one's unique personal experience of the issue, and that, as we observed before, means a loss of power to affect the condition.

Looking again at how Andy described his concern, one can see clearly the distancing and the impotence:

PT-6: Well, I just have trouble whenever I have to make a decision about anything. It seems as though I just go back and forth inside myself, and I never know what the right thing is. It's been that way for a long time. I would like to be more sure of myself, but I'm not. In fact, I think maybe it's getting worse.

Valuing

Still holding that rock, one is next likely to find it a nuisance or perhaps a source of some interest, to feel liking or disliking for it. Generally there is the notion that *the rock is* "likable" or "boring," and, though a moment's thought confirms that others might experience it differently, that is not the usual first reaction.

When Andy Campbell says of his hesitation that he hates it, that *it makes him* feel indecisive, it is clear that he is putting the power in the problem and the problem is viewed as though separate from Andy. Valuing responses of this kind maintain the objectification of the complaint.

SIGNIFICANCE OF THE PRESENTATION MODE

Use of the therapeutic opportunity. Thus far we have focused attention on how Andy Campbell and other patients describe their presenting concerns. This is Andy's chief activity during his first conversation with Dr. Nathan. In the weeks and months which follow he returns to that topic repeatedly, of course, but he also addresses other matters. Nevertheless, with exceptions, most of the time Andy deals with issues which he believes important to his life and well-being. Often these issues are implicit; sometimes they are explicit. How he deals with them is an important expression of how Andy takes hold of and uses the therapeutic opportunity to make his life different.

Blanche Nathan, as Andy's therapist, frequently considers inwardly and occasionally calls to Andy's attention this central matter of his use of therapy. She notes how genuinely Andy takes into himself the issues he addresses, how responsibly he assumes they are parts of himself, and whether he has a sense of and draws on resources within himself.

PATTERNS TENDING TOWARD THE OBJECTIVE

Segment 9.2
> (Some time has passed. Andy has become more involved in the therapeutic work, and he—without realizing it—is beginning to grasp the issues of his therapy in changing ways.)

PT-11: Sometimes I think things are going better, but then other times I'm not so sure. It's so hard to know. Like, for instance, I was trying to decide whether to trade in the old car yesterday, and. . . . Well, Janet says that it's really silly for me to still drive my old Chevy, but I think it's got a lot of miles in it yet. I'm no mechanic, of course, and . . .

TH-11: You seem to be debating with yourself right now as you tell me about it.

PT-12: Yes. Well, it's not quite the same. But I see what you mean. Why do I keep doing that? Maybe I just am afraid to take a stand. Maybe I want Janet or somebody to take responsibility for my decisions.

Note: Once again I'm using a sequence of excerpts from the same
fictional therapeutic partners. This has the advantage of suggesting context, but it is not meant to prescribe that actual therapeutic work should so systematically move along this scale.

Associating Functionally

If one imagines continuing to hold the small rock in one's hand, it
is likely that an idea of how it might be used would occur: "This
would make a good paperweight." In this mode, there is some recognition of the more individual and personal nature of one's reactions.
For example, another person might think, "I could throw this rock
and hit something with it." There is an implicit recognition that
individual differences are possible.

Speculations about the motivations underlying one's concerns lie
in a middle zone between objectification and subjectivity, though
closer to the objectifying end of the continuum. Patients vary in the
extent to which the individuality of their complaints is accepted.

Segment 9.3
PT-12: Yes. Well, it's not quite the same. But I see what you mean. Why do I
keep doing that? Maybe I just am afraid to take a stand. Maybe I want
Janet or somebody to take responsibility for my decisions.
TH-12: You think that may be why you have so much trouble with deci-
sions?
PT-13: I don't know. Maybe. Why do most people have that kind of prob-
lem? You must have had others before me with this kind of problem.

Although Andy shifts quickly back to objectification, such speculations may be important to movement toward claiming power in his
life. The therapist will want to note the extent to which the functional
association is arrived at abstractly or grows out of true inner recognition. Cues to this distinction reside in the communication level at
which the patient is working and the other kinds of associations (see
below) which emerge concurrently. Patients who find ideas about
possible functions of their complaints while working at the critical
occasions level are more likely getting in better touch with the meanings of those issues. On the other hand, detached speculation is
typical of the routine or contact maintenance levels.

When patients distantly speculate about their concerns—
"maybe . . . ," "could be that . . . ," "I wonder if . . . "—I am inclined to say something to teach the futility of doing so:

Better avoid the "maybe's" if you can. They're quicksand and when your lively mind starts on that path you can get totally lost in possibilities without having any notion which are solid and which are not.

Associating Causally or Analytically

Speculations about causes or attempts to find the components of one's concern are similar to functional associations in many ways. The difference is that seeking causes may have the merit of leading to inquiry into the patient's unique history, as contrasted with seeking for generalized functions.

Also, in causal inquiries the rationalistic approach involves intent to use one's capacities in one's own behalf. The difficulty is, of course, that this is often carried out impersonally, as if the subject were a mechanical problem — for example, a stopped-up sink or a car that won't start. Rationalistic analyses or causal theories are interesting and provide a trap for the unwary therapist, for they can lead one to sterile cognitive formulations from which no apparent emotional or behavioral changes result.

Segment 9.4

PT-14: I've been doing a lot of thinking about why I have so much more trouble coming to a decision than do most people. Or at least I think I do. You've never said? (Pause) Well, anyway, I've been trying to think about it, and I remember that my father was always topping me when we'd have a discussion about anything.

TH-14: How do you mean?

PT-15: Well, like one time I was saying how I wished we had different pillows on our beds. I think I must have spent the night at a friend's house or something. Anyway, I said I didn't like foam rubber and wished we'd get some down pillows. I felt kind of proud that I knew the difference. And than Dad said, "Do you know where down comes from?" That really pleased me because I had just learned about that and so I was ready for him. "From ducks," I said. And then he just smiled and said, "And from what part of the duck?" and I didn't know, and I felt like nothing, and my brother just laughed and laughed and kept saying, "What part of the duck? What part of the duck!"

TH-15: You felt really put down.

PT-16: You bet. I hated him right then. Well, not really "hated," but . . . well, I suppose I did for a while. I hated my brother too, but of course, I got over it. Still, I wonder is that isn't the kind of thing that made me hesitate to ever say anything flat out.

Typical of this cluster are speculations about causes and recounting of memories or other events in a search for clues to "solve" the issue. Andy's memory of the embarrassing incident with his father and brother may well be accurately pointing to one of the contributing sources, but the recalling of the incident is not *in itself* likely to produce a significant change in Andy's persistent indecisiveness.

Detailing History or Life Events

It is useful to note that in Andy's account of the incident with his father and brother there is an implicit question: "Is this what *caused* me to be so indecisive?" The power is implicitly in the incident from his past, not in Andy, the person presently giving the account. Andy, today, is seen as a victim of the event (or of his father's insensitivity), just as though Andy had a crippled leg which he could trace back to an automobile accident which occurred some years before.

This kind of causal thinking dates back to Freud at least; although Freud in time came to the recognition that "Insight alone is not enough." Yet, distressingly, it is still implicit in a lot of psychotherapeutic writing and practice, and it is the usual lay view of psychotherapy. Those who have worked with patients in depth and over some length of time usually recognize that knowing the initiation of a pattern is not sufficient to produce therapeutic change—just as knowing what pushed a stone over a cliff is not sufficient to stop its fall (to use an objective image about a highly subjective matter!).

All the forms in this cluster share a duality in that they may be superficially similar to more subjective forms when one attends solely to the explicit content. When Andy tells of the incident with his father (Segment 9.4), he has begun to mine his subjectivity but his perspective is still that of finding "what did it to him." In contrast, had he been immersed in his feelings of indecision and his distress about them and then come upon the same memory, a very different psychological event would very likely have occurred: He might have experienced a flooding of emotion, but more importantly, the memory would not have been presented in isolation (like digging a splinter out of a finger). Instead it would have been part of a broadened awareness, which might have centered around the indecision, the distress, relations with his father, or some other nucleus, and which would provide an opening to much more than the immediate issue.

The difference just described is one which therapists accustomed to looking only at the manifest and explicit will have difficulty perceiving. To recognize the critically significant meaning in that difference, the therapist must employ her own subjectivity, her intuition.

PATTERNS TENDING TOWARD
SUBJECTIVITY

This cluster of ways patients grapple with life issues has in common that the issues are, at least implicitly, recognized as lying significantly within the patient himself. The externalizing and objectifying of the two prior clusters are markedly less as the patient seeks within his own experience for what will aid him in making significant changes in feelings, outlook, or actions.

Segment 9.5
> (Andy Campbell and Blanche Nathan have become an effective team now as they have persisted through the minor triumphs and the discouraging defeats of the usual therapeutic course. Today Andy is in a low time.)

PT-17: Blanche, I just don't seem to be making any headway lately. For a while it seemed as though we were getting some place, . . . well, you know, maybe not to any final answers, but. . . . Anyway, I can't seem to think of anything today. I've been sitting here just jabbering nonsense as far as I can see, and . . . (sighs).

TH-17: Pause just a minute, Andy, and breathe. You're running out of air.

PT-18: Okay. (He leans back and slows and deepens his breathing, having been instructed in this before.)

TH-18: (After waiting for three or four of Andy's deepened breaths) Now, just become aware inside of your body. Let your thoughts do whatever they need to, but turn your attention to just how you feel right now physically. (She waits again.) Now, find out where in your body there is tension of any kind, and see whether you can relax it, let go of it.

PT-19: (He wriggles into a more comfortable position, loosens his belt, and stretches his legs briefly.) Mm-hmm, that's better.

TH-19: (Again waiting briefly) Now listen to your gut, listen in your belly, your heart, your lungs. Find out what's going on, what you need to talk about now. Don't say anything until you get a real sense of what needs to be said from your body, not your mind.

PT-20: (Eyes shut, breathing quietly but deeply, silent a minute or two at least) I'm feeling sad. I didn't know that! It's in my chest and in my eyes. Like I want to cry or something. It just seems so sad. I'm not sure what, but there's something that makes me feel bad.

TH-20: Um-hmm.

PT-21: I don't know what it is, but . . . (eyes swim). I feel so tired . . . tired of always being such a . . . (tears quietly sliding down his cheeks) . . . such a klutz. I don't want to be the way I am. (Voice stronger) I really don't!

Bodily Awareness and Associating

Andy has learned access to the accumulation of subjectivity which resides in our bodies. Much of this storehouse is available to us when we open ourselves to it, and—as in the example—may bring fresh perspectives to our confrontation with the issues of our lives.

It takes a degree of sophistication about one's own nature to let go of the familiar body-mind separation built into much of the everyday, objective way of treating ourselves and each other. Use of this maneuver with patients lacking that sophistication is unwise and futile. It is best to wait until they have begun to appreciate the difference between inner awareness and outer thinking-*about* themselves. Premature instruction of this kind often means increasing patient resistance and making it more difficult to use this resource later on.

Describing Dreams and Fantasies

Practice varies widely among therapists regarding the place of dreams and fantasies. Some see such materials as messages from the unconscious which are coded and must be deciphered by therapist or patient; others find it more helpful to encourage their patients to use them for associational stimuli.[4] By placing dreams and fantasies in this cluster of forms tending toward subjectivity, I compromise between these extremes.

Patients also vary widely in their readiness to recall and work with their dreams and fantasies. They often require coaching to make best use of them. Encouraging patients who have achieved a measure of acceptance of their own subjectivity to report dreams or to allow spontaneous fantasies to come into their awareness often provides openings to further inner vision.

My practice is to ask for a careful telling of the dream or fantasy, followed by a relating of all spontaneous associations that the patient can discover. Usually at this point I will have noted some words or images that seem to be particularly poignant or which were spoken in a manner suggesting affective loading. I feed these back, asking the patient simply to allow them to trigger whatever they will; meantime I kept alert to intercept any tendency to move toward objectifying or logically analyzing the material. This sequence usually will trigger additional material, which can then be cycled one or more times. I pick up unwitting double entendres, puns, and slips of speech and process them similarly.

Helping a patient get to the point of being able to work as I've just described is usually a time-consuming process which is concurrent with helping him incorporate his concern and recognize his own power to do something about it. When a patient spontaneously and fully works with his fantasies and dreams, he is really working at a truly subjective level (the last cluster) where the form termed "spontaneous fantasy" occurs.

An aside about the significance of dreams. Dreaming is ultimately a mysterious process and one which seems essential to life and well-being. As may be expected in one who puts central attention on subjectivity, I feel the dream epitomizes the nature of the subjective. No dream can be fully remembered, fully recorded, or fully understood by our waking, conscious minds. The dream clearly is an expression of a state of consciousness much larger than the usual way we experience our being. Many and shifting images, sensings of multiple layers of meaning, a kaleidoscope of feelings, and intuitions of significances for our waking life—these hint at a realm which is ours but about which we know far too little of its scope, powers, and how to access it. I often use patient dreams as examples of the greater resources latent within them and of how they need to be open to unbidden inner awarernesses.

Emotional Associating

In Segment 9.5, as Andy gets to his pain and sadness over being in his own eyes "such a klutz," he is associating emotionally to his own life issues. Often, as in the example, patients are helped to discover their emotional associations through becoming more aware of their bodies. Among the many possible other routes, recounting current life experiences with openness to discovery is often helpful.

Segment 9.6
PT-22: Janet and I went to see a movie the other night. I can't remember its name. It doesn't matter anyway. The point is that there was this one scene that just stuck in my mind. I can't see quite why, but it just comes up in my thoughts now. Shall I tell you about it?
TH-22: Just the scene as it comes back now.
PT-23: Well, this guy is standing outside his house in the early morning, just

watching the sky get brighter, and not doing much. He got up early for some reason and walked out there, and his wife and kids are inside asleep, and he's just watching the sky. (Pauses, swallows, catches his breath) I feel kind of choked up right now when I'm telling you about it. It doesn't make any sense, but . . .

TH-23: You're interrupting your own chance to find out about what this means to you by constantly criticizing what you're feeling and saying it doesn't make any sense.

PT-24: Yeah, I suppose so, but I can't figure out any reason for feeling that way. I'm a city boy and never lived on a farm like that, and I'm not married, and . . .

TH-24: You seem determined to prove how wrong your feelings are — and without really giving yourself a chance to discover about them.

PT-25: No, I don't want to do that. Wait a minute. Let me see if I can get that scene back. (He leans back, shuts his eyes, sighs.)

TH-25: Slow now, Andy. The man is standing there as the dawn is coming. (Her voice is soft, slightly dreamy.) His family, his wife, his children are asleep in the house behind him. He's just standing there.

PT-26: (Voice deep in his throat) Just standing there with his family asleep. His family . . . his family. I don't have a family. (Catches his breath) I don't have a family, but . . . but I want to have one.

TH-26: You don't have a family, but you want to have one.

PT-27: (Opening his eyes and looking very steadily right at therapist) Yes, I want to have a family, and I'm tired of being alone and on the outside of life.

Recognition in Process

Another mode, somewhat arbitrarily placed in this cluster, has to do with times in which the patient becomes aware — of his own accord or from the therapist's well-timed interpretation — of how some issue is being enacted in the therapeutic hour itself. I say this is arbitrarily placed here because so much depends on whether the recognition is chiefly a detached one similar to another descriptive observation, a somewhat aware acknowledgment corresponding to a causal association, a realization having the quality of an emotional association, or a deep insight arising from truly subjective discovery. The example which follows portrays the third of these possibilities, an emotional association.

Segment 9.7

PT-30: I thought after I was here last time that I would tell Janet we should get married now and quit waiting for . . . for whatever we're waiting for. But then . . .

TH-30: But then . . .

PT-31: Well, when I saw her, she was full of plans for our trip next month, and besides I didn't feel as sure or . . .

TH-31: You weren't sure about getting married?

PT-32: Well, yes (pause). I mean I think it's what I want to do, but somehow. . . . It seems as though it's time for me to settle down, and I know she wants to, but . . . but when I'm with her. (Pause) Oh, damn! Here I'm into it again.

TH-32: How do you mean?

PT-33: Well, like right now. I'm so indecisive I can't even talk about it straight here. It just keeps . . . I mean I keep seeing another side to things and . . .

LARGELY SUBJECTIVE PATTERNS

In Chapter 1, I stressed the importance of recognizing that the ultimate domain of depth, life-changing psychotherapy is the patient's subjectivity. Now, as we turn to examine ways in which patients work with their life concerns within that domain, what we attempt is an impossibility.

It is impossible to describe anything like a standard set of modes for patients to use in exploring their own subjectivity. This difficulty arises because of that very individuality of subjectivity which we have repeatedly mentioned. But more fundamentally it arises because it is not possible to specify *how* one is truly subjective.

"How to" is for objective tasks. In that area we can say things like, "First, lay out the various parts of the gadget in this way. Then pick up the feathered gizmo and insert its threaded end in Aperture A and give it a half turn counterclockwise. Next. . . . " An analogy of limited validity is to say that we can teach patients how to start, drive, and stop their cars, but we cannot teach them how to get the inner motivation to go any place.

The most we can do in the subjective realm is describe patterns that others have found helpful for getting more in touch with their true subjectivity. Then we can encourage our patients to use these as starting points for their own efforts. To say it differently, we can provide our patients with directions for how to get set for inner exploration, but we cannot tell them how to carry that process forward.

The truly subjective parts of the process are carried forward within the fastness of the individual psyche. Whatever objective or explicit instructions we can give will be short of the mark, may confuse more than aid, and may lead to enactments of supposed subjectivity that are actually counterproductive therapeutically.

Spontaneous Fantasy

Segment 9.8

PT-34: Blanche, I feel stuck. I suppose I'm not really trying hard enough, but. . . . well, I . . . (pause). I don't want to get caught into that now. (Pause) I'm trying to stay with my thoughts and not chop myself up, but I don't seem to be getting anywhere.

TH-34: You're so watchful about what you're doing that you can't really think about what you want to say.

PT-35: I know it! I know it, and I hate it, but how do I stop doing that?

TH-35: Let's see whether I can help you get beneath that self-consciousness: Settle back on the couch and really let yourself go so that the couch carries your weight.

PT-36: (Lies back and starts deepening his breathing) Um-hmm. Okay, so now what?

TH-36: Let go, Andy; you're still pushing.

PT-37: (Sighs heavily) Okay.

TH-37: Now just be quiet for a bit and watch the screen in front of your inner eye. Don't try to think of anything. Don't try to visualize anything, but let yourself be open to any imagery that spontaneously comes to you. When it comes, you will need to wait a little to begin talking. Let some images form, and then just quietly tell me what you see.

PT-38: (Silent two minutes) Nothing much. Just a kind of misty emptiness. (Pause) Seems as though there's a big fog, sort of. (Pause) Can't make out what it is, but there's something in the fog, something darker and solider (pause).

TH-38: (Softly) Mm-hmmm.

PT-39: I don't know what it is, but it's sort of moving. It seems comfortable. I mean, I feel kind of comfortable about it. It doesn't seem frightening or anything. It's getting closer now, and I want to see it better. (Pause) Oh! I see (pause).

TH-39: Mmmm?

PT-40: It's me, or it's sort of me, but it's not me too. I know that doesn't make sense, but . . .

TH-40: (Quietly, firmly) You seem to need to break up your imagery by criticizing yourself.

PT-41: Uh-huh. (Pause) It's like a me that might be but isn't . . . at least right now it isn't. I feel that it's like I'm looking at a me that could be . . . could be different . . . more sure of himself, myself. It's still pretty vague, foggy, but . . . but I think it's getting clearer. I mean the image . . . or maybe I mean that I'm getting clearer . . . know more about how I want to be.

It is impossible to specify what form such imagery will take. Sometimes it will be as positive as Andy's experience; other times it may be frightening, anxiety-evoking, or discouraging. Sometimes the images will be sharp and the action clear-cut; other times everything remains vague and indecipherable. Usually, if the patient can yield to the flow of inner, undirected awareness, there will be material of pertinence to his current concerns. But that's an important "if." The whole key to using spontaneous imagery is helping the patient truly open himself to what may issue into consciousness.

Of course, there are times when the patient cannot allow imagery to occur, and then the therapist needs to estimate whether there was true readiness for this sort of inquiry, whether her induction effort aroused resistance—conscious or not—and whether the inability to find imagery is itself an expression of where the patient is in dealing with his current issues.

A word of caution. Two sorts of circumstances are contraindicative for the use of spontaneous imagery: First, patients with poor ego structure, in the midst of extreme anxiety or depression or confronting extratherapeutic crises, are generally not well served by this suspension of usual objective-coping processes.

The second group of patients with whom one must use discretion in encouraging spontaneous imagery are usually effectively functioning people who plunge gladly into the pool of fantasy and can scarcely be lured out. I do not mean that they become autistic. I mean they readily find imagery and fantasy which they tell extensively and in therapist-entangling detail. A whole therapeutic hour can pass in this way; rich pictorial and dramatic vistas are presented, and very little genuine therapeutic inquiry occurs. With such patients, after a maximum of ten minutes of such material, it is well to call for consideration of what the imagery is expressing. This may lead to discovery that a resistive function is being served under the guise of subjective exploration.

Free Association

Freud's "basic rule" was for the patient to say whatever came into his mind without editing, considerations of propriety, or other restraint. Since estimates are that most of us can think at about the rate of 800 words per minute but can only speak at 125–150, this basic rule is a manifest impossibility. However, the idea behind it is a useful one, and some patients use it well.

Segment 9.9
TH-44: Andy, today I'd like you to try something a little different.
PT-44: Okay. What?
TH-45: I suggest you use the couch again today. Get settled on it now. (Waits for patient to do so) Now, just let your awareness be open, without your conscious effort to guide it. (Pause) Now, try to just tell me whatever comes into your consciousness. Just describe it and move on to whatever else appears. So far as possible, let yourself be simply a channel for whatever in you now wants to be expressed in and through you.
PT-45: I don't know whether I can do that. It seems as though I can't think of anything, or there's too much, or . . .
TH-46: That's fine, Andy. That's what's coming through right now. Just let it keep coming.
PT-46: Yeah, well, uh . . . (pause). Uh . . . I can't think what to say. Everything's sort of vague, and there's no clear thought, and . . .
TH-47: Uh-huh (tone of acceptance).
PT-47: Uh, this seems sort of pointless. I mean, I can't seem to do what you want. (Pause) Hmm, I'm still trying to do what you want! There it is again. I'm always trying to do what people want. I'm tired of that, but I . . . I wonder . . . I wonder what it would be like . . .
TH-48: Ummm?
PT-48: If I just listened to myself. I don't think I know what that means. Like now, I'm supposed to just be listening to myself, you know? And I'm not doing anything. I'm just wasting time. I don't really think this is working, Blanche . . .
TH-49: (Quietly, firmly) Keep going, Andy; you're already doing it.

The excerpt illustrates a frequent difficulty at first: The self-consciousness induced by the task may make the patient doubt its utility. But the excerpt also illustrates that given reasonable encouragement and firm, friendly insistence, the patient unwittingly is soon dealing with the issues. The prerequisite necessity is for the patient to have some appreciation of the necessity of subjective exploration and readiness to commit himself to the effort.

Using a couch. I find it valuable to have a couch or reclining chair available for my patients, and while I suggest its use from time to time, I never require it. Our habits of mind-set are so different for times when we lie on our backs and think about how our lives are going from what they are when we sit (usually face-to-face) in conversation with someone. Obviously the former position—once self-consciousness is past—is much more facilitating of subjective exploration. (About a third to a half of my patients recline frequently and less than a third never.)

Concern-Guided Searching

What I am calling "searching" is a way of tapping into the same natural capacity which Freud recognized with his basic rule of free association. This innate capacity of human beings is that on which we call whenever we meet a situation to which we need to respond but for which we have no preexisting well-practiced response pathways.[5]

Concern-guided searching is a developed form of free association. Recognizing the impossibility of a patient's saying all that comes into consciousness, a touchstone is required to serve as a way of selecting from the abundance that is potential. That function is fulfilled by the experience of *concern*.

Concern is the experience of letting oneself really care about some life issue, of being willing to invest oneself in it, and being ready to work to bring about desired changes. (Chapter 11 deals further with this important concept.) Its value is as an empowering and guiding force in the therapeutic exploration of one's subjectivity.

Three conditions are required for effective searching to take place: (a) The patient must identify a life issue which he wishes to explore more deeply and fully and describe it to the therapist completely— and often, repeatedly. (b) The patient must be as deeply immersed as possible while carrying out this description—remaining at the critical occasions level as much as he can. (c) The patient must maintain an expectancy of discovery, a readiness to be surprised.

Segment 9.10
PT-51: You know, Blanche, I think we've gotten some handles on my indecisiveness, and I know it's a whole lot better these days, and yet . . .
TH-51: Yet . . . ?
PT-52: Yet I feel that some way we're still missing something.
TH-52: Uh-huh.
PT-53: Like Thursday when we were talking about my Dad and how he would top whatever any of us said, I kept feeling as though that was

not quite the point. I still have that feeling, but I don't know what is the point either.

TH-53: Just follow that feeling . . . the feeling that there's something else, something you need to tell yourself.

PT-54: Well, I've tried to think what it might be, and I just don't. . . .

TH-54: Trying to figure it out will just get in the way of what you need to do, which is to listen inside of youself.

PT-55: (Pauses, silent a minute or so) I think of that scene I told you about at the dinner table, when my brother and my Dad got in the big fight . . . well, not a real physical fight, but still they were so mad. (Pause) I didn't quite know what I thought. Each of them wanted me to be on his side, but I couldn't do that.

TH-55: Um-hmmm.

PT-56: Don, my big brother, grabbed me by the arm and said something like, "Come on, have some guts, tell him what you think!" But I was too scared. Dad said, "Let him alone. You're a bully." That made Don even madder, and he started shouting at Dad that he was an even bigger bully. I was so scared they'd really start hitting each other . . . or me.

And go gradually Andy finds another root of his hesitation to take a stand. By this time, he is seeing that his concern is more than that single issue. He has come to recognize how often he sacrifices his own views to be liked by or at least acceptable to others, how much he feels starved for having his own way of being, and how much anger is stored up inside of him. This anger is nearing the surface now, and that is adding to his fear of getting any deeper into his feelings.

HELPING THE PATIENT MOVE TO DEEPER
WORK

The moral of this chapter is not that every patient should work at the truly subjective levels. Not every patient should; not every patient can; indeed, many cannot. The level needed for any particular patient will depend on a number of considerations — nature of the presenting problem, readiness to make a long-term commitment, soundness of ego functioning, amount and depth of change sought, for example.

We have already observed that some people should be discouraged from the loosening of reality contact that the deeper levels require. Such patients may have insufficient ego strength or may be in life stress situations which call for immediate, practical responses. If it becomes apparent that such a patient is having difficulty going deeper and yet needs to do so to deal with his life better, the therapist may foster movement a few places along this scale rather than pushing for a major change in functioning. Thus, a person who is functionally associating and thinking about the causes of his concern is best helped by being encouraged to become more aware of his body sensations and the associations linked to them. Later, if this works out well, he can be invited to experiment with reporting and associating to dreams and fantasies.

Even patients who seem likely candidates for depth work should not be pushed toward truly subjective levels abruptly. The therapist does best if she forms an impression of the levels at which the patient is ready to work and then gradually encourages movement along the scale a cluster at a time. Sensing where the patient is and what his needs are at any given point is the essence of therapist artistry.

Why Didn't Blanche Help Andy Make a Decision?

That's the question that some people ask. They feel that therapy took the long way around the barn to deal with Andy's difficulties. To be sure, some good practical counseling aid might have led to Andy's making a decision about marrying Janet. But then he'd very likely be back to square one when the next important decision came along—where to live, whether to have a baby now, etc. Only by helping Andy get into the underlying soil from which the indecisiveness springs can a more fundamental change in this pattern come about.

That underlying soil has been seen in traditional psychotherapeutic doctine as the "cause," the historic source of Andy's symptoms. We certainly learned some of the events which clearly helped to teach Andy to be cautious about declaring himself, but just knowing those would not end the pattern. It was only as he became fully aware of how being indecisive served him currently, of how it was part of his way of defining himself in his life nowadays, that he became able to reduce this pattern.

"Reduce" is not the same as eliminate. Basic patterns such as this—often called "character" patterns—seldom are totally eradicated in psychotherapy. Rather, the patient sees how his pattern functions but sees so much more in addition that he is no longer captured by it. This larger vision of himself is the essence of therapeutic change and improved life functioning and satisfaction.

CONCLUSION

This chapter has dealt with the ways in which patients take hold of the concerns which bring them to therapy and the issues which are linked with those concerns. The initial presenting complaint may be foremost throughout the work or it may soon fade into the background or disappear altogether. However that may work out, at any point the patient is working on some concern, and how he does so is of central importance to the whole enterprise.

For the patient who is suitable for deeper work, the first step is to help him work at whatever level he is most immediately ready to use. As he does this for a time, he may spontaneously begin to deepen his engagement. Of course our patients don't just work on one of these levels at a time; they vary over a range. We note where they are most of the time, when they're most immersed, and what they can reach on occasion only but toward which they are moving.

How does patient treat his inner life, his subjectivity generally? These same levels apply in varying degrees to talking about intentions, wantings, fears, and all the other aspects of subjective life, including relations.

Here is a sampling of areas in which these dimensions may be useful.

- What bothers patients about themselves.
- What bothers them about others and objects.
- How they tell about experiences, dreams, etc.
- How they talk about therapy itself.
- The form in which they ask questions of therapist.
- The way in which they express immediate feelings.
- How they ask help.

A PSYCHOTHERAPIST'S JOURNEY

The man who, in his time, did as much to change the world as anyone, Isaac Newton,[6] once wrote, "I do not know what I may appear to the world; but to myself I seem to have been only like a boy playing on the seashore, and diverting myself in now and then finding a smoother pebble or a prettier shell than ordinary, while the great ocean of truth lay all undiscovered before me."

What an astonishing, humble statement from one so profound and of such original vision. I hope it is not presumptuous to borrow his metaphor; it is apt for our purposes here also.

The great ocean of the subjective lies all undiscovered before all of us. We wade in its shallowest waters, we wander along its shore, but we dare not, we cannot, venture out into its depths or its far reaches — for we are still children.

We do not know much of this ocean, although it is our archaic home or, perhaps better, the medium out of which we were spawned. Out of the infant's subjectivity perhaps we come "trailing clouds of glory." We have assumed that infancy was a blank slate, but more and more studies of infants by biologists and physicians suggest otherwise. The striking conceptions of William Emerson[7] seem to document the presence of a high order of consciousness while the fetus is yet in utero.

Such notions have, until recently, been dismissed out of hand. In our most chauvinistic of epochs we have denied all realities that fail to accord with the current, scientistic, objectivist view. Centuries of Eastern spiritual wisdom, the millenia-old, traditional beliefs of peoples in "undeveloped" cultures, the observations and speculations of many who do not adhere to rationalistic dogma — all these we have dismissed as superstition and unworthy of serious attention.

The subjective is a vast ocean. As we make our first dives into it or timid voyages on it — as this book describes — we are likely to find that our familiar world is called into question.

These things I assert:

One: We do not truly know our own identities. We are much more than our conscious awareness. We do not know how to access or bring to use much that is latently ours.

Two: If we can revise our sense of identity to include what is not conscious or objective (i.e., to truly incorporate the unknown and the subjective), we may begin to gain access to more of our potential. Our need to deny the unknown acts to keep it unknown and inaccessible.

Three: The runaway preoccupation with objectivity in our times and our culture is a genuine cancer which may very well destroy our species and even our planet. It is a growth, not toxic in itself, which so intrudes on other, healthy processes that it cripples and destroys them.

The demand to make everything objective (and explicit, a form of objectification) destroys much that is ineffable and subtle.

Earlier generations believed in a god who knew everything—including what lay "in the hearts of men." This meant that we could not escape responsibility for our thoughts and intentions as well as our deeds. Liberated from that external responsibility, we have been slow to pick up intrinsic responsibility.

Four: Despair has been the most frequent route to tapping the unrealized potential within us. When tapped, it has resulted in paradigm shifts and other creative outcomes.

Perhaps the imminence of Armageddon may bring us to the despair needed to jump past our prejudices. Perhaps only the despair of worldwide cataclysm can do that. Can it occur while there is anything to save?

Five: Fully recognizing the deeper, more inclusive, more fundamental role of the subjective means establishing a whole new paradigm—not only for psychology, but for science; not only for science, but for being human; and, perhaps, not only for being human, but for beingness itself.

CHAPTER 10

A Basic Approach
to the Resistance

The client comes to life-changing psychotherapy in order to change her life. What she brings to therapy to be "worked on" is her way of being alive. What life-changing therapy must do is to aid the client in changing her way of being alive. But the way the client is alive is—much more than she recognizes—the basis of her sense of who and what she is and what her world is. Therefore, when therapy becomes truly life-changing, the client feels her identity, her world—in short, her life—is being threatened. Not unreasonably, the client resists the therapeutic effort.

Significant depth of subjective involvement is required to make possible the explorations and confrontations which are the core of life-changing psychotherapy. Therapist sensitivity and skill in using powerful methods while providing the support of a meaningful relationship are the essentials of attaining that depth. This chapter displays one such approach, founded on the pioneering work of psychoanalysis.

More than in the other chapters, this presentation of a method for working with the resistance is sectarian in that it grows out of my conception of the nature of human personality and of the rationale for psychotherapy. I attempt, however, to present this approach so that those with somewhat contrasting orientations may still profitably draw on it.

ONE OF FREUD'S most important contributions was to identify resistance and to recognize that it was of central significance to the therapeutic effort. "When we undertake to restore a patient to health, to relieve him of the symptoms of his illness, he meets us with a violent and tenacious resistance, which persists throughout the whole length of the treatment," he wrote.[1]

It is unlikely that Freud was the first to discover that his efforts to help were being deflected by the very person whom he sought to aid and, many times, that this was the very same person who had come asking for that assistance. Surely physicians, priests, teachers, and

173

many others had encountered this paradoxical phenomenon from humankind's earliest days. What Freud, the prototypical depth therapist, did that was uniquely important was to accept resistance as an integral—even central—part of the enterprise rather than to dismiss it as poor motivation, wickedness, or stubbornness—the more usual prior interpretations. For a person as jealous of his contribution and what would be given its name as he, it is revealing that Freud wrote, "There is no psychoanalysis which is not the analysis of the resistance."

DEFINING "RESISTANCE"

This important term may be defined in several ways and at several levels of clinical interaction. It is used in significantly different ways by therapists and theorists of various persuasions. I will offer a basic conception and then show some of the ways it is manifested. Here we begin by recognizing a general use of this term: "You caught cold because your resistance was lowered," we are told. Resistance to disease is a familiar concept. This use of the word makes evident that resistance is a healthful process native to our bodies—and perhaps more than bodily alone.

Resistance is a name for those impulses in the client which seek to reduce threat and for those processes through which the client enacts such impulses. Obviously, so conceived, resistance is a universal, normal, and even desirable part of the way in which we deal with our experience. That is an important recognition to keep in mind. Who does not seek to reduce threat? The sequel questions are the distinguishing ones: What is perceived as threatening and therefore to be resisted? How are the threats reduced? At what cost?

Freud saw resistance manifested in his analysand's failure to follow the "basic rule" of free association and in the client's failure to accept the interpretations advanced by the analyst. Despite many modifications of theory and practice (including much less emphasis on the basic rule), many current therapists and analysts retain the view that resistance is the client's defense against the therapist's interpretations. In my view, that can be a resistance, but I also believe that it may not be.

Resistance is not the same as client opposition, antagonism, or hostility. Clients may argue with therapist interpretations vociferously and with great presence; they are not resisting as I am using the term. Clients may be furious with the therapist and make it perfectly evident, and so long as this is not a screen for avoiding presence, I still do not see them as resisting. Now, of course, these two instances are overstated to make the point. It is seldom as simple as resisting or not resisting. It will be evident, however, that I am conceiving resistance differently from the traditional psychoanalytic view.

Resistance is the impulse to protect one's familiar identity and known world against perceived threat. In depth psychotherapy, resistance is those ways in which the client avoids being truly subjectively present—accessible and expressive—in the therapeutic work. The conscious or unconscious threat is that immersion will bring challenges to the client's being in her world.

Resistance is shown as the client holds off deep immersion in the therapeutic work by objectifying herself and maintaining a surface orientation. Resistance is the counterforce to the pull to subjectivity, the need to avoid genuine presence in one's life—whether in therapy or out of it. Resistance, so conceived, results in inauthentic being.

Resistance Dimensions[2]

To aid our grasp of the resistance's significance and prepare us for thinking about working therapeutically with it, I will now spell out a series of dimensions which are involved in this pervasive clinical phenomenon.

Interview resistance. The first evidence of resistance usually occurs in the initial contact with client.

> Nan was five minutes late to her first appointment. She made a perfunctory but uninvolved apology. For her next three appointments, she arrived an average of eight to ten minutes late. When she came to her fifth interview nearly a quarter hour after the time, the therapist pointed out the pattern and asked Nan's thoughts about it. She laughingly dismissed the matter, describing her busy work schedule and assuring him she'd do better in the future. The therapist didn't press the point but he felt a lack of real engagement with Nan on it.

Our first recognition of a resistance pattern often comes about in this way. We feel deflected or note that the client has drawn back from involvement or recognize that in some way we have lost the main

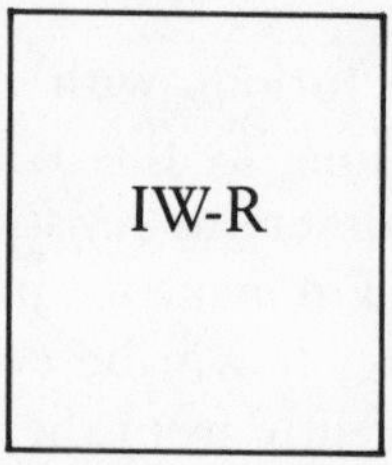

```
┌──────────────┐
│              │
│              │
│     IW-R     │
│              │
│              │
└──────────────┘
```

Figure 10.1. Interview Resistance Seen as an Isolated Phenomenon of the Conversation.

thread of our inquiry. We may think of this as "interview resistance," and we often see it at first as an isolated matter. Figure 10.1 thus puts it in a little box.

Life-pattern resistance. As therapist gets to know client, he discovers that the interview resistance is not an isolated event but that repeatedly the client shows this pattern. Clearly it is a well-practiced part of her response repertoire. Then it becomes evident that the patterns being enacted in the consulting room are part of the client's usual way of being on the outside as well. The following example is exaggeratedly obvious, but still quite representative.

> After being only a minute or two late for the next two sessions, Nan is again consistently late for her appointments. She always has excuses. When questioned about this pattern, she tries to dismiss it as insignificant: "My work schedule is just too busy." "I've always been the last one to arrive (laughing)." "Has nothing to do with therapy; it's been going on since way before I started with you and will probably go on the rest of my life."

Nan does not readily accept that her continual tardiness is a resistance because she is sure it's a way of being that exists independently of therapy. Of course; that's the point: The discovery that the life-pattern resistances are operative outside the consulting room makes plain the importance of bringing them into the therapeutic discourse. The in-therapy resistance is no longer to be seen only as an isolated matter, a troublesome but unimportant habit; now we recognize it as a segment of a larger life pattern. Figure 10.2 puts the interview resistance within this larger framework.

Life-limiting processes. The next step is the crucial one that gives resistance its importance to depth therapy. Working together, the

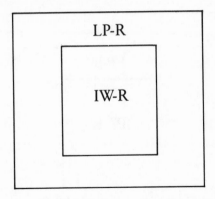

Figure 10.2. Interview Resistance Is Seen to Be an Aspect of Life-Style Resistance.

therapeutic partners find that there are other life patterns which also operate to keep her from immersion in herself, which interfere with her self-discovery, which pervade her life outside therapy. In other words, it becomes evident that the life-pattern resistances are intrinsic to the distresses in the client's life which, directly or indirectly, may have led to her coming to therapy.

Moreover, we come to realize that these patterns are not separate difficulties but form a constellation which acts to limit the client's world (including her self-concept), to let her feel that she is safe and able to manage her life. This is sometimes referred to as the "transference neurosis," in that it represents in miniature in the office the larger neurotic gestalt which is disabling the client's life. The recognition of this constellation of patterns which so limits the self-and-world concept of the client is a recognition of immense significance, as it helps us understand the deepest function of the resistance, to recognize its positive aspects, and to orient our therapeutic interventions in a way which is most apt to be successful.

I will first of all illustrate this point and then discuss its significance further.

> Nan's therapy gradually brings out her need to fill every moment with activity, her near panic when she finds herself without something she "needs to do." When she entered treatment, she shamefacedly confessed her secret obsessive ruminations. These were something that frightened her and which she hoped therapy could relieve. Now it becomes evident that she needs these thoughts to fill her mind whenever she has an unoccupied moment. Similarly, her lateness is a way of making sure she will never have to wait for anyone or anything and thus be faced with emptiness.

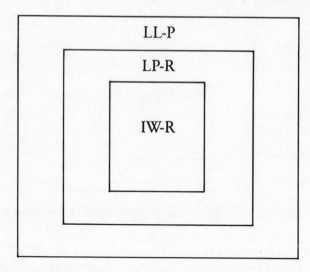

Figure 10.3. Both Life-Style Resistance and Interview Resistance Are Discovered to
Be Subsets of the Life-Limiting Processes.

In this example the patterns have been stripped of their actual
covering and complicating aspects in order to show the skeletal way
the concerns which trouble our clients are manifested in the interview
and in their life patterns generally. Now the larger frame (Figure
10.3) which encloses the interview resistances and the life pattern
resistances confirms that what we are disclosing is important to the
client's life more generally.

The self-and-world construct system.[3] Each of us must develop or
construct a conception of who and what she is and of what her world
is, how it operates, and how she can make her way in it. We come to
have some notion of our own strengths and weaknesses, our own
needs, the dangers which particularly threaten us, and the kinds of
things or states of being we will seek or avoid. The potential world is
immense; always we must make some compromise with possibility to
secure the liveable.

Rollo May[4] has described how we shrink the world to proportions
within which we feel we can be safe. Some of us retreat to a very small
space; some seem always to be opening up new possibilities; most of
us settle for a comfortable but limited world and only occasionally
explore new alternatives.

Nan found in therapy that her flight from solitude and her need to
be continually occupied were pervasive influences in her life and that

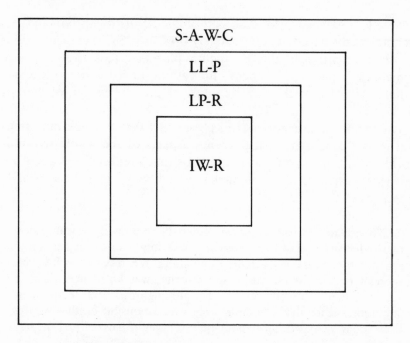

Figure 10.4. All Resistance Forms Are Demonstrated To Be Structures in Client's Self-and-World Construct System.

they significantly disrupted her relations with others and the quality of the work she performed. Unable to risk pausing to take stock, she took the more superficial and immediately available choices in most life situations and so was not able to work at what could have been her true level nor to maintain relationships that were other than brief and casual. She had known those lacks; now she could begin to face the emptiness from which she had so long fled and through that confrontation to reclaim the rest of her potential.

This self-and-world construct system is, of course, much broader than the resistive functions; it includes as well the constructive, functional structures which make the client's life possible and provide the fulfillments which that life yields. We see, therefore, that it is the embracing framework within which the resistance patterns are set. It is abbreviated as S-A-W-C in Figure 10.4.

Summation

It should now be apparent why this concept of the resistance is such a critically important one. Recognizing the resistance discloses a therapeutically central aspect of the way the client identifies herself and structures her world. The pathologic or distress-producing elements thus displayed are immediately present in the therapeutic hour for direct attention by the therapeutic partners. This gives the work immediate impact on the client's life (as contrasted with work which requires transfer of therapeutic gains to the client's out-of-therapy life).

The further significance of this perspective is that it calls our attention to the constructive, life-serving aspects of the whole self-and-world construct system and reminds us that the resistive aspects are only that—aspects. The structures to which they adhere have positive aspects as well.

> When Nan was young, she was the baby of a family that included two older sisters and her parents. These four had formed a warm group before Nan unexpectedly came along. When Nan was five, the younger of her sisters, the family favorite, was killed in a boating accident. Nan probably saw her die, although this is not certain. In any event, she felt that in some way she was responsible for the tragedy. Even today she speculates about how she might have caused or prevented it.
>
> Nan says the family tells her that she changed radically thereafter, becoming withdrawn and irritable. She remembers night terrors and waking fears throughout her childhood, and she still has occasional nightmares in which she struggles to protect herself or her own children from vague threats.
>
> In our work Nan comes to memories of learning to depend on reading until she fell asleep, of keeping very busy during waking hours, and of setting herself mental problems to do whenever she had idle time. All these ways of forestalling fearful, self-blaming, and anxious thoughts have continued in various forms. She says now that she thinks they were all that kept her from going crazy or committing suicide in her lonely and distressed high school years.

THE CLINICAL ENCOUNTER WITH THE RESISTANCE

It is time to move from the conceptual level to the clinical events through which the resistance is manifested and in which therapy seeks to reduce its constricting effects. First a variety of examples demonstrate the protean potential of this life process. Then we examine functions the resistance serves. These two steps prepare for detailing therapeutic procedure for working with the resistance.

Typical Resistance Patterns

The examples which follow will bring out the ways in which the resistance interferes with the client's being fully present and immersed. These are, as we have just seen, the ways in which we often first become aware of these patterns. However, the therapist needs to recognize that he is not the opponent of the resistance and is not seeking to defeat it. Instead, he hopes to find the constructive aspects and reinforce those while helping the client reduce the crippling aspects.

> Alice asks many questions about the therapist: "Are you married? . . . Where did you grow up? . . . Is your work satisfying to you?" When this persistent curiosity is reflected back to her, she protests as though accused of impropriety. "I'm just interested in you. You know so much about me, and I . . . I thought it would help me to be more relaxed if I knew more about your background. I don't mean to be nosy. I hope you're not annoyed with me."

The therapist notes that Alice's questions often interrupt her immersion, seem to transform the interview into a social exchange, and usually come when Alice is about to get into uncomfortable material. Clearly, the questioning is one form Alice's resistance takes.

> Charles is exceeding committed to therapy; so much so that the idea that he is resisting would dumbfound him. He comes to each session with a list of things he wants to "work on" or with a carefully written out dream. He listens respectfully and intently to whatever I say, and he often expresses appreciation of my help.

Altogether an ideal client? No. Charles keeps such tight control of the content and level of our work that it remains an academic exercise in which he seeks to be the star student. Whenever I try to get Charles to be open to the uncontrived, the unexpected, and the impulsive within himself, he finds himself blocked, impatient, and subtly resentful.

> Linda is a therapist herself. She is interested in learning more about depth therapy as well as in getting help with "some personal issues," as she terms them. From time to time the work on these personal matters is interrupted by the professional motivation which prompts Linda to ask questions about my intentions in raising a particular issue or in

phrasing my interventions in the way I do. At other times, Linda regrets that she is not a better client so that my task with her would not be so difficult.

Linda is very sincere and completely intends to make herself fully open and invested in her work. She knows about the importance of getting subjective depth, and she watches herself continually to see whether she is getting there—just as she watches me to see how I try to help her. The results, of course, are that Linda makes herself an object of study, and her true subjectivity remains unavailable. When this is reflected to her, she readily agrees, laments her resistance, and tries harder than ever. She is unwittingly adroit in getting me entangled in trying to help her try not to try so tryingly.

Eddie is in misery; many sessions are filled with his descriptions of his anxiety, pain, and need for help in getting control of those feelings. Frequently we need to set a time to stop work before the end of the hour so he can go through a number of steps to regain equilibrium sufficiently to leave, drive his car, and meet his other obligations. He lives in daily fear of being overwhelmed by his panic. Several times he finds it necessary to phone me for support and the reassurance that I am still here and concerned about him.

Eddie is not weak; he conducts his business effectively, meets and deals productively with many people, and returns again and again to the work of therapy. Yet that work is also the site of the tremendous threat under which he truly suffers. He hates his own fear, but he cannot will it not to be; much therapeutic work will be needed to help him accept it so that we can redirect and ease it.

Other, familiar patterns are being pleasing, argumentative, complaining of injustices, overly rational, flooded with feelings, seductive, oppositional, confused, passive, affect-blind, without wants or needs, overly attached to therapist, or excessively dependent.

It is evident that anything that the client says or does can serve resistive purposes, just as almost anything the client says or does may also express her health and wholeness. Depending upon our purpose at any particular point, we may attend to the resistive or the healthful aspect or to both.

Some Functions of the Resistance

Attending to the resistive aspects of client participation, we can identify different functions which resistance serves at various times:

- Reduction of openness in self-disclosure.
- Keeping the work objective, readily defensible, or impersonal.
- Postponing disclosing feelings and thoughts until the client has "previewed" them.
- Keeping control of the direction, intensity, or quality of the therapeutic work.
- Avoiding directly experiencing need, wanting, or other emotions, especially when they are directed toward therapist.

INTERVENTIONS INTO THE RESISTANCE

The modes of working with resistance which I will describe rest on certain assumptions:

- That the client is genuinely motivated to change, although that motivation may not be available at this point.
- That simple verbal reporting (feedback) to the client about a resistance pattern is not likely to be effective.
- That displaying to the client the fact of and psychological cost of a resistance is a key to helping the client change it.
- That awareness growing out of repeated occasions of immediate experiencing in some depth is apt to have an impact.
- That awareness of single resistive patterns is less effective than recognition of constellations of patterns in relation to the deeper need structures they serve.

From these observations we can develop a series of steps to help the client begin to relinquish the resistances.

Tagging

First, the client must be aided in recognizing the importance of getting some depth in the process of inner exploration. (Chapter 2 described this essential process in detail.)

Next the client needs help to become aware of patterns that interrupt her inward searching. This usually means that initially the therapist must try to identify to himself one cluster of resistive responses which seems most prevalent and accessible to the client's awareness. Then he needs to bring it repeatedly to the client's attention. Here are some typical examples:

- You're feeling confused now.
- You just changed the subject.
- Now you've switched your attention to me and away from yourself.
- You're wishing I would tell you what to talk about now.
- You've lost the train of thought.

Tagging the resistance is a matter of again and again pointing to the resistive pattern as it is occurring. This means that the pattern chosen for therapist attention must be one that is manifested frequently and is interfering currently with the client's inquiry into her own subjectivity. This means also that it is usually best to select only one such pattern for attention at any given point. Later, when several patterns have been identified, each for a period, then more than one can be tagged.

I said that the therapist must repeatedly point to the resistance selected for attention. "Repeatedly" means just that. With accelerating frequency the therapist needs to point to the client's dependence on this way of managing his in-the-moment experience. The first interview in which the therapist does this, he may take three or four opportunities to tag; the second interview it needs to be eight to ten times, and before too long it should be nearly every time that the behavior occurs. Therapists may feel diffident about putting on that much pressure, but if a resistance pattern is correctly and frequently tagged in this way, movement to deeper levels is very likely to occur.

After the tagging has proceeded even a short time—and especially if the client is beginning to understand how it is interfering with her work—it is helpful to add words which remind the client of the frequency of her use of this resistance:

- Again you find yourself confused.
- Did you notice that you changed the subject once more?
- Here we go again: moving from your inner work to focus on me.
- We're back to trying to get me to direct you, aren't we?
- Once again, you've lost the train of thought.

It will be noticed that these examples vary in the amount of interpersonal press they carry. Therapists will want to modulate that process in terms of the state of the alliance and the extent to which the client is committed to inner inquiry and can hear the thrapist as genuinely trying to support that effort.

Teaching the Effect of the Resistance

As the client becomes aware, through the tagging, of how frequently she relies on the pattern, the tagging needs to be extended to show how it affects the work. This usually means pointing to how the resistance causes the client to objectify herself, to decrease emotional involvement, or to otherwise lessen subjective centering. Notice that the effect involved here is immediate and limited to what is manifest. At a later stage the motivation of the resistance will be disclosed, but to do that now will frequently result in an unavailing discussion, or even argument, about whether the suggested, but assertedly unconscious, intention was indeed the cause of the blocking.

Segment 10.1 illustrates how this process may go.

Segment 10.1
Client: Betty Stevens; Therapist: Carlton Blaine
CL-21: I've been thinking lately about what I told you about my father and how he changed when I went through puberty. I don't know whether that's my imagination or if it's really the way it was.
TH-21: Standing apart from it as you are, it's hard to get any farther.
CL-22: Yes, I know. But when I try to get into the feelings, I just get all mixed up.
TH-22: Are you mixed up now?
CL-23: Well, not right now, but it's close. Wait a minute. (Pause) Okay, now when I think about it, I remember how kind he used to be when I was younger, and I feel kind of teary, wishing he would have stayed that way.
TH-23: He was so good to you then.
CL-24: Oh yes, but then . . . when I was 12 or 13, well, it began to be different.
TH-24: Then it began to change.
CL-25: Yes, but I can't remember much about that. I mean I *know* it was different, but I can't really get the feelings back. (Pause) No, when I try now, I just find all sort of thoughts coming in and I get confused. That's what always happens.
TH-25: So, again your confusion keeps you from knowing what you need to know.

Segment 10.1 demonstrates two important points about the handling of the resistance: The client is already becoming aware (CL-21) of the resistance pattern, confusion, but the therapist does not attempt to teach its effect until that effect is actual in the moment (i.e., TH-25, the teaching response, comes after the client is experiencing the blocking, CL-25, not when client is only *talking about* it, CL-22).

Teaching Needfulness

As recognition of the resistance pattern comes to the client, it is usually desirable to begin to teach her that the behavior is not simply a bad speech habit or an instance of carelessness but a motivated action.

CL-26: Well, I'm not getting confused on purpose, you know. I can't help it.
TH-26: You sound as though I'm accusing you of doing something wrong.
CL-27: Yes, I mean, no. I mean, I know you're trying to help me, but I can't help it when I get confused.
TH-27: It's hard for you to see that in some way you might unconsciously be using your confusion.
CL-28: Why would I want to do that?
TH-28: Well, let's let that question wait a bit. For the moment, tell me, are you confused right now?
CL-29: No, not now.
TH-29: Now we're not into your inner living but standing outside, so to speak, and talking about it.
CL-30: Uh-huh. Yes, that's right.
TH-30: Okay, now try to get back inside. Can you get in touch again with the wishing for your father's lovingness that you had when you were small?
CL-31: (Settles back into the chair, closes her eyes, and sighs. She is silent for a time. Then she sighs again and opens her eyes which are misting now.) Yes. Yes, that feeling is always there it seems. You know, I saw Dad at Christmas, and he's looking so old now, so old and so frail. It makes me sad.
TH-31: (Softly) Just stay with the sadness.
CL-32: I wonder how many more Christmases we'll have. Since Mother died, he just doesn't seem to have the will to keep trying. I wonder if he thinks about how we used to be, he and I. I wish we could talk about it. I wish . . . I wish . . . oh, I don't know what I wish. (Sits more erectly) I don't know. It all gets muddled up.
TH-32: Getting muddled up is another of your confusions. How they stop you from knowing what you need to know about your own feelings!
CL-33: Yes, they do! I never thought of it that way. But what can I do about it?

It is important to note that once again the therapist has made certain that the client was subjectively ready for the resistance interpretation before offering it. To have made this suggestion when she first asked for it (CL-28) would have been not only futile but would have made it more difficult later to help her recognize the effect of the resistance.

Demonstrating Alternatives

The client's question (CL-33) seems to ask for a next step in helping her with the resistances, but the therapist may note that there is still a defensive quality to this. If that is so, he will do well to delay going on to the next step until the client has begun to be more spontaneously aware of the intrusion on her work and more directly looking for a solution. (Indeed, she may of her own accord recognize what is needed if the tagging and the teaching about the effects have gone well.)

Segment 10.2 imagines that more work has been done so that now the client is moving toward this place of genuinely seeking what to do when the confusion resistance occurs.

Segment 10.2
TH-41: You're feeling stuck again.
CL-41: Well, I don't know what I'm supposed to do if I'm confused. I just am confused.
TH-42: That's just all there is to it?
CL-42: Your question just confuses me more. What else could there be? What else could I do?
TH-43: Your confusion comes in right away to keep you from looking deeper into yourself.
CL-43: (Sadly) Yes, it does.
TH-44: Just stay with the confusion. Feel it, experience it any way you can.

The introduction of such a suggestion (TH-44) needs much greater sensitivity to the client's readiness than does tagging. This is because the suggestion calls for a change in the client's conscious intention. The confusion, in this case, has been seen as something unwanted; now she is being counseled to approach rather than reject it. This step is often a difficult one for clients, but with gentle but insistent encouragement they can learn to take a different attitude toward the resistance. This is important progress, for it is part of bringing in a changed internal climate in which client energies are less divided and conflicted.

In Segment 10.2 the client is encouraged to go with the confusion, since it is a subjective experience. Had the resistance pattern been different, say, client trying to reason her way out of some internal issue, therapist might then have recommended staying with the feelings which the reasoning was aborting, as in Segment 10.3.

Segment 10.3
Client: Beatrice Broyles; Therapist: Herbert Drake.
CL-1: I have been trying to get at this persistent feeling of fright that I have so much. I can't seem to figure out what's causing it.
TH-1: Once again you're trying to "figure yourself out" as though you were a puzzle.
CL-2: Well, I don't really mean it that way. I'm just sick and tired of feeling this way, going around scared of something I don't even know what it is.
TH-2: You know it when it's what you're feeling though.
CL-3: Yes, I do. (Sighs, sad) I know it then, and I hate feeling it too.
TH-3: You sound closer to the feeling now than you were a minute ago.
CL-4: Yes, I suppose so. But what I want to know is why do I have to have this miserable feeling so much?
TH-4: You don't seem to think actually feeling it here is much help; you'd rather analyze how come you have it.

As the therapist's first comment in this segment (TH-1) makes evident, the client has repeatedly attempted to work out logically the basis of her anxiety. This pattern has been reflected back to her before, but apparently she doesn't yet understand the therapist's doing so as more than simply correcting word choice (CL-2). Thus, she goes right on into some more "figuring," although she is careful not to use that word again.

Nevertheless, the therapist has planted a suggestion (TH-3) and has disclosed a secondary aspect of the resistance, dismissal of the experience (TH-4). He will need to return a number of times to both of these and other, related elements in the client's resistance to her feelings. This will be done gradually, moving the resistance identification forward from being incidental, as it is here, to being central, as in the following example (which would probably occur after quite a bit more work with the resistance had intervened):

Segment 10.4
CL-11: Well, I just think that if I could work out why I have these feelings, then I could change them.

TH-11: Figuring things out, working them out—these are the ways you've tried to get your feelings to change for years now. How's it proved out?

CL-12: Uh, I know. There I go again, sounding as though I could solve my emotions like they were arithmetic problems. I really know that doesn't work, but I just don't know what else to do.

TH-12: You learned to try to figure things out, and it works for you in many places, but it doesn't work when you're trying to get into yourself, to understand your own experience more.

CL-13: That's for sure!

TH-13: Figuring things out keeps you from having your feelings, your inner thoughts of all kinds. Do you think you could try just staying with those feelings and thoughts without figuring anything out, just let them emerge?

CL-14: Hmm. I don't know. (Pause) I could try. Let's see, I was feeling kind of . . .

TH-14: (Interrupting) Wait, wait a minute. Take time to get into yourself or you'll be right back into *working on* yourself instead of *being in* yourself.

The therapist is beginning here to teach an important lesson (TH-12): The resistance pattern has served the client well in the past, has positive values, but it has become compulsive and escaped the control of her intention. With this comes the opportunity to teach the client that she does not have to abandon control if she becomes more open to herself and to the therapist. Such therapist comments as the following aid this recognition:

- "Your need to figure things out goes into gear before you have a chance to decide if that's what will help."
- "To let yourself have your feelings here and when you're with yourself doesn't have to mean that you have to have them anywhere at anytime. You still can choose."
- "To you it's been as though not depending solely on your reasoning was making yourself an emotional slob. That's not very reasonable, is it?" (said with a smile).
- "Of course, you need control; we all do. The trouble is you've only known how to control by slapping your feelings in prison."

Segments 10.3 and 10.4 also illustrate how a resistance pattern may not always be evident in the same words, even though its process is the same. Whether client speaks of "figure it out," "find out why," "analyze the basis for it," "reason it through," or "use logic," she is clearly making her experience—and thus herself—into an object to be objectively analyzed. The therapist helps when he recognizes the same underlying effect of various resistance expressions and points out that commonality.

Teaching the Function of the Resistance

In Segment 10.4, the therapist begins to show the client (TH-12) that the resistance pattern is not a random thing but an intentional part of the client's repertoire. The next step consists of helping the client discover that the behavior that is blocking her is also serving her in some way. This is an important step but one that needs to be done with tact, lest it be heard as an accusation that the client is consciously interfering with the work, as happened with the earlier client in Segments 10.1 and 10.2 (CL-26 and -34).

In various ways, the message needs to be gotten over that the resistance pattern has served the client, that it is not necessarily wholly a bad thing, that it is now getting in the client's way at times, and that the client has the possibility of changing the pattern when she determines to do so.

Loosening and Replacement

As the work of tagging repeatedly, demonstrating the effects of the resistance patterns, and beginning to suggest alternatives goes on, subtle changes will likely be occurring in the client's self-exploration in therapy. The compulsive, unconscious hold of the resistance pattern will begin to loosen; at times it will be less constricting and occasionally it will not occur at all.

Another likely and important development may be that the client becomes more aware of the centrality of the subjective and how therapist interpretations of the resistance clearly are designed to protect it. With that recognition the client may see that, despite her conscious intention to explore fully and openly, there are unconscious impulses that impede that work. She may also begin to identify her own resistances and to experiment with hanging in through them, keeping in touch with her inner experiencing to some extent even as the resistance operates.

Freed to find the values in the resistive behavior and not feeling that she must abandon all control or limits, the client begins to open new areas of herself to her own and the therapist's understanding. This facet of the work may go on with greater and lesser intensity at various periods throughout the course of therapy. Other work will, of course, be carried on concurrently, but always the need for maintaining significant depth (usually "critical occasions" level) is the criterion to decide relative emphasis between work on the resistance and other tasks.

So far I have spoken of resistance patterns as though each existed separately. Nothing could be less true. These patterns are interwoven with each other and are layered over each other. The work of peeling back these layers is a distinguishing aspect of depth psychotherapy and is essential if genuine life changes are to result. Segment 10.5 illustrates this in a highly condensed fashion.

Segment 10.5
Client: Hal Steinman; Therapist: James Bugental[5]
    (Hal has been trying to get a deeper understanding of his nearly ungovernable feelings of rage at his son, Tim. He knows now how futile is his attempt to reason himself out of these, but he doesn't know what else to do. In this segment, he moves unusually quickly through several resistance layers.)

TH-21: What comes to mind right now as you think about yourself and your relation with Tim?

CL-21: Just the same things I've told you before. [The first level of resistance at this point. He is not distinguishing between factual report and inner exploration.]

TH-22: Say them again, if they really and spontaneously come to mind right now.

CL-22: Oh, Jim, I don't like to be stubborn, but I've tried this again and again, and it just doesn't do any good. (Dispirited, edging on impatience) I don't know why he makes me so mad. I can't really talk with him at all. [A second layer, discouragement, which hints of a possible third, anger.]

TH-23: Well (persisting, encouraging), just give it a try now. And maybe I can tune in with you and see better how it goes when you try to think about it.

CL-23: Okay (dubious, resignedly). Well, I just think to myself what might be the reason I . . . [Third layer: reporting past experience rather than expressing immediate process.]

TH-24: No, wait, Hal, don't tell me about it. Just do it right now. Think out loud so I can hear what it's like inside of you as you work on it. Just let me listen in, but you think your own thoughts for yourself.

CL-24: Well, I wonder if maybe we've got one of those Oedipal things going and I resent Tim as another male in the house, but that seems nonsense to me. Then . . . uh . . . I think probably I never had a chance to through my own adolescent rebellion . . . because of the war and all, and so I resent Tim's doing it. But if so, I don't get any big flash of light or ringing bells or anything. (Pause) And then I'll think I'll go read some more of Eriksen and see if I can come up with a better idea, but I'm really not very optimistic. [Fourth layer, objectifying himself.]

TH-25: Hal, you're still standing off and looking at yourself as if you were another person and you had to think up possible explanations for what he, this strange person, does.

CL-25: Yeah, I suppose so. (Troubled, not so sure) Well, I wonder what the hell's the matter with me. I know that I'm going to drive Tim utterly away or cause one of us to do something really bad if I can't get a hold on myself pretty soon. I get so damn frustrated with myself I'd like to kick my own ass for the way I act sometimes, and . . . [Fifth layer, self-punitive stance.]

TH-26: Hal (interrupting, urgently), when you're not treating yourself like a puzzle to be figured out, you're acting like a tough drill sergeant cussing out a dumb recruit. Don't you ever just think your own thoughts for yourself on your own side?

CL-26: Well, yes, I guess so. (Really troubled now, sensing the problem more than he has before, anxious to do well) I mean, sometimes I feel really sad and kind of sorry for myself. I try not to dwell on that. It doesn't do any good, and I really can't waste the time. [Sixth layer, self-pity.]

TH-27: Wow! Hal, if you're not a dumb recruit to be cussed out, you're a poor inept slob to be pitied. You really don't have much chance just to be Hal, the person in the midst of his own life, trying to work things out as best he can, and feeling a lot about the people in his family and their lives. No wonder it's so hard for you to change things the way you want!

CL-27: Ugh! I don't like that. I mean, I think I really understand what you said this time, but I sure don't like your pitying me. [Same level: self-pity]

TH-28: Pitying you! (Anger not feigned but probably not as strong as I'm letting it through) You dumb jock, I'm not pitying you. But I surely can feel a lot of fellow feeling for you. That's a damn hard place you're in, whether you know it or like it, or not. I know because I'm often there myself.

CL-28: (He's silent for some time, digesting this. Then his voice is subdued.) I read you. And thanks.

How wonderful! It just seldom happens so neatly (and of course this is abridged). Still, this interview occurred after six months of three interviews a week during which a great deal of preparatory work had been accomplished.

UNDERSTANDING THE DEEPER PURPOSE
OF THE RESISTANCE

Note: This section presents a view of the dynamic source of the resistance—a view having roots in existential, humanistic, and psychoanalytic psychology. Up to this point, the therapeutic procedures have been relatively theory-free and thus available to therapists of varied orientations. This is less so for the following paragraphs.

As the client becomes familiar with the workings of her resistance needs, she is learning at the same time to see them as parts of herself, not as alien introjects, and to recognize that she has a measure of choice about them and the possibility of more modulated control of their operating. This multifaceted recognition contributes to the client's feeling of progress and motivation for the difficult work ahead.

The transitional step from work directed solely to reducing resistance to work with underlying neurotic structures is the step of helping the client disclose the deeper purpose of the resistance. To understand the meaning of this important step, we begin by stepping back a bit from our close concentration on clinical procedure.

The Self-and-World Construct System

When we think about our situation as human beings, we recognize that we are continually engaged in trying to make effective connections between the two worlds in which we dwell, the subjective and the objective.

One of the central ways in which we make these bridges is to develop and continually tend the self-and-world construct system. If it is solidly anchored at both ends, then our life experiences generally work out fulfillingly. If, however, the match between the system and either our internal or our external realities is faulty, then we experience anxiety and other distress.

The self-and-world construct system, as we have seen, defines what and who we are and the nature of the world in which we live. If I define myself as a person of generous and loving nature who cares about others, and all of my experience confirms this view, well and good. But what if I fly into a rage at one of my children? What if I take unfair advantage of another person? In other words, what happens when I go against that self-definition?

When incoming experience of myself or of the world does not accord with the way I define myself and my world, then I may do any of several things: I can recognize the mismatch and set about amending my construct system to make it more realistic. I can experience the mismatch at a preconscious level but find it too upsetting to my construct system and so repress the event. When experience is repressed, kept from consciousness, then it must be kept out by some means. Here the familiar "defense mechanisms" of psychoanalytic theory are very descriptive — projection, denial, and other distortions are used.

Depth psychotherapy, however, calls for exploration of the client's subjectivity, which includes those parts of the subconscious which are conflictful. This task directly threatens the repressed disjunctures between one's self-and-world definitions and one's actual experience. The resistance comes into play to forestall the confrontations, which seems too upsetting to endure.

In brief, the resistance seeks to preserve the way the client has defined herself and her world and therefore the very identity of the client herself. It is a life-preserving impulse — although one which has escaped aware control.

Examples of resistance functions. Here are some instances of client resistance patterns and the underlying purpose they served in protecting self-and-world constructs[6]:

> Laurence was always busy, always achieving. He saw activity and achievement as the basis of his identity and feared desperately not having them.

> Jennifer was a stickler for the rules, for doing things the right way, and for being extremely accurate in whatever she said or did. Eventually, when she acted on her feelings impulsively, we found how certain she had been that she was unlovable because she felt so fallible.

> Frank was argumentative, angry, and abrasive. He was convinced that only by fighting could he make any place for himself. He feared caring about anyone else because he doubted the feeling would ever be returned. Then, in therapy, he had to face his loneliness and the possibility of relating without anger and distance.

> Louise needed to please so much that she didn't know whether there was any self within her. She feared conflict and felt it would destroy

her. She had to come to terms with her own angry and rebellious feelings.

Therapeutic Disclosure of the Purpose of the Resistance

I said above that other therapeutic work is going on concurrently with the analysis or reduction of the resistance. That other work needs to include the gradual eliciting of the client's self-and-world construct system.

More on the self-and-world construct system. Of course, the therapist's understanding of the client's ways of seeing herself and her world is not something that can be attained by direct questioning. It requires quiet observation of what is implicitly demonstrated in the client's self-report, in her relating with the therapist and others, and in what she chooses to discuss and not to discuss in therapy. One of the most important areas needing exploration is what the client believes would be overwhelming threat. Gradually the therapist forms some impression of what the chief attributes are in the client's way of seeing herself, in the client's value system, in the client's way of conceiving the world in which she lives, in what she believes to be the sources of power or effectiveness, in what she seeks to gain or to avoid, and so on.

This is a process more similar to painting a portrait than to making a collection of related objects. The general outline often comes first, then some particular aspects are roughed in a bit more while others remain virtually untouched. In time, changes must be made as new observations amend earlier impressions. No final completion is to be expected; human beings are far too subtle, multidimensioned, and in process for that to be a realistic goal.

The existential crisis.[7] As the interrelated tasks of disclosing and working through resistances and developing an understanding of the client's self-and-world construct system advance, they inevitably will converge. There comes a point at which it is imminent that there will be a confrontation of the fundamental disjunctures between the client's construct system and what is being disclosed as the resistances roll back. This is a time fraught with potency for life change—and with grave dangers if poorly handled.

Simply but starkly conceived, what must occur is for one or more ways in which the client has been in her life and in her world to die in order for newer and more healthful and authentic ways to emerge. What must die may be a cherished way of identifying oneself ("I've always seen myself as fair and considerate of others, but now I have to face that from time to time I am quite selfish and even occasionally destructive,") or it may be coming fully into a dreaded possibility ("I've always thought if my cruel and vicious fantasies were known, it would destroy me or at least end any hope that anyone would want to know me, and now I am telling someone about these fantasies").

The word *die* is a dramatic one, of course, but it best captures the depth of this crisis. Clients often have dreams, fantasies, and even impulses about death and dying at this point, for they intuitively know the death that must occur. If the therapist is soundly present to the work and to the person who is doing the work (client, not therapist), there is little likelihood of any enactment of these impulses. But they are important to the working through and must be respected as such.

I will not here attempt to detail all that goes into handling what has been called "the existential crisis," the crisis of existence. Suffice it to say, if the therapist is attempting to work in this mode, he will want to inform himself well before this point, and he will need to proceed here with marked dedication and sensitivity.

The essentials at this stage can be listed: First, the therapeutic alliance needs to be strong and assured for the client's support. Second, the client's own pace for making the confrontation and working with it should be respected, so long as the resistances which erupt are identified as such. Third, the therapist must maintain firm respect for the client's autonomy and avoid inappropriate intrusion on the working through of the confrontation. Reassurance, suggestions for action, or interpretations are seldom appropriate. Finally, the therapist needs to monitor and handle his own countertransference and personal responses to the confrontations, for these will often have an impact on him as well.

A PSYCHOTHERAPIST'S JOURNEY

Like the social-climbing offspring of immigrants, psychology long sought to be a "real science," free of the taint of its ancestry in philosophy and metaphysics. It refused to speak the ancestral language of "spirit," "soul," or even "will," although the family name kept the embarrassing prefix "psyche," which translates as each of those un-welcome terms.

To be sure, much of academic psychology has sought to divorce itself from philosophy, but it has only taken up with the exhausted mistress of nineteenth century physical science. That reductionistic and deterministic view has largely been discarded by the present generation of physicists, as those who study human beings should have done long since.

These thoughts occur to me as I think about the inexorable convergence of depth psychotherapy and the realm of the spiritual.[8] I do not strongly identify with "transpersonal psychotherapy," feeling, as I do, that the human includes all that of which humans are capable and therefore all that realm that we can in any way comprehend.

But to return to the point of my musings. As I become truly aware of the arbitrariness of our definitions of ourselves and our world, it is an overwhelming realization. I, just as most of us, grew up thinking the objective world firm and independent of observers. This new realization opens dimensions which I can only speculate about, never explore more than its most accessible edges, and certainly never know fully. I am, willy-nilly, thrown into a twilight zone, in which my dimmed sight can only indistinctly recognize the old familiar land-marks, now irrevocably changed. This, like it or not, is and always has been the domain of the spiritual, however that term may be employed.

Sidney Jourard urged the readmission of the word *spirit* into our psychological vocabulary.[9] I use "spiritedness" to point to the dynamic which expresses our subjecthood. Being subject means being an active element in existence, means being a power that transforms the potential into the actual, means being a seer and not the seen, a doer and not the done to, an actor and not the acted upon. Being subject means that we do not look for that which causes us to do—as we might when trying to understand why the rock rolls down the hill; rather we recognize that the subject is the initiator—the person who pushed the rock over the hill.

Spiritedness is the force of our being which impels us forward into life. Our spiritedness is expressed in our having orientation, direc-tionality. Human beings are always in process, going somewhere, doing something. Human beings, human subjects, are never empty, truly inert. Chapter 12 carries this conception further as it identifies spirit as a name for the dynamic which impels our intentionality.

When, as therapist, I support my client's peeling back the layers of resistance, we come close to an encounter with raw spirit. When together we truly recognize the openness of being (deriving from the arbitrariness of all definitions of world), there comes a trembling moment of recognizing ultimate freedom. Of that moment, Alan Watts wrote, "Where he thought to find the specific truth about himself, he found freedom, but mistook it for mere nothingness."[10] This astounding recognition is too easily passed over without permitting its full meaning to hit us (and possibly upset our comfortable worlds.)

It is impossible to forecast what the client will do in that moment. The possibility, though remote, of suicide is certainly there, as already noted. The possibility of a major life change is equally there and somewhat more probable: a change of career, divorce or marriage, a move to a new setting and lifestyle.

From such moments, and many others, I have come to realize the limitations of the deterministic view. Clients, realizing to whatever degree they can the openness of their possibilities, overthrow our best predictions, advance or retreat, choose newness or cling to old ways, and use the therapeutic opportunity well or poorly — all ultimately in terms of their own inner spirit or lack of it.

The client's autonomy does not absolve us therapists of our responsibility to do what we can to challenge our clients to use the therapeutic opportunity fully. We must keep perspective and maintain humility before the final autonomy of the client. If we therapists are open, we are continually surprised as we recognize anew that what has been poured into our clients by their lives is but part of what issues forth from them. The more fully they have confronted their resistances and their choicefulness, the more surprising are apt to be their elections.

All of which is to say that subtly my clients are converting me from a dedicated agnostic into a kind of believer who does not know what it is he believes but daily becomes more convinced that there is that something more in which we do well to believe and on which we do well to rest our efforts. Once again the *something more*!

SECTION V

Intrapsychic Processes

CHAPTER 11

Concern: Source of Power and Guidance

It is astonishing to realize how seldom have our clients actually taken significant intervals of time to think and feel through their distresses and what might be done about them. It is astonishing until we look in the mirror and ask ourselves the same questions. How often we all postpone the serious and broad-scale contemplation of our lives' courses. Meanwhile, we keep our heads down as we busy ourselves with "practical" and immediate matters.

Clients may report years of frustration and pain and tell of endless hours of trying to solve their problems. Still, when we ask what is the main issue, what attempts at solution have been made, what further avenues they want to explore, and similar questions, we often meet with vague answers, confusion, and reports of intentions never carried out. By spotlighting client concern as a central matter requiring thrapeutic attention, we provide a framework for the client to undertake in a serious, committed way that long-delayed self-exploration.

This chapter defines client concern in terms of four aspects of principal importance for the therapeutic effort: pain, hope, commitment, and inwardness. Each of these facets is described in terms of how it may be optimally mobilized and focused. It is my belief that client concern provides the chief impetus for our work and the most reliable guide for the directions it must take. Finally, therapist concern is identified as the needed complement to client concern; together they form a powerful dynamic for the work.

A CLIENT COMES TO psychotherapy because he is concerned about his life in some way. When I say that, I am using the word *concern* in a special way. Although it need not always convey a dysphoric mood, it has some of the other qualities we associate with worry, problem, complaint, symptom, or similar terms.

DEFINING CONCERN

Concern is a name for the attitude and emotional set of a person who seriously considers his own life and the course it is taking.

Concern is a constellation of feelings, thoughts, and intentions which is organized by an evaluative-anticipatory perspective on one's experience of being. Concern may eventuate in efforts to bring about changes in one's way of being, in the circumstances or relations of one's life, or in the inner orientation of one's living.

Concern in relation to other processes. Earlier pages led us from the exchanges of the therapeutic conversation (presence and press) to the ways of guiding and recognizing meaning in the subject matter (the forms of paralleling) to the avenues which bring us deeper into client's subjectivity (the objectification-to-subjectivity ratio and the handling of the resistance). Now we have arrived at the first of two perspectives on processes which are only partially and infrequently conscious for client, concern and intentionality. This level is as far as we can go with our purpose of building bridges between the external aspects of life and the subjective. Beyond this point we must operate almost completely by intuition and inference.

Concern and intentionality are powerful conceptual and therapeutic tools precisely because they are the most direct ways we have for observing and affecting the client's mode of being in and managing his life. Therapists who fully comprehend these processes and have developed the sensitivities and skills to use that comprehension are able to influence their clients in profound ways. This, then, is an undertaking that calls for a high level of personal and professional responsibility.

THE FOUR FACETS OF CONCERN

As we have seen, concern is a subjective state which has cognitive, emotional, and intentional aspects and which is manifested when client soberly considers the course of his life. So conceived, concern, as a unity or gestalt, has four chief facets: pain, hope, commitment, and inwardness. Ideally, when the client comes to psychotherapy all of these subsystems of his concern are "go". Practically, this is rarely the case. Indeed, if it were so in a particular instance, one might question whether that client even required therapy—so powerful is fully mobilized concern. The usual situation is that some aspects are manifest (often, the pain), and others are submerged or only incompletely available. As we now examine each of the facets, we will be thinking about how it may be brought to bear more effectively on the work to be done.

Understanding the Client's Pain

When thinking seriously about how his life is going, the client may experience emotional distress, anxiety, or actual physical pain. He finds that too often significant aspects of his way of being bring him hurt, sadness, or disappointment. This pain is many times the most conscious and significant impetus to the client's decision to seek professional help. By itself, however, it is not sufficient to carry the task through.

Clients come with pain of many kinds and intensities, and sometimes the pain is masked when they first enter our offices. Therapists may need to remind themselves of this when a seemingly comfortable client dismisses his concern. Generally, we do well to assume that the person who asks our help is hurting and is hurting sufficiently to have overcome a number of obstacles to be sitting here now.

Yet pain cannot be taken for granted, nor can we let it govern our work. Simply to reduce pain is not therapy. Pain is a natural signal that something has gone wrong with the human system and needs attention. Simply quieting pain is as unwise as pasting cardboard over a persistently flashing red light on the car's instrument panel.

Over time, the therapist will come to understand the client's distress in terms of its intensity, the forms it takes (nagging worry, pervasive anxiety, obsessive thoughts, rages or other outbursts, or physical distress), its history, any changes that have occurred in it, and how the client himself views it. This is a gradual process, not a formal inquiry.

In the following the client is describing his pain; it will be seen that the explicit description is only a part—in some ways, the smaller part—of his presentation of that anguish.

Segment 11.1[1]
Client: Laurence Bellows; Therapist: James Bugental

> (Laurence is a business executive who comes to therapy because inexplicable and unpredictable episodes of severe panic are disrupting his life. In an earlier intake session some of the details of therapy arrangements were handled; now he is here for his first regular therapy session. In the first few minutes he handled some further details of the business arrangements; now, having completed these, he seems to be in distress.)

TH-11: You're having trouble trying to say something right now, I think.

CL-11: I read a story the other day on the plane from New York. A story about the Amazon. . . . Travel magazine the hostess handed me. . . . There was a story in there. . . . On the whole it didn't amount to much, but there was this kind of aside about the natives. They, uh . . .

TH-12: (Abruptly I realize that he's fighting a terrible battle within himself. I don't know what it is, or much about it, but I can feel the intensity like a wave of energy pushing against me.) You're in the midst of some kind of struggle right now. Why don't you let the story go for the minute and see if you can tell me about that fight that's going on inside of you?

CL-12: (Composure draining away. His face is tight, so deliberately masked that it hurts to see it.) Yes, well, I want to tell you about this thing I read. . . . I mean I got the first insight I've had into. . . . I find it very hard to talk about this, because I'm afraid it will provoke the same thing that happened on the plane. Ughh! It's amazing how physically painful this is.

TH-13: What happened on the plane? (A simple factual question may help him get traction.)

CL-13: I had one of the those panics. (He sits very still, waiting, listening within himself.) I read this item in the travel magazine, and then I suddenly found the feelings building up in me. I didn't know whether I could hold on. Felt like the plane would just open up and drop me from forty thousand feet or something like that. Almost wished it would. Managed to down a couple of stiff martinis and finally it eased. Had another drink to keep the thing down, wine with dinner, and brandy after. By that time, I was able to relax and watch the last half of some stupid movie I'd had in front of my eyes all along and hadn't been able to focus on. Damn well could become an alcoholic doing that. Hmmm. Those panics are the worst experiences I've ever had. (More composed now, telling the event has helped.)

TH-14: Can you tell me about the item in the magazine now?

CL-14: Hmmm. Yes. Yes, I believe I can. Sorry to have such a time of it. Well, it was about the. . . . Oh! It does start up again inside me so quickly when I think about the story. Hmmm. Well, let's say it. These Amazon natives get ahold of one of their enemies, and then they smear his body with honey, and they stake him out right in the path of the army ants. And the ants . . . thousands of the bastards . . . the ants just eat the man alive. Uhhh! Mmmm. My God! (His body squirms in his chair.) They eat him alive! Just imagine how he feels, what he thinks, as they take all those little bites! Awghh!

TH-15: Awful!

CL-15: My God! Just imagine it. It's impossible. A man would go insane. I would. I hope I would. I hope I would just lose consciousness—not be aware of what was happening. I know I'm probably a physical coward. . . . No, I can think of some times when I wasn't—but that's not the point. Whether I'm a coward or not, there's something about that story that is worse than just the physical suffering. (He is gripping the arms of the chair and struggling almost without awareness of me.) Hmmm. It's those little ant bites. It's seeing one's own flesh disappearing, one's own body just dissolving away into the ants. . . . Awghh! Oh, God damn it, I don't want to go into another of those panics. I don't think I can take it.

Laurence's account on the verbal level is intense and highly meaningful, of course, but it is only part of what he is expressing. As he tells about his pain, he enacts its torment in a way words can only suggest. His body's posture and movement, his facial expression, the general muscular tension, his constricted throat, his voice's pitch and the disappearance of the well modulated tones so evident earlier, and many, many other aspects combine to scream his pain.

Comprehending the pain is not necessarily a cognitive grasping of it. At this point neither of us knows what causes Laurence's pain; neither do we know what will trigger or relieve it. We don't even know what therapy can do for him. Yet, in a very real way we appreciate that pain; empathically, we know it in our bones. We now sense how it grips him, how it interferes with his otherwise smooth functioning, what he does sometimes to control it, and how desperately he fears it.

It is significant that though the first interview with Laurence occured nearly six weeks before this session and his busy schedule prompted his delay in beginning, when the panic—the form his pain takes—hit, he called at once to ask for the earliest possible time. His concern was chiefly in terms of that pain, and the other aspects of that concern were less promptly available. (An excerpt from that initial interview is given later in this chapter.)

Understanding the Client's Hope

The decision to seek psychotherapy usually signals that the client has some measure of hope that life can be better, but it does not always mean that. The hope may be conscious and, sometimes, quite specific—"I want therapy to help me use my creativity so I can get out of this crappy job I'm stuck in now"—or it may be vague or only implicit in the way the client presents his pain (as was the case with Lawrence in Segment 10.1).

Some clients explicitly deny hope, insisting that they no longer have any such feelings, but their being in therapist's office suggests that they may be self-deceived. In still other instances that base too is undermined ("My wife insisted I come see you, but I don't think you or anyone can help me"). Finally, there are some clients who come, consciously or unconsciously, with apparently the sole intent of proving that nothing will make them different or better. They seem to want to be able to say, "Well, I tried therapy, and it didn't help a bit." I find the last group easier to work with than those who truly only come because of pressure from someone else.

The desire for a changed life experience is often heightened by the pain, but it is not synonomous with it. Surprisingly to the novice, clients may be truly pain-racked yet have but little available hope. Often depressed people feel they have made so many hopeful starts only to be disappointed that they resist hoping any more. Instead they try to resign themselves, to seek distraction, or to suppress the pain. With such people the therapist faces the necessity of aiding them in reconfronting their pain in order to disclose the hope which has been suppressed with it.

Saying this another way, the denial of hope is a resistance which must be dealt with as are other resistances (see Chapter 10) and which requires careful therapeutic management to avoid precipitating client flight. This is not something to be accomplished in a single session, nor is it a task that can be done in isolation from responding to the client's general presentation of himself.

Segment 11.2
Client: Dick Davis; Therapist: Gladys Johnson
> (The excerpt which follows comes about three months into twice-a-week therapy with a client presenting a history of chronic, moderate depression. For nearly two months, and with increasing frequency, the therapist has been identifying to the client ("tagging") times when the client withdraws into objectifying himself or elaborating on his complaint that he is hopelessly different, unfitted for this world. This session has been going on about five minutes, and the client is making his familiar self-description.

CL-1: I feel as though I'm an alien, like I got put on the wrong planet. Other people seem to be able to make it, but some way, I just can't. Other people seem to be happy about their lives. I just hate mine.

TH-1: Miserable.

CL-2: Yes, it is. I don't think I'll kill myself. Oh, I've thought of it often enough, but somehow that doesn't seem like something I'd do. So I just live in this constant state of blah.

TH-2: What do you think about this way of living?

CL-3: I hate it! I don't like feeling this way. Do you think I enjoy it?

TH-3: You seem pretty complacent about it.

CL-4: Well, what can I do about it?

TH-4: What *can* you do about it?

CL-5: I don't know. What would you suggest?

TH-5: Suggest for what?

CL-6: So I could get out of feeling this way all the time.

TH-6: Is that what you want?

CL-7: Of course that's what I want. Wouldn't you?

TH-7: You know, that's the first time in the three months we've been talking that you've said directly that you want it to be different. Do you think it ever will be?

CL-8: (Sullenly) I don't know.

TH-8: (Challengingly) Where did you go? Where's the energy you had a minute ago? You were really here then. Now you're sliding back into your old, familiar black hole.

CL-9: Oh, It's all so hopeless.

TH-9: "It's" not hopeless, but you are afraid to hope.

CL-10: What's the use?

TH-10: You're all cozy back in your cave of saying there is no use hoping because nothing will ever change.

This response to hopelessness has the best chance of being effective if it comes when a solid therapeutic alliance exists and when it is given out in accelerating doses rather than all at once. The therapist must continue to mix support (Th-1) with drawing out the hopelessness (TH-2, -4, -5) and increasingly direct confrontations (TH-3, -6, -7, -8, -9, -10). The therapist will have to work this path many times, over many sessions, before this resistance layer will roll back, but it will roll back in most every instance if the therapist is sensitive, persistent, and not punitive.

Mobilizing Client Commitment

Therapy that intends being life-changing is a demanding and expensive undertaking. It is expensive in terms of time, intrusion upon client's life, emotional energy, and, for most clients, money. A significant commitment must be made by the client if any significant result can be sought. Many clients need help in recognizing this fact of life, however.

Life-changing psychotherapy which seeks to aid clients in major ways is long-term, usually frequent (two to four times a week), and intensive. Although major changes are often what clients want, too frequently they are unprepared for what it requires of them. Even when they don't consciously and explicitly want so demanding a program, the issues they present often require it. If therapists act responsibly in undertaking to work with them, this must be faced at the earliest appropriate point.

I phrase the timing in this conditional manner because oftentimes the client cannot really understand the necessity until he has been helped to be more fully in touch with the other elements of his concern. So many clients seek to add therapy onto an already full schedule and emotional economy. It just won't work. Add-on therapy is inevitably shallow therapy with shallow results.

Therapist and client both need to recognize that life-changing psychotherapy is an enterprise which demands appreciable commitments of the currency of one's vitality in its several forms (money, time, energy, emotions, thought). Figure 11.1 graphs a hypothetical client's distribution of his "vitality capital" as he enters therapy. The many investments of that capital compete for any extra resources. Consciously or not, some portion has been set aside for psychotherapy. This I can generalize: Whatever the amount allotted to therapy, it is not enough!

Facing the demands of life-changing therapy. Think about it: The commitment required for life-changing psychotherapy must, obviously, be life-disruptive. Does that seem extreme? It is. Consider further: When a client seeks a significant change in his experience-of-being-alive, he asks that very experience-of-being-alive be changed. If he limits what he invests in therapy, he limits the extent of change that can occur in his experience-of-being-alive.

For any change to occur in a long-standing life pattern, a client must be prepared to invest significantly and to experience disruption of his usual life routine. This investment is, by no means, only one of money — although that can be appreciable. Segment 11.3 shows how the need for commitment can be handled in an instance in which money is not the issue.

Segment 11.3[2]
Client: Laurence Bellows; Therapist: James Bugental
(This is the preliminary interview which occurred six weeks before Laurence

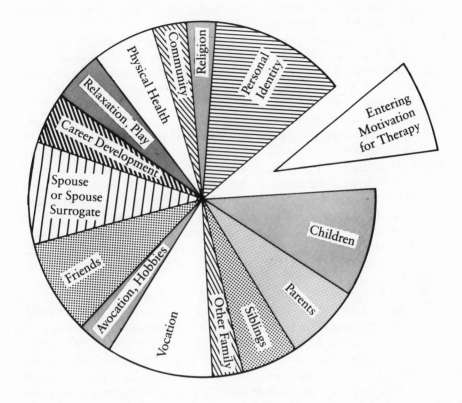

Figure 11.1. Hypothetical Distribution of a Client's "Vitality Resources" and the Extent of His Readiness to Invest in Psychotherapy.

began therapy formally (in the session of which Segment 11.1 is an excerpt). The segment below comes toward the end of this preliminary meeting and before I have presented my treatment recommendations. Typical of Laurence is this take-charge maneuver.)

CL-1: I travel a lot, you know, and it will be hard for me to set a dependable schedule, but of course I'll do what I can to give you notice whenever I have to be away. Now, this is a Tuesday morning. Would you like to see me every Tuesday morning that I'm in town and at ten, as this morning?

TH-1: Mr. Bellows, if we decide to work together, I will want to see you at least three times a week and preferably four, and you will need to arrange your affairs so that you rarely miss a session. (Let's get this thing straight right now. He wants to dismiss his terror as a minor matter. I'm damn sure it is not. Must have been challenged by the smooth way he took over, and so I'm having to reassert myself!

Amused. But it's probably just as well anyway. He needs help to take his pain and his life seriously.)

CL-2: Four times a week! (Consternation, but a bit overdone, I think.) I really don't see how I can manage it with my commitments, but . . .

TH-2: (His pause is well calculated to get me to offer some adjustment. He *is* skillful in interpersonal dealings, no doubt about it. Best just to keep quiet and wait.)

CL-3: Well, if you think it's really necessary . . . I could try to work out three interviews a week for a month or so, I imagine. I mean, you know your business, I suppose, and . . .

TH-3: (He's nettled—a little dig in that "I suppose." Yet he's beginning to let himself think more seriously about the prospect and needs of therapy. Don't want to play games with him; he's really in great pain and terror, and I don't know much about him or why he suffers so.) I'd be willing to try three times a week, as long as we made those times regularly. But, Mr. Bellows, let's level with each other. This is not a matter of a month or so, if I can make any judgment knowing as little as I do about you.

CL-4: How long a period do you estimate, doctor? (Level, careful.)

TH-4: That's really almost impossible for me to say at this time. I hardly know anything about you yet. And, frankly, even when I know more, it will be doubtful how well I can estimate the total time you'll want to work with me. I put it that way because it will always be fundamentally your choice whether you continue or leave. What I can tell you is that most people with whom I work continue their therapy between two and three years; although some, of course, stop sooner and some keep going longer.

CL-5: Two to three years. Hmmm. This really is quite a different matter than I had anticipated, and I'm not sure. . . . (Pausing, contemplating, not quite so smooth now)

TH-5: Yes, it is a major undertaking, Mr. Bellows. It needs to be thought of as one of the major events of one's life, for what we attempt to do here is to reexamine the whole course and meaning of the way you're alive.

CL-6: Well, yes, mm-hmmm. But that seems much more comprehensive than I think I require at this time. I'm sure it would be quite worthwhile, if one had the time and resources. Hmmm. Yes, quite worthwhile. (Considering, hesitating)

TH-6: But you wonder if it is what you want to undertake right now.

CL-7: Yes, you see, I'm very busy right now . . . can't really see taking off three or four mornings a week—even if only for a few hours—right now. Hmmm. Yes. (Thinking) Do you really think such a comprehensive program is required simply to alleviate these episodes of panic which I described?

TH-7: Mr. Bellows, I frankly have very little idea of what may be required for that purpose. I have barely met you. I will be glad to talk with you six or eight times, if you like, and then together we'll reassess what may be indicated. (He brightens, starts to speak, but I push on.) But I don't want to mislead you. My educated guess is that at the end of that time I will make the same recommendation I have just made—for two reasons: First, I very much doubt that those panics are some peripheral or isolated problem separate from the rest of your way of being. Thus to get into what brings about the panics, we will almost certainly open up other parts of your inner experience. (His eyes are tightening slightly; no other evident reaction.) Second, I believe significant, lasting changes only come from this kind of thoroughgoing inquiry into a person's life. Now in regard to this second point, you should know that there are a number of other competent people in this area who do not work as intensively as I do, who do not believe it is required, and whose names I'd be happy to give you.

CL-8: Yes, well. Hmmm. I appreciate that and your candor, Dr. Bugental. (Stalling, thinking rapidly) I suppose what I'd better do is take some of those names and then consider all that you've told me over the next few days. I can then call you toward the end of the week or the first of next week.

TH-8: That seems like a good plan. As I said, if you do go ahead with me, this undertaking needs to be one of the major events and commitments of your life. Certainly you don't want to plunge into such a program without careful thought.

(And so we wind up the hour. I give him three names, and we politely shake hands and bid each other goodbye.)

Helping the client make the commitment. Several features of the therapist's work in this segment demonstrate ways of educating the client to the reasons for such a demanding therapeutic contract:

- It is important to remember that we are seeking client commitment for a fairly long-term and quite heavy program. Therefore, persuasion and salesmanship are not appropriate because their results will wear off if there is only a shallow inner conviction on the client's part.
- The most influential tack is to help the client feel that his pain has been genuinely heard, that a program is being offered which will seek to help him move from the pain to the hoped-for state, and that the therapist is ready to join the client in this program.
- Candidly recognizing the size and demands of the program puts it in scale and aids the client in making an informed and meaningful decision.[3] (To potential clients for whom financial considerations are more important than they were to Lawrence, I am likely to amplify

this point—beyond TH-5 and TH-8: "This needs to be thought of as one of the major undertakings of your life and one of the major expenditures. Only purchasing your home and perhaps one or two other items will be as expensive in money and as demanding in time, energy, and emotions.")

- Although it was not needed for Lawrence, it is sometimes helpful also to point out the long history of the concerns which bring the client in and to contrast it with the therapeutic program. For example: "You've told me that you've struggled with this matter for most of your adult life (or most of your life), which, given your age, means at least 20 years. Now we're proposing in three 45-minute (or 50-minute) sessions a week for two or three years to offset that amount of backlog! That's a pretty big order, and it will take all you can bring to it and all I can bring to support your work."

- Similarly, with people who want to come only once a week, it is sometimes useful to point out the contrast in more current terms: "You have told me how very full your schedule is and how little time you take for yourself. Now you're talking about trying to make a dent in that busy week with less than an hour a week. I think you can see that is not a very realistic proposition, and I certainly don't want to join you in such a self-deception."

Arousing Inward Orientation

Life-changing psychotherapy is therapy which inquires into the bases on which one identifies who and what one is and the way one believes the world to be. Obviously these are not matters that can be grasped effectively when the client explains his experience in terms of other people (spouse, parent, employer) or external agencies (God, fate, heredity). A desired therapeutic outcome will depend heavily on the client's genuine acceptance of the primacy of inward exploration and self-renewal.

It is clear that clients who want the therapist to change others or want the therapist to tell them how to change, manipulate, or appease others are not going to engage fully in the kind of therapy we are describing. What may not be so obvious is that some clients who come with this unsuitable motivation can be helped to redirect their focus and to look within themselves. Some of these people are simply naive psychologically; once they have discovered the world of their own subjectivity, they become engrossed and quite adept at working there. Others who similarly want the focus to be on persons not present in the room are so threatened by what they imagine will happen to them that they use this shield. Some of these people are equally accessible to our work, once we have helped them feel that their fears are accepted and that they will not be forced into the dreaded areas without support.

As with all of the aspects of concern, inwardness is vulnerable to suppression and repression. To avoid looking into oneself by denial is a primitive defense, but certainly a frequent one. This fact does not make it any less serious as an issue for clients who need and seek major therapeutic aid. In unlayering this resistance, we will frequently find psychopathology which is heavily laden with guilt, blame, and shame. In such cases, the effort to mobilize inwardness for the support of therapy will very likely prove to be a crucial part of the total therapeutic course.

Segment 11.4
Client: Gus Campbell; Therapist: Helen George
CL-1: I can't understand her. Honestly, I can't. She is always talking about feelings and stuff like that, and then she tells me I have no feelings, and that's just not so. I have feelings just like anybody else, but she doesn't believe it and says I'm all brain. All brain! How do you like that? Just because I don't want to spend all my time simpering around over someone's baby or how Mrs. Jones has a bad back or some other stupid thing like that.
TH-1: It makes you mad to be told you have no feelings.
CL-2: Well, of course, it does. Wouldn't you be hurt if someone said that about you?
TH-2: And it hurts you. Seems like you have some feelings right now.
CL-3: Yeah, Oh, I have feelings all right, but she won't be satisfied until I break down and cry or something.
TH-3: You're mad and you're hurt by her telling you that you have no feelings. Can you get with those feelings that you're having right now?
CL-4: How do you mean, "get with" them? I'm feeling them right now. I think I need to tell her she just doesn't really hear me. She ought to listen better.
TH-4: When you try to get with your feelings here, you find yourself almost immediately thinking about her and what you could do with her.
CL-5: Yeah, maybe if she would just simmer down. You know, she is always fretting about something. Boy, if that's having feelings, count me out. Just this morning she was getting all worked up because the garbage collectors hadn't picked up all the stuff we put out. That's a nuisance, I agree, but to hear her go on, you'd think they had spread the stuff all over the front porch.
TH-5: You're feeling strongly again right now.

CL-6: Well, not too strong, but it just seems to me that she's no great advertisement for having feelings. She was on the phone to the refuse collection company and telling them . . .

TH-6: (Interrupting.) I want to know more about that feeling you're having right now.

CL-7: I told you. She was getting all worked up about the garbage collectors, and . . .

TH-7: Wait, I want to interrupt you again to help you see something: You get your feelings inside of you all tangled up with what triggered those feelings. That trigger is outside of you. Now see whether you can get back into what is going on inside of you.

CL-8: Yeah, well, like I said, she . . . she gets so hot about so many things. (Pauses, uncertain)

TH-8: Got away from you again, huh?

CL-9: Yeah, I guess so. I don't think I know what you want.

TH-9: Uh-huh, Gus, I think you're right, you're not quite sure you get what I'm driving at. But that's important that you recognize that. I think some of the trouble you're having with making things come out the way you want may be tied up with the fact that you don't know what I mean when I ask about what's happening inside of you.

A bare beginning. It will be many sessions yet before Gus can begin to look inward, but at least he's taken the crucial first step of beginning to recognize that there is something he is unaware of that may be important to him.

The therapist uses several steps to help Gus be more ready to hear her when she makes an interim summary (TH-9): She shows understanding of the client's frustration (TH-1, -2, -3) and in the process gives a measure of support by pointing out that Gus does have feelings (TH-2, especially). That support, however, is tied to the first effort to direct attention away from Gus's wife and toward his own inner processes (TH-3). Gus is not ready to use this yet, but it probably subliminally prepares the way for the next steps. Gus, who just doesn't understand about being inward, quickly goes back to his wife (CL-4), but the therapist uses that very fact to point out the pattern (TH-4).

On the surface, the client is simply persevering on a familiar topic, but the therapist is planting seeds which will grow into self-questioning about what Gus is doing. Thus the therapist again calls his attention to his feelings that are being manifested in the moment (TH-5), and before they can be lost in a long complaint, she follows up with two moderate confrontations (TH-6, -7). The fact that she twice interrupts him to make these points will add impact and bring Gus closer to considering the point she is making. This effect is demonstrated as Gus starts to slide back into his familiar recital but now realizes — probably for the first time and quite incompletely — that he is doing so. Helen shows sympathetic understanding (TH-8), which also implies that Gus is now working to stay more inward. The client then more genuinely confronts his unfamiliarity with looking into and disclosing his inner experience (CL-9). Once again the therapist responds supportively, but this time she links the support to the concerns which Gus has previously presented, thus giving it motivational support.

Summary on Mobilizing Concern

Insofar as broad generalizations are possible in an art form as subtle and complex as depth psychotherapy, one that holds good far more often than not is this: The first order of business in this therapy is to assess the extent to which all aspects of the client's concern are available and brought to bear on the work. The second order of business is to disclose and reduce the resistances which keep any aspects of concern from being so directed.

These tasks may be accomplished in a few months or may require literal years. It is exceedingly rare for all four aspects to be fully present immediately, and there are many fluctuations in their contributions throughout the therapeutic course. Some clients seem ideal at the outset because all aspects of concern apparently are favorable, but all too often the unwary therapist finds some time later that one or more of them was more verbally cited than authentically engaged.

It will be evident that concern, as I am advancing this concept, is intimately related to the notion of levels of presence. The fully concerned client is most apt to be fully present. Defects in the mobilization of concern are likely to be manifested in limited immersion in the work. These are two ways of working with the same client issue. They are not identical but closely linked and mutually facilitating.

Concern provides the impetus for the client to cooperate and stay with the work when promptings to oppose, resist, or drop out are triggered. Concern fosters movement to deeper communication levels and supports genuine immersion. It is concern which is centrally influential as the client moves from objectifying himself to more truly subjective exploration, and it is concern which helps guide that inward searching. In brief, psychotherapy finds in client concern two crucially important elements: an energy source and a lodestar by which to steer.

THE GUIDANCE FUNCTION OF CONCERN[4]

While many psychotherapeutic schools would agree on the importance of working within the client's subjectivity, differences are likely when it comes to selecting what issues within that subjectivity should receive the client's attention. Some views postulate universal issues — e.g., the vicissitudes of sexuality, individuation, object attachments. In such instances, the choice is often clear. Others look for certain psychological processes — affective clusterings, intrapsychic conflict — with similar results.

My own belief is that fully mobilized client concern is the best compass for guidance of the work. In the ideal circumstance, the client's very involvement (concern) with his life magnetically draws him to the matters needing his attention, without his needing to "draw back" to judge which of several possible topics to take up. This process proceeds largely unconsciously in the fully immersed and genuinely concerned client.

It is chiefly as presence lessens or there is a slacking off of some part of the client's concern (e.g., trying to please therapist, wanting to disguise an unflattering self-report) that the client becomes uncertain how to proceed. Yet every therapeutic journey has times when the client, for whatever reasons, is at a loss as to direction. Often, at these points, the client looks to therapist for guidance, "What should I talk about? . . . Should I tell you about my dream or about the argument with my wife?"

Typically, my answer to such questions is along these lines: "You have the only valid compass, so look into yourself and see what (or which) really matters to you right now." Sometimes I link that up with a reflection, "You seem to feel that I know what's important to you better than you do. That's a startling idea. Do you really believe that?"

Helping Clients' Contact Concern

Client concern, as a guiding process, is not the same as client complaint, the problems with which the client is currently struggling, the emotions which may be gripping him, or what the client would *say* most concerns him. Client concern is his felt sense, his organismic awareness, of what is genuinely most meaningful or most needful of his attention at this particular moment. Therefore, this concern cannot be arrived at by logical processes; it must be the product of intuition or inner discovery.

Clients need help in learning to be aware of, listen to, and be guided by their sense of concern for their lives. Here are some snapshots of how this aid can be provided: (Each of these collapses into a response or two what might well take many exchanges spread over time. None of these is by itself a valid formula for eliciting genuine concern.)

CL-A: I don't know what to talk about this morning. Nothing much has happened since we talked the other day.

TH-A: Good! Without an agenda, you will be freer to get in touch with yourself at a deeper, more important, and more immediate level. Just take a moment now to get better centered in yourself. (Pauses, waits, may give relaxation and centering suggestions) Okay, now see whether you can feel how your life is going these days. Don't tell me about it yet; just feel the general sense of it. Then, when you are ready, talk to me about what you find inside yourself, what is really important to you, what you want to think about and feel about in relation to your life.

CL-B1: I started to tell you about the fight my husband and I got into this morning, but then I thought of how I've been feeling so constantly tired and unhappy lately. I don't know which would be best to tell you about. What do you think?

TH-B1: Donna, you've got the only roadmap; I can't tell you. Wait, that doesn't mean just go ahead and grab something. Take a minute, and see what happens when you reach down inside yourself where you really live and where you want to make your life better. Then from that place decide how you really want to use our time now. It might be either of those topics, or it might be something else entirely.

CL-B2: (Silent briefly) I don't know whether I know what you mean. I don't seem to find anything when I do what you said. I just keep going back and forth between those two things.

TH-B2: It's hard at first to get in touch with that deeper place inside you, but you'll get the hang of it after a bit. For today, just try once more and see what thoughts or feelings you have about what I'm asking you to do. You'll have something about that for sure.

CL-C1: So I went back and told them what I thought, and they said it was a lot of crap. I don't know why people act that way. After all, I was just trying to be helpful, but you know how people can be.

TH-C1: So what?

CL-C2: (Startled) What do you mean?

TH-C2: Just that: So what? So why tell me about it?

CL-C3: Well, I thought you should know what I have to put up with.

TH-C3: Why? Does it matter?

CL-C4: Of course it matters (irritated tone).

TH-C4: It didn't sound like it. Fact is, you sound more involved now than you did when you told me about what happened with those people.

CL-C5: I don't understand you. What do you want?

TH-C5: I want to hear about what really matters to you, to your life, to what you want to change for yourself.

These kinds of interventions have in common that they call for significant talk from the client but do not tell the client what topics to deal with. They do not tell the client for two very good reasons: First, the therapist can rarely know just where the client is subjectively and what he is ready to grapple with at the moment, while the client has a unique access to such material and can learn to get in touch with it. The other reason is that one of the most important outcomes therapy can give a client is increased inner access and assurance.

Often, when a good working relation exists, the use of surprising and abrupt phrasings (TH-C1 to C5) has the advantage of breaking up familiar patterns that may be functioning mechanically.

Hidden Collusion With Client

When therapy has been going well for some time and then becomes stale and unproductive, there is often a hidden—and quite possibly unconscious, on both sides—collusion operating between client and therapist. I will not try to elaborate fully on this here, but it is worthwhile to point out a likely source of such an impasse: the unrecognized agreement to allow one or more aspects of the concern to drop away.

For example, Del had made good progress for more than a year when subtly the pace changed and our sessions became heavy and profitless. Only after far too many wasted hours did it dawn on me that we were working together to quiet the pain and fear which had once made our sessions tense and often uncomfortable for both of us. Now we were enjoying being undisturbed in that way, and we were avoiding reawakening the feelings, even though they were not by any means worked through.

THE THERAPIST'S CONCERN

We speak of the relationship between client and therapist as an "alliance," that is, a joining of forces. The alliance consists of two energy systems being brought into concert to accomplish purposes important to both. Our discussion of client concern made evident the power of that process and its irreplaceable function of guiding the client's inner exploration. Now we need to recognize and examine the therapist's complementing concern. Here too we will recognize that concern is not the same as worry or anxiety, that it is closer to motivation or intent.

Just as it was helpful to identify four facets of client concern, we can recognize four matching facets for the therapist:

Client Concern	*Therapist Concern*
Pain	Need
Hope	Vision
Commitment	Presence
Inwardness	Sensitivity

Therapist's Need

It is so crucially important that the therapist find need fulfillment in her work that if she does not she should leave the field. The idea of being helped with one's life by an impersonal, uncaring therapy machine operator is repugnant to most of us. Moreover, it is very likely that such an effort would be countertherapeutic.[5]

The therapist's need often is for financial compensation, as the work supports her living. This is an appropriate need, although too often therapists find it distasteful and regrettable. It is neither of those. We live in a culture in which money is one of the major dimensions of everyday life for therapists and clients alike. If the therapist has no monetary needs, as sometimes happens, that is a handicap which needs direct attention. Failing that, the therapist will be out of touch with a powerful influence on her clients' lives.

Is money demeaning? Whether it is ideally desirable for psychotherapy to be a commodity with a price, the fact is that for the most part it is that. Moreover, when a client does not have to pay that price—or a personally significant portion of it—he is apt to be less invested in the work. This is an old truth of our trade which we

question when new to the field but which bitter experience relentlessly teaches again and again. The existential reality of the penetration of the psychotherapeutic by marketing values and attitudes is
such that therapist and client must recognize this fact and address it
in their work from time to time.

Of course, if money is the only need the therapist satisfies through
her work, then she is apt to be shallowly invested and to find it hard
to remain committed through the inevitable stressful and repetitive
periods of the work. The result can be a limitation on the potential
that therapy can realize or, in other cases, unnecessary prolongation
of therapy.

Other satisfactions. Happily, most therapists engaged in depth
psychotherapy find it satisfies other needs: One of the foremost of
these is the deep satisfaction of having a part in seeing a person with
whom one has made a deep relation claim his life anew, realize his
powers more fully, or come to greater peace within. Psychotherapy
does work, sophists to the contrary notwithstanding. Seeing it work,
knowing one had a significant part in its working, is a richly rewarding experience.

There are other need satisfactions that therapists find: Through
their practice they actualize inner potentials for disciplined and effective interaction with others, for developing and refining their creative
and artistic gifts, and for making meaningful contributions in their
communities. For many of us, the sense of having a privileged seat at
the human drama is a reward of great value. Similarly, the shared
gratifications that are possible when one works with congenial, stimulating, and dependable colleagues are very fulfilling.

In sum, therapists ought to feel that important personal needs are
being satisfied through their work. When they no longer feel that,
they are in genuine danger of becoming stale, repetitive, and insensi-
tive. It is a professional responsibility of a high order that at such a
time one should seek further personal therapy, collegial consultation
and support, a sabbatical period, or further training and supervision.
Failing to take one or more of these courses successfully, one should
change his professional post to one which makes less of an emotional
demand.

The therapist's need complements the client's pain—thus the urgency of the last paragraph. We cannot be casual when people in pain
come to us for aid. When we can join our needs with the impetus of
their pain we have the possibility of enriching both our lives.

Therapist's Vision

As client and therapist work together, the client's hope will be stimulated and, desirably, it will begin to be fulfilled in some part. Concurrently, the therapist is evolving, quite without conscious contrivance, an inner sensing or image of the person that is latent within the client. This evolving vision of the client's potential must not be confused with a countertranferential projection onto the client; rather, it is the therapist's intuitive recognition of the way the client can be if their work together is optimally effective.

The difference is that the "vision" is not a matter of specifications of what the client *should* be or do—e.g., allowing her son more freedom, changing his job to a better one, writing that book. Therapist's vision is more generic or primary—e.g., lessening of self-criticism so that he can think and relate more spontaneously and happily, letting her empathy give her more sense of relatedness and reduce her isolation, freeing his will to confront some of the constraints on his living.

Saying it differently, the difference between the projected goals for the client and the evolving vision lies in the orientation of the former toward external and visible changes, while the latter often has more to do with emergence from subjective limitations. Here is an example drawn from work with an exceedingly compulsive and often angry woman:

> In the therapeutic hours I frequently find that I have two strong and quite contrasting feelings: I feel weary and impatient with her endless interruptions of her own lines of thinking, with her continual starts and stops that are the results of her relentless criticism of herself. Yet along with that impatience I have feelings of sadness and sympathy. These come from my image of Jennifer as a woman who yearns to dance but who lurches on crippled legs. For under the frustrations of her continually trying to say and do everything exactly right, she is a gentle and warm person who genuinely wants to love and be loved.[6]

Therapist's Presence

To be genuinely present is no small matter. Especially when one operates by a preset plan for the work or with the fixed idea that one knows all that needs to be known about a client, boredom can become a real problem. When that is the case, presence is one of the first casualties of the non-engagement. (Lasting life change is a later victim.) Rogow quotes an analyst who says,

You're like a sleuth trying to find out what happened. Maybe you can find out in six months, and the rest of the time you spend trying to get the patient to understand what you have found out. In the trade you hear the statement: "It took me one month to analyze the patient and it took him three years to learn that." When that's the case, the rest is kind of routine.[7]

Clearly these sad messages come out of a very different perspective on and experience of psychotherapy than we are concerned with in this book. Therapists who find their contacts with clients routine, repetitive, and boring can scarcely be truly present. One may hope that in the time since the collections of Rogow's cases, those therapists have retired to stamp collecting or sunshine cruises and have not been replaced by their own kind.

Full presence means being truly accessible and appropriately expressive. One must be able to be reached by the client's experiencing, by the feelings, impulses, strivings, and retreats elicited in the hours. A supervening theoretical system is a screen admitting only that which fits the system, with the result that the therapist becomes more present to the system than to the client. The truly present therapist uses her empathy in a disciplined fashion to allow the client's experience to evoke resonances within her, resonances which then combine with her intuition (or stimulate it) to provide moment-to-moment attunement to the state of the alliance, the trend of the client's flow of awareness, and the needs of the overall development of the work.

Therapist's Sensitivity

The primary instrument brought to the support of the client's therapeutic efforts is the therapist's trained, practiced, and disciplined sensitivity. In many ways, this sensitivity is akin to a musical instrument which must be carefully prepared, maintained, tuned, and protected. With experience it can make possible the detection of nuances of feelings and meanings that would quite elude any attempt at explicit documentation, the drawing of inferences which are intimately in harmony with the client's subverbal experiencing, and the phrasing of interventions in terms exquisitely fitted to the client's needs, both in the moment and long-term.

This sensitivity is not solely a matter of education or supervision, although both may contribute importantly to its evolution, It is a product of life experience; thus, it is more difficult for a younger person to develop it—more difficult, but certainly not impossible, as some very intuitive and empathic younger colleagues demonstrate. Generally these are people who have had more than usually varied (and, often, difficult) life experiences.

To be sure, age may produce a rigidity which is the opposite of sensitivity, and in any case, age is no guarantee of its development. Sensitivity, such as is here called for, is the product of varied and meaningful human contacts, of exposure to the esthetic dimensions of life, and of firsthand encounter with the existential conditions of one's own being. And of something more.

SUMMARY

Concern is a built-in potential of human beings. Life experiences sometimes so crush or contort one's inner sensing that for all practical purposes, no real contact with that inwardness is possible. People severely so afflicted are frequently diagnosed as schizophrenic; less severely they may be seen as obsessive-compulsive.

But in the reasonably healthy person, the experience of concern is possible, even though it may be unrecognized and latent. It is a sad commentary on our culture—and particularly, our educational institutions—that the pressure for objectifying has cut so many of us off from access to this life-important talent. Therapy which awakens the client's concern for his own life makes a significant contribution to that life thereby. Therapists who learn to enlist their own concern fully gain significantly for their own lives.

A PSYCHOTHERAPIST'S JOURNEY

Is psychotherapy a science or an art? I have made clear where I stand on this question from the title of this book. Others still seek Freud's lost El Dorado of the perfected science of human behavior. I care less about the behavior and more about human experiencing. What we have are two fields uncomfortably living together in the same words—psychology, psychotherapy. The marriage is not working out well.

If psychotherapy is a science, as science is usually conceived, this chapter is nonsense. Such science seeks to be objective, to reduce the effects of individual differences among its practitioners (to zero if possible), to be dependably repeatable in its processes and products.

To such a science the concern of the therapist is irrelevant except as it is confined to following the treatment manual without variation.

The art of psychotherapy, on the other hand, insists that what goes on inside the therapist, the artist, is crucial to the whole enterprise. Therapist concern is not simply a nice, humane embellishment; it is more central to the work than the words the therapist speaks.

The difference between these two perspectives is highlighted by another quotation from Rogow, whose survey of psychiatrists and psychoanalysts turned up many who mentioned the "passivity and boredom" of their work as problems. One, a training analyst, advised a younger trainee:

> Do research, teaching, psychotherapy, group therapy, family therapy, ward therapy, music therapy. Develop some hobbies. Do *anything*, but don't do only psychoanalysis or you'll die of boredom when you get to 45.[8]

It is easy to blame such therapists as unfeeling and mechanical. What is more to the point is to recognize that, when one takes a completely objective view, therapeutic conceptualization and procedure are likely to be structured in advance; then the work itself is scarcely more exciting than bus driving.

The Distinguished Janitor Theory

For a time, realizing how true to our experience was this placement of the power of therapy in the client, my colleague (and the subject of this book's dedication) Alvin Lasko and I conceived what we called the "Distinguished Janitor Theory of Therapy." The gist of this notion was that we would find a janitor—or other unskilled person—who appeared mature, confidence-inspiring, and professional (in a word, "distinguished") and instruct him to sit with clients, listening intently, nodding frequently, and restricting his input to "Uh-huh," "Yes," "I see," and "Tell me more about that." We speculated that he would have a high success rate.

Looking back now, I estimate that we were only half right. There was an important truth in our theory, but it was incomplete, and that incompleteness makes a difference in both the number of people we can help and the depth of the therapeutic result that those people can attain.

The truth in our theory was that clients carry the crucial potential for changing their lives, that hardly anyone exercises that potential fully if he is unsupported in using it, and that simply putting one's concerns in words and having them respectfully attended to by another person has immense influence in helping a person use his own powers.

The omission from our theory was therapist concern. We assumed that good intentions and an appropriate manner were the main ingredients needed for therapeutic work. I know now that those ingredients are valuable and that some work can be done with those alone —indeed, is being done by thousands of professionals, subprofessionals, and lay people who give this useful aid to clients and friends. But I also know now that there are many other people whom these limited tools cannot reach or whose deeper needs cannot be brought forth and worked through with benign manner and attitude alone.

Therapist concern brings a greater range and depth of impact to the service of clients' own healing/growth potential. That greater power helps clients who cannot at first risk letting their needs be fully known or who cannot penetrate their own resistances, to cite two examples. Only with the sensitivity and presence that therapist concern provides can these people be aided to disclose (to themselves principally, to the therapist, secondarily) the core of their life issues. Only with the involvement and perspective that a therapist's need and vision provide can such clients be supported in the painful and terrifying self-confrontations necessary to major life change.[9]

Ours is not the ultimately crucial contribution to the life change our therapy can provide; that is the client's right and responsibility. Ours is, however, a highly significant and respect-deserving contribution.

CHAPTER 12

Intentionality and
Spiritedness

Only human beings, so far as we know, have the heavy responsibility and remarkable opportunity to participate in the cosmic function of creating actuality and to do so with some measure of consciousness. Each moment we must select from the infinite storehouse of the possible that which will be realized (made real), in the process consigning to irrevocable oblivion imense banks of what will never be. We are so caught up in this task and so familiar with it that we forget to wonder at it or to recognize its astounding significances.

Among the most distinguishing capacities of humans is that of having intentions, of conceiving purposes and values, and of taking actions to bring some of these into realization. Therapists' work with these processes is aided by conceiving a sequence in which impulses emerge from the unconscious and go through a series of "gates" which prune many away to allow some to become part of actuality. Our description of this sequence emphasizes the gates through which intentions must pass to move forward and thus it displays ways in which the blocked purposes of our patients may be freed.

I propose four subjective stages in this process — unconscious roots, wishes, wants, and willed intentions — and three externalized phases — preliminary actions, actualization, and interaction. Of course, these are arbitrary inventions rather than discovered truths, but they are useful in aiding therapists in phrasing and timing interventions and in having realistic expectations for their patients

IN THE FOLLOWING paragraphs I present an imagined subjective monologue portraying the functioning of intentionality.

If I but listen, I can hear at all times the voice of what is potential within me. It calls out for fulfillment. It speaks of how it might be, of what I have dimly sensed and briefly experienced. It tells me of how I

226

might, if only things would work out, feel within myself. I yearn for a promised land, but mostly I see it only from afar. I hunger for an ease within, and at times it comes — magically, it seems — and then it is too soon gone. I recall moments of fully functioning strength, and I search for how I may feel that way more and more.

The voice of what is possible within me speaks only the language of subjectivity. It does not know the tongue of the outside world, of other people, of workaday activities and requirements, of vocation, church, school, laws, elections, clocks and seasons, money and schedules, and all that great confusing realm in which I must daily make my way.

I stand in the doorway between the two worlds, urged on from within by that insistent voice of my subjectivity yearning toward greater realization, while at the same time confronting that outer panorama of opportunities and demands. I know so well how unlimited is the hungering and how very limited are my perception and my power.

So I am compelled to be a kind of translator. I listen to that inner voice whose archaic language I have always known but never spoken. Then I look at the outer world, which uses quite a different language, and I try to translate the one into the other. Early in my life I learned that there are few true cognates, that the two languages do not share a common structure, and thus that there are few direct parallels between them. Each translation that I make of an inner prompting into an outer course of action is inescapably a guess, a gamble. Which external steps, what goods, which events will most nearly equate to those inner promptings? I risk that if I do thus and so, if I am with a certain person, if I achieve such and such a result — if I but bring about some particular state of affairs in the external realm — then the inner feelings for which I long will result.

Sometimes I do well at these translations; sometimes poorly indeed. The task is so much harder because so many people, for so many reasons of their own — some neutral, some benign, and some antagonistic, have tried to tell me how to make the matchings. Parents, friends, con men, teachers, advertisers, salespeople, churches, political leaders, philosophers, and many, many others have insisted that seeking this or avoiding that would satisfy the internal hungering. But so often they have been wrong or only partially right.

Moreover, I have found that the translations that worked well one time do not necessarily continue to do so the next. It is so evident that I and my efforts alone do not determine the outcomes. Contingency continually intervenes and spins the wheel to make formerly satisfying matchings no longer fulfilling and to surprise me with unexpected events when I had thought I was safely on known ground.

So I try to make my doing and not doing effectively serve my inner wanting through the experiences I have in the events of my life in the outer world. Of course, necessity does not let me wait in that doorway. I am constantly, like it or not, propelled into making choices. As Pascal said, "You have no choice; you must place your bet." So I bet my life over and over again.

HUMAN BEINGS BE-ING HUMAN

Just as all matter reduces to energy, so it is with us: We are, in our deepest nature, processes, not things. We are humans, be-*ing*. We are the *ing* of our doing. We are not what we do, but the do-*ing*. We are not what we think, but the think-*ing*. Gordon Allport once remarked, "Structure is the secretion of process."[1] Life, process, is always moving on, always *in process*.

Saying this another way, human life is importantly characterized by intentionality. "Importantly" because intention is a central element in the direction our lives. Just as our lives are ultimately process, so the processes of our lives express our intentionality. In simplest terms: Intentionality is the meaning we create/express by our living.

Our beingness impels us into do-*ing*, act-*ing*, relat-*ing*, and so on. Only by *ing*-ing can we express/experience our be-*ing*. Unrealized potential is dead. We seek to actualize our potential, to give actual life to what is otherwise dormant. We all have many potential lives, only a limited portion of which will ever be actualized to any extent. The form of our lives is that which we bring from the mists of latency into the light of actuality.

It is a lifelong struggle to wrest direction of our being from other forces and into harmony with our intentions. It is a struggle because external forces seek to direct us, because within ourselves there is such competition for control, and because the sense of personal identity which we need to guide us is itself incomplete. Personal identity is always in the process of being formed by the very business of making these endless choices. We are, so to speak, constructing the vehicle even as we attempt to ride in it and steer it. And, moreover, we must construct it of materials we pick up as we go along.

As an aside, we may note that what children need in order to have meaningful lives is not education as we know it today, not discipline if that means being taught to rely on someone else's opinion of what is right, not limits or permissiveness or good models or avoidance of bad companions or any of the other familiar injunctions of childrearing. Each of these is commendable under some circumstances, but none of these is *the* essential. What is essential to a meaningful life is a developing sense of personal identity. Most of us spend our lifetimes seeking that, and inevitably we achieve it most imcompletely.

And then, in our older years, that personal identity (that ego or self) is what we must learn to relinquish — through transcending it or through confronting the reality of our ultimate deaths.

THE INTENTIONALITY SEQUENCE[2]

Our understanding of intentionality and thus of dispiritedness is aided by a model of how impulses may arise and evolve toward and into actuality. Table 12.1 shows this model sequence. Of course, this is not the only way of conceiving this important process, but it provides a useful and clinically proven framework for working effectively with what our patients are confronting.

Subjective Phases

Intentionality. Impulses to be and to do arise in the realm of the unconscious. We can speak of this as our "intentionality." Rollo May, Irvin Yalom, and Leslie Farber[3] are the most seminal, current thinkers

---

TABLE 12.1
The Intentionality Sequence

Phase	Characteristics (Examples)
Intentionality	Unconscious source of impulses (Instinctual, organic, social, etc.)
Wish	Spontaneous, fanciful ("I wish I could fly like a bird.")
Want	Hopes, yearnings, desires ("I want to learn to fly some day.")
Will	Plans for oneself, intentions ("I will learn to pilot a plane soon.")

. . . The gulf between the subjective and the external . . .

Action	Preliminary, tentative, try-out (Calls the airport training school.)
Actualization	Making it actual, a part of one's life (Takes and completes pilot's training.)
Interaction	Shiftings among many other intentions (Gives up golf to have flying time.)

© James F. T. Bugental, 1978, 1982

---

about this centrally important human process. May says, "By intentionality, I mean the structure which gives meaning to experience. . . man's capacity to have intentions."

Wishes. From this pool of potential, some impulses emerge as generalized "wishes." A wish is usually a rather nonspecific, loosely envisioned seeking toward experience. It is not tested against reality: "I wish we were in Southern France this afternoon." "I wish I had wings so I could fly like the gulls." We wish easily, widely, and transiently. Nevertheless, wishes are important in providing our deeper seeking with a route to possible actuality.

Wants. Some wishes are tested against reality, and those that survive may be termed "wants." A want is an impulse toward experience which has been examined for its reality. "We cannot suddenly be transported to Southern France this afternoon, but we can — and do — want to plan a trip to France sometime next year." Our wants provide us with menus of possibilities. That word *possibilities* is the cue; we do not act directly upon our wants.

Willed intentions. This array of wants leads us to the task of relinquishment. "Every choice is a thousand relinquishments," some sage has observed. We must make the life-and-death decisions which will do so much to determine the courses our lives will take. These choices we term "willed" intentions. Willing means killing off some possibilities so that others can be on our agendas for ourselves. Books and journals arrive in numbers far beyond my ability to peruse. I want to read all of them, but many will never be opened. Some do survive to go on a growing pile of those I intend to read. Note the future orientation: "I will read those soon."

Externalizing Phases

Action. The next step in this sequence marks a major transition from the solely subjective and implicit to some form of external actuality. I pick out one of the waiting books, open it, and read several pages. So doing I have taken an "action" and entered a whole new realm. "Action," however, here means only a preliminary step.

This leads to a new choice point: I started to read this book but now find it not on a topic I want to pursue. The sequence, insofar as the impulse to read this particular book is concerned, aborts at this point.

Actualization. On the other hand, perhaps the book indeed deals with what I want to learn about, and so I read it fully. This makes the reading of that book a part of actuality, and what *is* — an "actualization." It is manifestly important to distinguish preliminary and tentative forays into actuality from committed undertakings.

Interaction. Actualizations inevitably cause shiftings further back in the sequence. Because I am reading this book fully, three others drop from willed intentions to wishes. This is the final step, "interaction." Each actualized impulse sets in motion ripples evoking adjustments of other impulses.

The "Gates" Through Which Intentions Must Pass

As we trace the sequence impulses follow in this model, we recognize how they get winnowed so that relatively few survive. Now, of course, much of this elimination occurs preconsciously on the basis of well-learned habits of perception and judgment. We would literally be incapacitated if we had to make all these decisions consciously. Nevertheless, we need to recognize that this process is continually going on without our aware "supervision."

In the course of psychotherapy it is always essential to bring into consciousness the ways in which the patient is making these actuality/oblivion choices around certain key areas of her life. This is familiar practice in many perspectives, although, to be sure, not usually described in these terms or carried out in a formal way.

Especially helpful in working with patients who have issues in using their own capacities is investigation of the blocks to their carrying out their intentions. Table 12.2 lists the gates which must be passed. This way of considering patients' difficulties can often aid in locating where intrapsychic resistances to action are situated.

SPIRIT AND SPIRITEDNESS

In this section I will present an elusive but important conception: the notion of spirit. Sidney Jourard[4] proposed that psychology needed this addition to its vocabulary, and I think psychotherapists need it

TABLE 12.2
The "Gates" Impulses Must Pass to Attain Actualization

Phase	*"Gate" to Be Passed*
Intentionality	Is there some degree of consciousness?
Wish	Is it realistic?
Want	What will be relinquished to let it pass?
Will	Will some overt action begin to be taken?
. . . The gulf between the subjective and the external . . .	
Action	Will it be carried through fully?
Actualization	What else will have to change?
Interactions	

even more. Although the term carries with it the aura of religion and mysticism, the concept is too much needed to let one's prejudices (if they exist) prevent considering its value in our art.

The Dispirited Condition and Feeling State

The central "business" of human life is the translation of intentions into actuality as we try to have the living experiences which we believe we need and want. How we conduct that business depends, first of all, on how we define ourselves and our world, the self-and-world construct system which we described in Chapter 10. Impulses important to one's sense of being a known (to oneself) self in a known world need to attain actualization dependably. When this is not happening, anxiety is aroused, a backlog of intentionality work accumulates, and there is a deadening of vitality. This is the dispirited experience.

Dispiritedness is a term to characterize the condition of blocked intentionality and its accompanying feelings of dysphoria and (often) anxiety. Anxiety is an overlapping and somewhat more limited concept, in that it refers to a specific feeling state which may arise from a variety of influences.

Of course, I recognize that intentionality may also be impeded from the outside. In such instances dispiritedness is less likely to be part of the presenting picture. Instead we may see hostility, passive aggression, confusion, or psychotic decompensation. When imposed blocks to intentionality result in confrontation with unacceptable alternatives, then we may see these latter processes concurrently with dispiritedness. Concentration camps brought about this conjunction, making more understandable the often noted passivity of their inmates.

Expectancy and spiritedness. The arousal of expectancy is a concomitant of the approach to actualization. Thus, the closer an impulse is to attaining reality, the greater the resulting loss of spiritedness if that impulse becomes blocked.

Of course, this description is overly simple. Impulses do not exist or move separately; they are clustered, and there is often overlap among the clusters. My wanting to go to Southern France includes intentions to see some familiar and some new places, to live at a different pace, to eat wonderful meals — in short to do many things. In turn these impulses overlap with others — to revise our working sechedule at home, to have more time with special friends, and so on. When these impulse clusters have too many blockages and aborts, a spread of the dispiritedness results. If we don't get to make our trip, we find it harder to approach our usual activities with enthusiasm. (Of course, the reverse is also true: When we actualize important impulses, we find new zest in other areas as well.)

Relinquishment. Each of the gates that an impulse must pass if it is to be actualized is significant, but one of the most frequently troublesome for many people is that which distinguishes wants from willed intentions, i.e., relinquishment. It is hard for many of us — having lived in a time of rising expectations — to let go of possibilities, even though holding on to them may itself prevent desired actualities. Yet let go we must. I spoke above about how we must continually place our bets. The chips with which we bet are our hours, our opportunities, our hopes, our lives. Sometimes we win, sometimes we lose, but we want to win it all.

Actualization and relinquishment. Actualization and relinquishment are polar opposites: Actualization gives life, gives reality to possibility; relinquishment administers death. That death is a very real one. What we might have been but will never be, what we might have done but will never do—these are as irretrievably gone as a classmate killed in the war. Therapists need to remember that the deaths of invested possibilities evoke mourning, and grief work must be done. Genuine pain and sadness are involved, and time must be allowed for working-through.

Anger. There are further implications here which illustrate how these conceptions integrate a range of experiences: The dysphoria which is so characteristic of dispirited times is the emotional aspect of this work of relinquishment and grieving. Frequently related to this is anger or rage lying back of depression. That anger is a response to being blocked in important areas and to needing to give up invested perceptions or intentions. (It is useful to distinguish *dysphoria*, an emotional state, from *depression*, a clinical category. The former is often an appropriate response to negative experiences; the latter is an abiding condition only limitedly related to an intercurrent event.)

Inertia. A familiar element in the usual picture of depression / dispiritedness is inertia, the inability to bring oneself to act. Regnant impulses are blocked, and no vital substitutes are yet activated. Nothing seems worth doing. Yet this period of inactivity frequently serves a useful purpose. It provides time for realigning intentions, for making needed relinquishments, and for the grief work which may need doing so the person can undertake new intentions with emotional vigor.

Of course, much of what we describe is only incompletely available to consciousness. In intensive psychotherapy in which patient has learned to search within in an open way, these processes become evident.

Forced action. Some people who do not have such access to their inner living try—often with the well-meaning encouragement of family, friends, or even some psychotherapists—to "pull (themselves) together and do something." This kind of forced action, deprived of its roots in unconscious and deep intentionality, is seldom successful, rarely yields satisfaction for those who try it, and may actually be destructive, as it increases self-alienation. Those who attempt to bypass the blocked intentionality by this route often find their experience unsatisfying, false, or meaningless.

To say "seldom successful," is to recognize that in certain instances encouragement to action can be helpful. These are generally cases in which a depressed person already has largely worked through the relinquishments and grief but still hesitates to take the preliminary "actions" which begin the movement out of inertia. That working through may come about in any of three ways (or combinations of them): (a) as a natural but unconscious evolution which the intentionality system prompts, (b) as the result of concurrent therapeutic efforts, or (c) as a product of independent and disciplined self-exploration which may use skills derived from earlier psychotherapy. In any case, beginning to break out of the inertia can operate as the impetus to mobilize intentionality and return to inspirited living.

The Experience of Being Dispirited

The following is a self-portrait of an episodic depression written by someone who otherwise functions unusually well. Severity of symptoms is not the distinguishing mark of major depression. More important is how widely encompassing is the blockage to the ability to continue to bring intentions into actuality. The person who wrote the account below is able to act with effective intentionality in many areas of life, while yet being blocked in some significant aspects.

> I feel made of stone. My face is concrete. It hurts to move my mouth, and my eyes want to close. Everything is too light for the darkness I want to wrap around myself. My hands are heavy and move in slow motion. There is nothing worth doing; everything has been done before much better than I could do it anyhow. Why bother, when it is so difficult and so useless?
>
> All around me people are talking too loud and too fast. They expect me to "do something, do something." They are going faster and faster, and I am going slower and slower. Soon I will stop altogether. Then no matter how hard they pull or how loudly they shout, I will not hear them. I will not move.
>
> There was a time when I didn't feel this way, but now I can barely remember how I felt then. I know I did things and laughed and talked with my friends. Who are my friends? I don't feel as though I have any left. Not really. They want to change me, pull at me, make me feel different. But I am stone, granite — rock-hard to the core.
>
> This is a bad day. I don't want to talk to anyone or answer any demands. The best thing I can do is lock myself in my room and be alone. I know that if I don't do that I will soon find something to accuse them about — those others that I remember I used to love but whom today I hate.

Secondary reactions. Our culture judges any deviation from feeling good or being continually productive as wrong, sick, or evidence of a moral failing. These socially learned judgments are secondary and not to be confounded with the primary dispirited process. Such secondary reactions to dispiritedness may take many forms: blame, shame, guilt, and accusation of the self or others; anger, irritability, or provoking anger; isolation and withdrawal; and occasionally violence directed toward the self or others.

Tertiary reactions. Tertiary reactions also are often seen by psychotherapists. These take the form of nonpresence or detachment, in which patients distance themselves from the dispiritedness and its associated processes. Among the more common distancing tactics are overrationality, sardonic pseudo-humor, bitterness, helpless resignation, and undue dependency.

It will be recognized that the foregoing paragraphs are descriptions of the layering of the resistance (Chapter 10) when seen from its dynamic source. When we talk below about therapy of dispiritedness, we will be working in the opposite direction.

PSYCHOTHERAPY AND DISPIRITEDNESS

No true psychotherapy ever goes as neatly as the textbooks and theories describe; still a three-phase schema will portray the underlying strategy of therapy with depressed patients. In actual work the three phases overlap and are not as strictly sequential as is suggested.

First Phase: Presence

A frequent obstacle to therapeutic progress is the tendency of many middle-class, reasonably successful people to mask their true dispiritedness with detachment. They tell of their depression, but in a chatty, casual way. They report inactivity while inviting chuckles over the way they are. They describe the pressure of things to be done—absolutely necessary to do—but they observe that pressure and their lack of response from an impotent distance.

An early task of therapy, in such instances, is to deal with this lack of presence. Doing so identifies the detachment (tertiary reaction) as the outermost layer of the resistance. It must be frequently labeled as such and repeatedly brought forcefully to the patient's awareness.

Second Phase: Dealing With Secondary Reactions

As patients begin to let go of their detachment, attention needs to be directed to their secondary reactions—the ways in which they react to their own dispiritedness. This process involves identifying and reducing the blame, guilt, rationalizations, or whatever pattern is disclosed. In this work, catharsis of emotional blockage is important to freeing up the spiritedness and revitalizing the intentionality processes. The following account illustrates this reaction and the therapeutic work involved in dealing with it.

Beatrice is recently divorced when she enters therapy. Functioning well in her career, she complains that her relations with men are unsatisfying, that nothing she does has any meaning. Repeatedly she expresses determination to rebuild her life as quickly as possible in order to "get on with it." She says, "My divorce has been final for almost a year. We were in therapy before the divorce; so I've already done my crying. I just want to find another man and get my home established again."

Beatrice now sees her once challenging career as monotonous. Restless, she takes on a variety of activities, becomes president of a professional organization, adds another sport to her list of physical accomplishments. Still, again and again she is disappointed in her attempts to find satisfying activities and relationships with men.

Beatrice is trying to force herself to be at the "action" level, even though she is out of touch with her vitality, her spiritedness, and thus nothing in her system is working. She needs to go back, to go in, to stay down, and to be with her own grief.

In one session the therapist challenges Beatrice to let go, to enter into herself and say how it is in there. After a few minutes, she begins to describe what she experiences:

"I am in a cave deep underground, far from the entrance, very dark. I know I have to keep going to find the way out, but I see no light anywhere. I want to get out. It's such slow going, feeling my way in the darkness. I keep looking over my head, hoping for a trap door, a shortcut back to the light, but I see nothing. Then I hear a noise. It's the sound of birds. There are birds flying around in here. That pleases me."

The next weekend, for the first time, she chooses to be alone, to have her feelings. On Sunday she drives to the old house where she spent her summers as a child, a place and a time she connects with a sense of warmth and security. When she tells about it the next day she begins to cry for the home and family she lost in the divorce. Therapist cries with her.

Although superficially Beatrice's life is successful, subjectively nothing is working out because she will not face her own depression. The immobilized feelings of a depressed period terrify her. So she flees this darkness, taking her cardboard self out to do all her busy-ness. Since she runs from herself, she hungers in vain for closeness to someone else.

One-way intentionality. Work with people such as Beatrice has proven that the healthy flow of the intentionality process, the spirited flow, is one-directional—i.e., is from the unconscious through the intentional processes and so to actuality. When patient attempts to reverse that direction—to force action in the hope of evoking an inspirited fulfillment—the result is a dull, unrewarding enactment.

Third Phase: Primary Intentionality Blocking

When work with the secondary reactions has progressed sufficiently that patients recognize that they are reacting to their own dispiritedness, the therapeutic task is to encourage patients to accept the dispiritedness without complicating it. Only in this way can the relinquishments and grief be truly worked through so that the blocked intentionality can be reinspirited. This is more easily said than done. It requires continual alertness to the attitude and presence with which the patient experiences the life inertia. It calls for quiet confidence and steady presence on the part of therapist.

While helping the patient experience dispiritedness and avoid distracting responses to it, the therapist may recognize that the patient is beginning to confront a new kind of anxiety. Fears of non-being, death, the emptiness of the universe, of meaninglessness, or of ultimate aloneness may begin to surface. These are, of course, forms of existential anxiety. The presence of this anxiety often signals readiness for deeper therapeutic work.

Confronting Existential Anxiety

Existential anxiety, the anxiety of being, is anxiety that cannot be analyzed away. It can only be confronted as steadfastly as possible and then incorporated into one's being.

Earlier we described the fundamental importance of the ways in

TABLE 12.3
Estimates of the Basic Givens of Being

Basic Given	Confrontation
embodiedness	change
finitude	contingency
ability to act or not act	responsibility
choicefulness	relinquishment
separate-but-related-ness	a-partness*

*In the sense of being a-part-of and apart-from

which we define ourselves and our world. These ways are the constructs through which we order our being. They arise, usually unconsciously, as we experience the parameters or "givens" of existence. Various observers have suggested their own lists of these fundamental conditions; I find the five shown in Table 12.3 clinically and conceptually useful.[5]

This table proposes that each condition of being brings with it an inescapable circumstance, called a "confrontation," which each of us must deal with in some manner. Thus, the fact of our embodiedness forces us to recognize (or repress) that we are continually changing, that we and our worlds are continually in flux. The neurotic process frequently tries to arrest time, to insist on unchangingness, no matter how destructive that effort is.

In a similar way, our being finite means that we will die, that we cannot do all things, that we cannot know all we need to, that contingency is always our partner in determining the outcomes of our efforts. Those efforts express our ability to take action, the fact that we are not hapless observers, that what we do makes a difference, and that we carry, therefore, responsibility. That responsibility is linked also with our choicefulness, with our being able to select from a repertoire of possibilities, and as a result with our continual need to relinquish. Finally, our paradoxical circumstance of being at once related to but separate from all others leads to confronting our aloneness at times and at other times to accepting our being bonded to others whether we would or not, a condition given the name of "apartness."

A caution: When working toward the confrontation of these existential conditions, therapists must not get caught in patients' desires to "feel better." Of course, they are in therapy for that very purpose; yet pushing past what is authentic for them at the moment is destructive, not helpful. Thus, therapists have to be wary of rewarding good feelings and colluding in subtly punishing bad feelings. The temptation to intervene is strong for many of us, for there is the inevitable fear that patients may slip into pathological lethargy or get too discouraged and abort the work. Nevertheless, to try to urge our patients because of our concern is to undo work already accomplished and to betray our patients in a profound way.

If there is the opportunity—created by neither participant's interfering—at some point most patients discover a resurgence of intentionality. This renewal is frequently heralded by patients' coming to a kind of centered peace and inner quiet not known before. Once that state is attained, it is important for therapists to be firm but unintrusive until their patients are ready to move on.

A PSYCHOTHERAPIST'S JOURNEY

My quest to understand the "something more" in human beings was never only an abstract or scholarly one. It was strongly motivated by teenage periods of extreme anxiety around the inexorable fact of my death. Later, in graduate school, these feelings were renewed in the light of the atom bomb and the awesome possibility of world destruction. At that time, I found support and comfort in the Episcopal Church and in a new belief in God (after having been raised without any consistent religious instruction).

With time, these anxieties became less overwhelming, and the dogma of the church proved less than sustaining when my need was less critical, and I moved toward a comfortable, complacent agnosticism.

(This calls to mind my favorite bumber sticker: "My karma ran over your dogma.")

I am grateful for the support I received when I needed it so badly, but I can no longer find sustenance in a traditional church with its many to-me-irrelevant preoccupations of buildings, hierarchy, internal politics, fund-raising, and so many others.

"God" is, to me, one of many names for a manifest reality but a reality that is far different from the God of established churches. God is a way of pointing to the same immensity that words such as "The All," "Ultimate Meaning," "The Ground of Being," and many others designate. Perhaps it is best to recognize the ancient tradition that no one can know (or say) the name of God. This is so, not because it's spooky or forbidden, but because we cannot put a word on the infinite any more than we can paste a label on interstellar space.

The manifest reality is the astonishing fact of being itself in all its aspects from the submicroscopic to the immensity of intergalactic space. And equally astonishing is our awareness of this immensity. It is manifest also that we are not the pinnacle of all this wonder. We cannot comprehend (understand) that which comprehends (enfolds) us. We cannot even begin to comprehend ourselves to any degree. It is a ridiculous braggadocio which prompts us to claim we can and will reach ultimate knowledge or that we know more than any other agency in the universe.[6]

So my own personal journey has led me to look for a way of talking about that which is beyond my knowing, a way of speculating about what so clearly affects me and my work, a way of identifying the mystery that resides in the core of each person I know, each patient I work with, and myself. The term that I find useful that way is "spirit."

In Chapter 10, I described how this concept illuminates the further aspects of work with resistance. Affirming the validity of spirit in human life is a subtle but radical postulation: Until recently American psychology, with few exceptions, has treated the person as an object, as a reacting thing.

In contrast, the conception that the person is the ultimately active, initiating, or responsible agent, that what the person does is not completely explainable by an antecedent "cause" (e.g., parental teaching, conditioning, trauma, environmental contingencies) is central to the perspective of all that I have been presenting. I do not dispute that many of these influences may act on the person's awareness — both conscious and unconscious. It would be foolish to deny what is so apparent. But it is equally apparent (and it would be equally foolish to deny) that this is less than the whole story.

Saying it differently, I insist that action (overt or covert, explicit or implicit) is fundamentally produced by a person, not by some external "cause." Spiritedness is the force of our being truly subjects, and it is this which impels us forward into living. Our spiritedness is expressed in our having orientation, directionality.

Spiritedness is a larger concept than intentionality, but it embraces that important aspect of our being. Spiritedness is, of course, invisible. It is known only by what it moves — as is the wind by the waving of trees and grass. Yet just as the thrashing of the trees is not the same as the gale that presses on them, so the actions of our lives are not the spiritedness which motivates them. Intentionality is that aspect of spiritedness which is expressed in the particular intents and goals which we pursue. ·

All humans and probably most animals possess spirit, at least in some measure. With some, we know it only by its absence, and we accurately speak of such people as "dispirited" — the spirit has gone out of them. With others, we use phrases such as "spirited" or having "high spirits." Whatever surplus meaning those words have, there is no doubt that they do convey some meaning shared by all of us.

Most psychotherapists who have worked for years in depth explorations with their partners know this invisible but crucial element in human beings and know that it is not taught in graduate school and is pointed out only by the most exceptional supervisors.

The methods of this book do not reach spirit. (It will be remembered that Figure 2.1 diagrammed the levels of presence and needed to show an ultimate level only by the point at the center of the diagram.) These methods do, I believe, make it more possible for some of our patients to get through the obstacles which imprison their own spiritedness. That is a very wonderful thing, and I am content.

The Therapist as Artist

CHAPTER 13

The Therapist's Commitments

Commitment is an essential attribute of mature psychothera-
pists, just as it is intrinsic to being authentic as a person. Under-
standing the nature of constructive commitment provides thera-
pists with a perspective from which to view issues of role,
responsibility, and ethics. It also imposes on them serious obliga-
tions which need to be recognized and internalized.

This chapter defines commitment in existential terms. Readers
using other perspectives are, of course, free to make their own
interpretations, but all therapists need to confront the issues de-
picted. These are first displayed in a section devoted to position-
ing the concept of commitment in relation to other constructs,
such as authenticity, blame, and our existential situation.

Next we attend to the clinical significance of therapist com-
mitment, describing both affirmative and countertherapeutic as-
pects of five attributes of committed being. These are phrased as
committed being rather than as *commitment to, a distinction*
that preserves the center of responsibility in the therapist.

The five attributes of committed being are: (a) being commit-
ted in one's own participation as therapist, (b) being committed
in relation, with the patient's being, (c) being committed in rela-
tion to the patient's "family" (a term used with a very particular
meaning), (d) being committed in relation with the society of
which both therapist and patient are parts, and (e) being com-
mitted in relation to the mystery which enfolds us all.

WHAT COMMITMENTS IS it appropriate for a psychotherapist to
ask of herself? Should she be committed to her patients, to the cultural values within which she and her patient live, or only to her own
standards? Is it countertherapeutic to have *any* prior commitments?
These are important but too little addressed questions. This chapter
proposes a framework for thinking about them and then offers my
ideal for my own commitments as psychotherapist.

THE NATURE OF "COMMITMENT"

The great difficulty in working with a concept such as "commitment" is that it tends to become isolated from other ideas and from lived experience. Nothing could be more contradictory, for the very essence of commitment is that it links together the values and modes of our being and does so in a way that is grounded in immediate life. Mindful of this danger, I begin by proposing a simple conceptual framework for commitment and then demonstrating its operation in the day-to-day work of the consulting room.

Authenticity and Commitment

Viewed from an existential perspective, the good life is an authentic life,[1] a life in which we are as fully in harmony with the basic conditions of being human as we can be. Inauthenticity is illness, is our living in distorted relation to our true being. Psychotherapy is a means by which a person may seek to gain or regain congruence with the givens of being human.

Commitment is essential to authenticity. Recalling the description of the "givens" of being human in the last chapter (Table 12.3), it will be remembered that one of these was our ability to act or to not act. This confronts us with responsibility for our doing and not doing. An authentic acceptance of responsibility takes the form of commitment. The contrasting, avoidant response is blaming.

Saying it differently, commitment is an attitude, an emotional investment, and a determination to respond in a value-actualizing way. In terms of the intentionality sequence, commitment calls for willed intentions which are frequently translated into preliminary actions and, when necessary, into actualizations (which, of course, set in motion interactions in a widening ripple effect).

To say that I am committed to putting my patient's welfare ahead of most other considerations is easy. That commitment becomes a challenge when I must decide whether to see a patient in crisis at a time that is disruptive of my home life, when I must choose whether to give in to another patient's pleas for special treatment or work through the tantrums that will come if I refuse, or when I must insist that a third patient's frequent absences are countertherapeutic and not acceptable, even though he has "excellent" excuses for them.

The point is that true commitment is not an abstraction; it is an almost daily confrontation with what I believe and what I value and whether I can stand with my beliefs and values.

Commitment and Responsibility

Commitment is a courageous response to the existential anxiety that comes with our being confronted by our responsibility for how we act and do not act in our lives. It is the intent to stand forth as the author of our doing and to meet what this stance may evoke; thus, it contrasts with yielding to the dread of blame. Commitment is particularly important when we recognize our work as therapists as a controlled and demanding kind of doing and not doing in which we often feel the heavy weight of responsibility and where, not infrequently, we must marshall our courage to face what needs to transpire in our offices.

These too are abstract words, but therapists who work intensively and deeply know them as much more than that. There is a tightening in our guts, a speeding up of our thinking, and an intentness in our intuiting which are the living counterparts of these cool words. In the moment when a despairing person contemplates suicide, when a resistant patient threatens to act out violently, when a wife is considering breaking up a long marriage, when a man is about to abort his career, or when someone flirts with slipping over into psychosis—in such moments, *courage, dread* and *commitment* are no longer words but very concrete experiences.

We know how limited is our awareness of the consequences of acting and not acting, how incomplete is our appreciation of all that may be involved in any choice. Yet we must choose; we cannot withhold from acting since even not acting is an act, a choice. Moreover, if we are aware, we know that those actions and non-actions can have and continue to have consequences we do not want, consequences we surely would have prevented if we had foreseen them. We and others may be hurt by what was done or left undone. The word is a tough one, but it is accurate: We always carry some load of *guilt*. But saying that makes it necessary to be clearer about the nature of *guilt*, as I am using the term.

Blame vs. Guilt[2]

These two words are often used as synonyms, but to do so is to confuse our thinking. I will propose a way of distinguishing between *blame* and *guilt* which is theoretically defensible and clinically useful: A chief distinction between "guilt" and "blame" is that *guilt* refers to an emotional recognition of responsibility for my acting or my not acting, while *blame* is seen as an attribute of my being. "I am guilty

248   *The Art of the Psychotherapist*

that I acted prematurely with John and upset his careful plans," but, "I blame myself that I am selfish." This use of the term guilt is related to but not identical with the idea of "existential" or "ontological" guilt, the guilt that inheres in our very being and which arises because we do not fulfill our own potentials, do not act in terms of our own values and intents, and do not meet our fellows with full appreciation of their beingness.

Accepting the guilt of having produced outcomes that we regret is not destructive but freeing. It turns our attention from the past to the present and future as we consider how to make restitution and how to prevent the recurrence of such outcomes. Yet at times it can be heavy indeed to accept guilt when we face fully what it is that we have brought about. Consider the following example.

> Cindy, a psychotherapist, consulted me because she was continually going over and over her feelings about a patient who had suicided while in therapy with her. She told me the story of the tragedy in a manner which spoke clearly of many anguished rehearsals. She wept, and she confessed bitterly how she had let herself be inattentive to her patient's veiled threats. She came, without realizing it, for me to judge and punish her.
>
> This is not the place to recount the struggles of Cindy's own therapeutic course, the frightening times when she considered suicide herself (as a deserved punishment), or the eventual working out of her painful burden. The important point for our present purposes is that she had to recognize that she was so preoccupied with self-blame that she was rapidly becoming immobilized. As she was able to accept her guilt and reduce the blaming, she found that she could pay better attention to her current patients, could contribute some time to a suicide prevention center (as a kind of restitution), and could ultimately forgive herself and offer a more concerned and vigilant attention to those who sought her help.

When the load of responsibility seems too great, then one responds from dread. This may take many forms, but the common denominator is preoccupation with blame. This may be overt blaming: "I am this way because of my parents." It may be more subtle, "I can't help what I did; circumstances were against me." Or it may be quite disguised, "I spoke that way on impulse," or "I don't believe in lying so I'll tell you just how I feel." (To some, the latter statements may seem far removed from blame but analysis discloses that responsibility for what is said or done is projected away from the speaker's own center.)

Of course, what has just been said is far too either-or-ish. We are constantly expressing both our dread and our courage, blaming sometimes and being committed others.

CLINICAL DIMENSIONS OF THERAPIST COMMITMENT

Now, having provided this general framework for the concept of commitment, I will explain how I see that concept and its significance for the therapist and her interaction with patient. We begin by considering briefly two ways the word itself is used, transitively and intransitively.

Committed Being and Being Committed

The noun form *commitment* misleadingly suggests an act once accomplished and a condition thenceforth established. Realistically, it is more accurate to say, "In my encounter with my patient I am continually engaged in committing and recommitting myself." In other words, committing oneself is an ongoing process which must be repeatedly renewed.

There is a further implication: Borrowing a term from grammer, commitment may be used transitively or intransitively. For therapists the latter is the more suitable. I am not *committed to* something or someone; rather, I *commit* myself in my engagement with my patient. This usage makes *commitment* closer to *resolve* than to *invest*, in that it refers to a subjective decision within oneself.

We in the mental health disciplines are familiar with this word "commitment" in another context, where it has a contrasting significance: When we speak of patient being "committed to the hospital," we are describing something done to patient, an event in which he may be an involuntary participant. His relation to the hospital is that of an object to a subject. We may speculate that he is committed to the hospital because he is not committed in his own living.

When we use "committed" transitively, we generally imply this same loss of subjecthood, this same transfer of centeredness from the one committed to the locus of the commitment. Thus, to be committed to liberalism or to conservatism politically often means that labels or public leaders make the decisions for the committed one rather than that person himself. A therapist committed to a viewpoint

(Jungian analysis, psychoanalysis, existential-humanistic therapy) or an orientation (person-centered, object-relations) may easily slide into the same displacement.

The Therapist's Commitments

I will describe five therapeutic aspects of commitment. Each description is composed of two elements: the kind of committed being in the relation which is authentic and therapeutic, and the other forms of commitment which, while apparently similar, are actually inauthentic and countertherapeutic. I describe these in the first person as ideals I hold for myself, not as achievements I can claim.

First, I seek to be committed in my own being in the encounter with my patient.
As I meet my patient, I intend being a person in my own right, my own beingness. I intend to be accessible to his responses and emotions, to be inwardly resonant with him, and to be ready as appropriate to confront him with my perceptions. Committed being in the encounter means being, to the best of my ability, whole in my presence, risking myself and my feelings.

I am not so committed in my being with my patient if I practice so-called therapeutic detachment, if I deny my own involvement, or if I enact the fiction that all the patient sees of me is his transference.

The contrasting and inauthentic version of this first attribute of therapist commitment is one that new therapists unwittingly often slip into: If, when with my patient, I am *committed to* being a good therapist, a healer, an expert, or an existentialist, then I am not committed in my own being in the encounter. This is an instance, as my language has just indicated, of using the concept of commitment transitively. To be committed to being a good therapist may result in a portrayal of what I think a good therapist is and should do, but if my focus is on such a portrayal, I am lacking commitment in my own being.

The commitment of being authentic when with the patient is not license to self-disclosure, self-indulgence, or other supposedly spontaneous actions. In the '60s, a number of therapists became convinced that they only needed to be "natural" and "genuine," and patient would somehow be cured. This led to a chaotic situation which no doubt helped some, equally surely wasted the hopes of others, and actually damaged still others. Such therapeutic anarchy is far from my intent in this statement. Committed being with the patient means being aware, prepared, responsible, and discriminating in how I use my own powers.

Segment 13.1
Patient: Terry Black; Therapist: Jill Boswick

 (Terry is a patient with poor ego control who has acted out in destructive ways in the past. He has made as good a relation with the therapist as he is capable of at this point in his life; still it is tenuous and he often needs to test it. He alternates in his sessions among three modes: grateful dependency, unresponsive detachment, and angry demandingness. Today he is in the third: angry and challenging. On the surface, this centers around the therapist's refusal to let him continue to postpone paying for his sessions.)

PT-1: You just sit there like God Almighty and never say anything to help me. You just want my money and don't give a good goddam about what happens to me. Isn't that right?

TH-1: No.

PT-2: What do you mean, "No." Don't try to shit me. I'm onto your racket, and I'm going to get even. I'm going out in the waiting room everyday and tell everyone what a con game you're running.

TH-2: You're trying very hard to get to me, aren't you?

PT-3: Shit, I can't get to you. Nobody could. But I can get to the people who come to see you.

TH-3: You're so busy attacking you have no idea whether you're getting to me or not.

PT-4: Well, am I?

TH-4: Of course.

PT-5: How? Tell me how I'm getting to you.

TH-5: I'm feeling your anger and your desperation like you're pounding on me. They hurt, but they don't destroy me.

PT-6: Good! I'm pleased to know I can hurt you.

TH-6: You really want to make me feel about you.

PT-7: You bet! And when I start telling everyone in the waiting room about you, you'll hurt more, won't you?

TH-7: Terry, I want you to hear me now and hear me good. You can use your time in here to tell me whatever you need to, and we'll work with whatever comes out. It may not be pleasant for me, but I'll hang in so we can do what needs to be done . . .

PT-8: Yeah, yeah, but when I . . .

TH-8: (Interrupting, very firm voice.) Wait, Terry, I'm not through, and you better hear the rest: I will not stand for your disturbing other people who come here. Repeat, I will not stand for it, and I'll have you arrested the first time there's the least hint of your doing anything like that. Get this and get it straight, Terry: In here is your time and place, and there's lots of leeway. When you go out that door, you leave that privilege behind, and I will do whatever I need to do to protect the other people who come here to work on their own lives and to protect my own rights.

Segment 13.1 represents an extreme instance of the therapist's asserting her own position, being committedly in her own being. It may seem provocative, but with such a patient it is essential to stand clearly and unequivocally for what one deems important. If there is a wavering, that is apt to be even more provocation. Terry needs the modeling of someone who is centered (committed) in her own life. Moreover, the therapist must be prepared to follow through if the patient does not accept the limits she has set.

Unusually intrusive patients create other occasions in which the first form of commitment is important, as they attempt to invade the therapist's private life (through extended or late night phone calls, coming uninvited to the therapist's home, etc.). Of course, at times we need to be available at all hours to some patients, but this is usually an in-office or telephone availability. Patients, not in emergency, who need to test limits, are reassured and helped to form better ego control when the therapist has her own limits and can assert and enforce them nondefensively.

On the other side of the matter, there are occasions in which this commitment in one's own being conflicts with patients' legitimate needs: Therapist illness, change of career, domestic disruptions, vacations, and sabbaticals are instances. If one carries a usual caseload (20 to 30 hours a week), there is never a time when being away from the office will have no undesired impact on one or more patients. It is sad but true that the therapist's first obligation in these instances is to do what is necessary to preserve her own well-being. Failing that she will be less able to adequately serve all her patients, as predictable resentment will contaminate her work. It should be apparent from what I am saying generally that this is in no way warrant for callous disregard of patients' needs at any time. Moreover, in making such choices which adversely affect one's patients, one must accept true guilt and seek appropriate forms of restitution.

Second, I seek to be committed in my being responsive to my patient's seeking toward greater authenticity.

The focus here is the complement of the first attribute, looking now at the patient's side of our alliance. Often he will seek to involve me in inauthentic ways, e.g., satisfying his need for approval, for reassurance, for love, for punishment. My commitment directs me toward the person in back of any of these efforts and aids me in steadfast seeking for the patient's deeper center. When I am most so committed — and this varies widely — it provides a stable point which my patient implicitly employs to orient himself. In actual sessions this may take the form of a layer-by-layer analysis of the resistances (see Chapter 10) or a simple and persistent confrontation, such as "I can't find *you* in what you're saying."

The contrasting and countertherapeutic aspect of *commitment-to* comes about when I invest in a patient's inherent worthiness, goodness or potential. Often such an attitude seems so desirable and so humane that it is easy to yield to it. Particularly is this likely with the hard-to-like patient whom we are apt to persuade ourselves is a roughly hidden diamond. When this happens, we are often suppressing annoyance or anger by not meeting the patient as he is in the contact but redirecting attention to the imputed worth or potential.

Another way in which well-meaning therapists slide over into inauthentic relating with patients is becoming parental or sponsoring in a way which makes therapists the repositories of their patients' beliefs in themselves and of their hope or sense of worth. This seems so genuine and caring that it is often difficult for therapists to recognize that, if it is continued long, a dependency is being fostered which may ultimately have to be undone and which may very well take the therapeutic gains with it as it is shed.

To be sure, there are periods in which the therapist's belief in patients' latent potentials is a valuable resource (see the discussion of "Therapist's Vision" in Chapter 11). Those times need to be carefully monitored, and steps must be taken as soon as realistic to call on patients to take up responsibility for their own self-belief.

Segment 13.2
Patient: Gil Stratford; Therapist: Jean White
PT-11 It's been just the same this past week: Everything's gone wrong, and I can't seem to get my act together.

TH-11: Seems familiar, doesn't it?

PT-12: Sure does. I get so discouraged (sighs).

TH-12: You're really feeling down right now.

PT-13: Yes, yes, I am. If I didn't have you believing in me, I think I'd just give up.

TH-13: You want me to carry all of the hope for you?

PT-14: Well, you know. Right now, I just can't find anything positive inside of me. That's why I need you so much.

TH-14: It feels as though it's easier to have me carrying your hope than for you to risk having some hope yourself.

PT-15: I told you (protesting tone). I'm just way down. I can't find any hope now.

TH-15: I hear that, but I don't hear you really trying to find any feeling of your own for yourself. I'm ready to stand with you in these bad times, but I'm not able to do all of it for you.

PT-16: Are you telling me you feel hopeless about me too?

TH-16: You're twisting what I said. I think it's very hard for you to risk being with me in hoping you'll get out of these miserable feelings.

PT-17: (Grudgingly) Yeah, I guess so.

TH-17: It doesn't sound like you're picking up much of the load.

A bare beginning, but an important beginning.

Third, I seek to be committed in my implicit engagement with the patient's "family."

"Family" here means those persons who are significantly part of the patient's life. This usually includes some, but not all, of his family of origin and his conjugal family, as well as a few other persons. These are the people who strongly affect the patient and who in turn are likely to be significantly influenced by him.

The point here is that the patient is not separate from others but must be recognized as always living in a relationship matrix. It is all too easy for therapists and patients to slide into forgetting this reality to the cost of their work and of the patients' well-being—not to mention inappropriate injury to others in that "family."

Recognition and respect for the beingness of others need to be set against the subtle seduction of our patients to join them against the world. The patient, naturally, presents his own views of events and persons, and the therapist, wanting to be experienced as understanding and supportive, accepts these uncritically. Later, questions or confrontations which raise other perspectives may be experienced as betrayals. My work as therapist to or supervisor of other therapists has shown me this is a frequent trap for the well intentioned new professional.

The inauthenticity resides in the implicit teaching to the patient of an uncommitted and blaming stance in his relation to others and to the world. One cannot help a patient achieve genuine and authentic self-respect if there is indifference to the lives and needs of others in the patient's life space.

When working long-term with someone, I remind myself from time to time to consider the impact of our efforts on the others in the patient's life. Many times this occurs spontaneously as the patient describes interactions with those people. Sometimes, when it seems to me that a spouse is being severely threatened by changes and emotional flareups, I have watched for opportunities to suggest to the patient that the spouse be invited to a session in which we will give some perspective and support to him or her. These are always joint sessions (I would not see the spouse alone except under very unusual circumstances), and I try to have the patient take the major responsibility for informing the spouse.[3]

The inauthentic interpretation of this third aspect of therapist commitment is enacted when the therapist becomes—often without really recognizing it—committed to certain relations in the patient's life. The latter needs to be free to examine all of his relations, not in a blindly self-serving way, but in realistic evaluation. He may need to break off some relations, in which case the therapist's commitment calls on her to be concerned that it be done with suitable recognition of the other's feelings.

I do not subscribe to the old saw, "One analysis, one divorce." To be sure some marriages do not survive the clear light of realistic confrontation, but I admit to some satisfaction that my long-term patients have more often mended their intimate relations than broken them off.

There are delicate questions involved with this third attribute of being committed authentically. Should adult children who have adopted a homosexual life pattern "come out" to their parents? Should a married person confess an extramarital episode? Should children be fully exposed to their parents' conflicts? I have no general answers to such issues; the persons involved must accept responsibility for making judgments and for the possibility—however they decide—of giving or receiving serious hurt as a consequence of their decisions.

In contrast, when I learn that a patient is sexually molesting or physically abusing a child or a helpless elder, I have no hesitation about my stance. Quite aside from the increasing legal mandates (and, indeed, this was my practice before their enactment), I move in strongly to enjoin any continuation of these acts, to make certain that they have ended, and to secure legal enforcement if I am not assured of their ending.

This topic brings up an ethical and commitment dilemma: While obviously I support the intent of the laws mandating reporting of all such instances, I find them shortsighted and likely to increase the problems they seek to solve. To require the reporting of someone who has in the past engaged in abuse or molestation but who now seeks help to forestall any recurrences is to make it less likely that person will actually seek help. Such people then try to use "will power"—just as, very likely, they have before—instead of getting professional aid, and that route often proves futile. My commitments are such that if someone in this situation sought my help and I were convinced of his or her serious intention to overcome the impulse, I would risk ignoring the legal requirement. However, I would also accept the responsibility that, should our efforts prove unavailing, I would make a report to the proper authorities.

Fourth, I seek to be committed in my relation to society as the ground in which the patient and I have our being.

To make this fourth aspect of commitment understandable, I will examine the affirmative and the negative sides together: Erich Fromm[4] wrote of the human need for rootedness, something that I have too often overlooked in my therapeutic work—as I think other therapists also tend to do. Our identities as persons have their sources in society and our lives always occur in a social context, as essential as the airy medium we breathe. To be committed in my relation to society does not mean to be committed to any particular folkways or mores, institutions or governmental forms, or even to a particular culture. Folkways, mores, government, institutions, and culture are furnishings adopted by a particular form of society, but the basic fact that my patient and I are social creatures is not dependent on the forms of these furnishings.

This commitment means I cannot accept my own impulse or the all-too-ready tendency of many intellectual patients to explain our distresses, frustrations, and disappointments in terms of the "sick society" in which we live. To be sure, there is much that is pathogenic in our culture—as in any culture of which I have knowledge. But this only sets the terms of the task; it does not dismiss us from responsibility. This endemic social apathy of the intellectual is not a necessary product of society's ills but a neurotic flight from existential confrontation. My patient is—and I am—in an important sense personally responsible for what is wrong in society. We need to meet and incorporate that fact, not deny it and thus deny our own being in the process.

This point is easily misunderstood, so a few general corollaries may help: The sadly frequent modern credo, "I don't want to get involved," is the antithesis of what I am postulating. We are all involved, involved completely and for all our lives. If my patient and I are successful in our work together, then we emerge with renewed recognition of our involvement and our commitment. I wish that every patient who completes therapy with me would become a societal change agent, and I wish he would become such not from rejection of society and standing outside of it but from incorporation of society and participation in bringing about changes.[5]

Fifth, I seek to be committed in my relating with my patient in relation to Humankind and to the Mystery in which we live.

I write "Humankind" with a capital "H," knowing I might as well write "God" with a capital "G" or "The All." Probably it is most accurate to use "the Mystery in which we live." I'm not sure what I mean by any of these terms. They seem alternative ways of pointing I really don't know where but someplace it seems important to try to point. Certainly I don't mean a commitment to the gods of most formal religions or to some mystic transcendent principle which will displace us in the very responsibility I have been laboring to explicate. Perhaps what I can do is simply express my conviction that the authentic person recognizes his finiteness and, recognizing it, transcends it in some measure by seeking at least this sort of relation to what is beyond knowing.

In a practical way what this means for me is that I value and protect my own and my patient's sense of possibility, of the unknown, of the something more beyond our ken which may yet impinge on us. At times this means an openness to discuss his experiences which he feels to be instances of extrasensory perception, of mystical insight, or of being in touch with levels of human experience about which we know little or nothing. It means a candid openness on my part to realms of possibility which I can neither demonstrate nor refute. As appropriate to the stage of the work, I try to be straight with patients who inquire as to my views in this area, expressing my own interest, ambivalence, and, on occasion, speculations. I have but one conviction in this area: There is more to the human story than we have yet discovered.

IMPLICATIONS FOR THE THERAPEUTIC ALLIANCE

Long-term therapy of some depth inevitably involves times of warm communion and times of great stress—for both participants. Living through these together has a true bonding effect which is not always recognized by those who teach or practice more objective modes. Nevertheless, therapist and patient often have what can only be called a love relationship, which is by no means simply a product of transference and countertransference. Patient and therapists are two human beings, partners in a difficult, hazardous, and rewarding enterprise; it is unreal to expect otherwise.

Let me set this straight: I am not referring only to the currently popular preoccupation with sexual enactments between therapists and patients. These have been so abundantly and lip-smackingly dealt with that they require no further comments from me.

In describing inauthentic kinds of commitments above, I have pointed to subtle seductions to which the therapeutic relationship is vulnerable. These have in common the therapist's impulses to support, encourage, and otherwise endorse the patient's views of himself, his relations, and his life. Those are familiar and useful responses within limits, but too often they are insufficiently accompanied by confrontations of the patient with his responsibilities in these same matters. Since often the therapist is the patient's only confidant, there is an understandable reluctance to seem to play the demanding parent or admonishing teacher. Thus, it is all too easy to become solely the patient's defender and advocate. Well-intentioned as this is, it can be genuinely countertherapeutic and ultimately weaken the patient's own powers.

There are times when the therapist needs to make difficult and awkward confrontations, when she must refuse blanket endorsement of patient views and intents, and when she must oppose cathartic but inappropriate actions. Segment 13.3 provides an example of the handllng of such an incident.

Segment 13.3
Patient: Terry Black; Therapist: Jill Boswick

PT-21: I've been stewing all week about the way my old man treated me when I was just a kid. The bastard used to just get his kicks out of beating me up. It eats on me that he could just get away with it. In fact, . . . well, anyway, I keep thinking about it.

TH-21: You stopped yourself from saying something just then. How come?

PT-22: Oh, it's nothing (uneasily). Just didn't seem like I needed to waste time on it.

TH-22: You're sure anxious to get away from it.

PT-23: Oh, hell, Jill, you're always after me about something.

TH-23: Yeah, so what else is new? What gives, Terry, you're as antsy about something as I don't know what.

PT-24: Okay, if you want to know, I'll tell you, but don't say anything about it. My mind's made up. Okay?

TH-24: No, I don't give any promises in the dark.

PT-25: Shit! I thought you were on my side.

TH-25: You're sure jumping around to keep from saying whatever it is you've made up your mind about.

PT-26: Okay, so here it is: I'm going up there this weekend and kick the shit out of that old sonovabitch. Let's just see how he likes it.

TH-26: So you didn't want me to know that, huh?

PT-27: Oh, you'll probably get all mushy about it just because he's old now.

TH-27: How old?

PT-28: I don't know, and I don't care. He's had this coming for nearly 40 years, and I'm gonna love giving it back to him.

TH-28: How old, Terry?

PT-29: Oh, 66, 67, something like that.

TH-29: Think you can handle him?

PT-30: What are you doing? Kidding? Of course, I can.

TH-30: Of course you can.

PT-31: What's that mean?

TH-31: You're your father's son, all right—picking on someone who can't really defend himself.

PT-32: Yeah, let's see how he likes it.

TH-32: How did you like it?

PT-33: I hated it, and I want him to hate it too.

TH-33: And then?

PT-34: "And then" what?

TH-34: After you've beaten up an old man who can't fight you, what then?

PT-35: I'll feel a hell of a lot better.

TH-35: Will you? Take a minute and feel into that. Just imagine it: You've
left his house and left him lying there badly beaten up. Now what?

PT-36: I see what you're trying to do. Goddam bleeding heart is what you
are, Jill. Well, I still will feel a hell of a lot better.

TH-36: Terry, I know you say you will, and you may be right, but frankly I
doubt it. Anyway, I want you to hold off until we've talked it through.
Will you do that?

PT-37: I thought you were supposed to be on my side?

TH-37: Believe it or not, I really am. Let's take three times to talk it all over,
and maybe I can help you see that I am on your side even though I
think beating up your father is a dumb idea that will bring you more
grief than satisfaction.

PT-38: I don't know whether I want to wait that long. I really want to feel
my fist smash his nose right now.

TH-38: Three times, Terry.

PT-39: Oh shit, okay. Three times.

Jill's task during those three times is going to be to try to help Terry
see his responsibility in waiting so long to face up to his feelings about
his father and his own sense of impotence. She has, very likely, been
working on his overdependence on threat as a way of trying to get
what he wants, and now she will be hoping to link that up with the
present impulse to violence.

The question we're left with is: What if the three times makes no
difference in Terry's intention? Legally, Jill must report Terry's plan to
the police and to Terry's father. This latter step is a requirement
guaranteed to end the possibility of Terry's using help again now or in
the future. Whether Jill actually does report Terry depends on far too
many considerations for us to cover now.

Commitment and Society's Norms

The truth of this whole matter of commitment is that there are
likely to be times when that ideal conflicts with societal norms. The
approved and disapproved standards of our culture are not well syn-
chronized with human needs and realities. It is naive to expect that
there will always be a way to work out a congruent plan. When such
a disjuncture occurs, the therapist must confront the difficult choice
between staying with what is needed for the patient's reclaiming of
his own life and what is expected by the society.

These occasions open the therapist to possible censure when she
chooses to support the patient's needs against the folkways and

mores. It is often difficult—if not downright impossible—to document in explicit and publicly defensible terms the subjective considerations leading up to such judgment calls. Additionally, patients themselves may later be led by others to find fault with the very permissiveness which helped them free themselves.

Numerous examples of these kinds of issues are available: A patient of mine broke up a moderately expensive chair in my office in a release of long pent-up rage. Although we both felt good about the event, others have criticized it as fostering "acting-out." Another incident involving sexual feelings is by far the most frequently commented on in my book of cases.[6] Yet depth therapists know that there are occasions when such risks must be run.

Commitment as a value demands that the therapist examine her priorities and values, maintaining awareness of them and of the patient's long-term needs above—but not in defiance of—the more usual concerns our society teaches.[7]

SUMMARY

Commitment is one of the defining attributes of existential authenticity. So stated, it becomes evident that commitment is a way of being in the world; it is an ongoing process of being. Committed being may be set in contrast to the flight from responsibility into preoccupation with blame.

I have described my intentions as a therapist and as a person. I fall far short of their attainment, but I am committed in my constant recommitment to their pursuit.

A PSYCHOTHERAPIST'S JOURNEY

When I really grapple with the topic of commitment, seemingly so theoretical and abstract, it takes me into some of the toughest issues our world faces at a life-and-death, practical level. I will briefly sketch this:

Objectivity is the black plague of the twentieth century. That says it, but it understates the threat. The black plague only killed one in three in Europe. We contemplate killing all of us, all life, and our planet.

Objectivity is the name of the greatest threat our species has ever labored under. We are not likely to rival the dinosaurs for longevity as a species if we don't make a major recovery from objectivity.

War, of course, is the ultimate—perhaps exactly so—insanity of all, but it is by no means the only. War is a product of treating human beings as objects. Policies, territory, and economic advantage are more valued than lives and happiness when the objective view dominates.

Enough of our world's resources are being poured into war to materially improve the life experience of every person living in this world and to make possible a project immense beyond any precedent for dealing with all the world's social ills. We all need to pause and consider that incredible fact.

We need to learn to include the subjective in our lives, to take account of the inner experiences of people, to recognize that many truths are not such that they can be rendered explicit, unambiguous, or complete. Those same truths are essential to our survival, but we deny them because they are subjective.[8]

We have little if any idea how to live together with a subjective ethic guiding our lives. We can make some starts, but many of the possible ones are only theoretically possible. It is likely that many of them would be seen as UnAmerican or UnChristian or Unworkable or Unmoral or God knows what else.

Trying to pass laws that partake of the ultimacy of natural laws—which, themselves, are not truly "natural" or "law-like"—is a vain and destructive objectivist effort. We have learned to distrust human judgment, not recognizing that everything we do, every choice we make, every law we write, every part of our lives is ultimately resting on human judgment.

We mistake folkways for intrinsic truths. We mistake customs for necessities. We try to regulate where what we need is guidelines and latitude. Parole boards, governed by laws and rules intended to be humane, release unrepentent killers on us because the form of the law has prevailed over human judgment.

Democracy, egalitarianism, capitalism, communism, fascism, racism, nationalism, and all such are ultimately doomed to be failures because they do not solve the problem of objectivism. It is a problem that may, indeed, be unsolvable. If so, humanity is that problem. Our amphibian nature makes us the problem. We live in our subjectivity, but we must make our way in objectivity. We live in separateness, but we must survive in relatedness. These paradoxes are at the root of the human dilemma.

Objectification of human beings is the insanity that is the toxic pollution in the sea in which we swim, the world in which we try to live. We have been hypnotized from our earliest years to believe that it must be so. I want to say that which we learn not to say. I want to stand outside the universal post-hypnotic suggestion, and shout, "Wake up!"

Paul Tillich wrote,[9] "Man resists objectification, and if his resistance is broken, man himself is broken." We are in a broken world of broken hopes, and we may very well break the future of our species and our planet.

CHAPTER 14

Therapist
Artistry

This chapter brings together a number of strands to weave a conception of the therapist as artist. We begin by testing the practice of psychotherapy against seven characteristics shared by most art forms. Not surprisingly, it turns out that our field qualifies on all seven. Next we look at the person who is the therapist and speculate about the qualities and training desirable in those who plan careers in depth psychotherapy.

This leads to an examination of the stresses and rewards of lifelong commitment to the practice of depth psychotherapy. I conclude with a personal essay about the mystery within which our field and our lives are ultimately set.

OUR QUEST HAS SOUGHT avenues from the objectifiable, the external and explicit, to the client's subjectivity, a realm that extends far beyond the reach of words. Our fundamental assumptions have been that the most mature psychotherapists are more artists than technicians and that they bring to bear a wide variety of sensitivities and skills so their clients can release their latent potentials for fuller living.

These characteristics of virtuoso psychotherapists are not readily transmitted to their younger colleagues. To aid that transfer, I have presented an array of dimensions that point toward those elusive and ineffable resources.

It is difficult to make explicit what is meant by "point toward." Mature therapists doubtlessly use many of the kinds of considerations represented by the dimensions in this book. Equally doubtlessly they use many others as well. And still equally doubtlessly they seldom think about these dimensions in the ordered and systematic way that we have needed to use in presenting them here. Just as a great painter working on a major canvas is unlikely to think in detail about such matters as "blue and yellow make green" or the rudiments of the vanishing point, or as a master pianist spends little time on chord progressions when playing a concert—just so the virtuoso therapist has mastered these matters so that they are "second nature" to him.

When learnings of this kind are fully incorporated they lose their sharp edges and distinguishing names. Itzak Perlman doesn't play the violin; he plays music. Of course, when there is a need to review some aspect, then names and formal scales are helpful. The pianist goes back to reexamine her fingering on certain difficult passages; the painter experiments with new media and brings to bear knowledge of the properties of light and color.

The point is this: The dimensions in this book are not used in just these forms by master therapists. As I have set them out their chief function is to lead maturing therapists to such further perceptions as will foster their developing their own further potentials.

With this mission of our presentation in mind, let us examine the nature of art forms, with a view to aiding the developing therapist to recognize the task he has undertaken.

CHARACTERISTICS OF ART FORMS

Most, if not all, art forms—graphic, musical, visual, dramatic— share certain attributes, among which the following can be readily recognized:

- self as primary instrument
- open-endedness
- disciplined sensitivity
- highly developed skills
- a product of some kind
- self-determined standards
- identification with the work

Self as instrument. Probably the most distinguishing characteristic of an art form is that the artist herself is recognized by herself and others as the primary instrument for the expression of the artistic impulse. This is why it is expected that each artist will be distinctive, even though artists may be loosely grouped in schools or by media. We see that Chagall is different from Picasso immediately, and many can distinguish Stern from Perlman or Shostokovich from Stravinski. While each artist certainly seeks instruction, coaching, or other aids in refining her talents, it is manifest that the artistry is in the person, not in the vehicle of its expression.

Open-endedness. The art of psychotherapy is an incremental one. The artist-therapist goes through continual cycles:

- experiencing the phenomena of therapy at one level,
- becoming familiar and comfortable with that level,
- beginning to recognize previously unappreciated differences and similarities in the phenomena of therapy,
- consciously incorporating these new recognitions into experiencing the phenomena of therapy and so coming to a new level,
- becoming familiar and comfortable with the new level and allowing the new recognitions to be incorporated into the preconscious so that they no longer require focal attention,
- beginning to recognize new and previously unappreciated differences and similarities in the phenomena of therapy,
- and so on and on.

There is no end point, no final and complete mastery. Freud and Jung both continually changed and extended their observations until death; their disciples continue that process. Only those who aspire to priesthood in their traditions resist change. Beware that therapist who announces arrival at a position which needs no further change. He has lost his artistry and become a technician and is probably dangerous to his clients.

In summary, the key point is that mastery of the art of therapy is a continually evolving process rather than an end state, a matter of accepting—even welcoming—the constant challenge to move past where one is and to explore where one is becoming.

An Aside About the "Searching" Process

The process here described for the evolution of psychotherapeutic insight and artistry is actually a more basic human process. The same sequence characterizes those who live most fully and vitally. It is also very much at work when one writes about any human enterprise. In the writing of this book, I repeatedly find that the ideas I have worked out in advance become transparent when I am working on them again. Thus I find new components or applications or other developments coming into awareness as I write. This makes the writing process an exciting adventure; it also makes it a frustrating exercise in which I can never write at my growing edge but only one step back of that. If I try to write at that edge, I am faced with a terrible choice: to stop growing or to never complete the task.

Disciplined sensitivity. Just as we recognize that the ultimate artistic instrument is the artist herself, we see that the core of that instrument is the sensitivity of the artist. Without the capacity to learn to experience finer and finer distinctions or nuances of the medium—whatever it may be—all else will be futile. Musicians who have "perfect pitch," the ability to sing or recognize any note without aid, may not become artists, but if they choose that route they have a great advantage. The fine distinctions in colors that a painter can identify, the subtle intimations of feeling that an accomplished actor can convey, and the implicit drawing out of character that a skilled author can weave from words are other examples.

The psychotherapist must refine his capacity to pick up faint hints of emotions, to intuit changes in his client's intentions even as they are occurring, to sense what his client is ready to hear and use and what will be rejected, and, in short, to be the fine resonating instrument that we characterized in Chapter 11.

A product of some kind. We can recognize with Gray that many a "mute, inglorious Milton" lies in many a churchyard, but it is only the Milton which overcomes that mutism that earns the accolade of being called an artist. In Chapter 12 we saw how taking the decisive step of actualizing one's impulses made a crucial difference in one's exercise of her spiritedness. The challenge to actualize one's art in some fashion, to put oneself on the line and say "This is my work," is a step that some gifted people fear to take. Certainly there are those who could otherwise become virtuoso therapists but who fear to commit themselves to the uncharted depths of human subjectivity and so remain safely on the shore of technique and limited goals. Theirs is an aborted artistry at best.

Self-determined standards. In the final analysis, only the artist can judge his work, for only he can know the inner inspiration and how well it has been realized. A friend of mine, standing in a room with many of her paintings around the walls, once told me, "Some day I will make a painting!" What she meant, of course, was that deep within her she knew what she labored to produce and that she hoped in her lifetime at least once to achieve it. This is the essence of artistry. If one's self-imposed standards are too stringent, the artistic impulse is stifled; if they are too loose, the impulse is drowned in mediocrity.

Therapist-artists produce their work for audiences chiefly of two, their clients and themselves (although, most always there are a number of others who think they see that product and who do not hesitate to pass judgment on it—spouses, children, parents, friends, coworkers, for examples). This small panel means that inept and irresponsible therapists may produce poor work with only limited likelihood of discovery, and it means that some of the finest artists of our craft may be unknown to us. Those of us who write books may be better artist-authors than artist-therapists for all anyone can tell.

Identification with the work. The artist makes her identification with her art such that it is part of her and she is part of it. To make this tie between who one is and what one does is to dedicate oneself and one's life. That means a wholeheartedness which enriches the work. It can also mean a kind of "attachment" which may make it difficult for the person to move on to other parts of her life or to relinquish the work when her personal evolution calls for that step. A friend who had made a national reputation as an authority in his field told me on the eve of his retirement that he feared that he would be as though dead if he did not continue to produce in his field.

SELECTING AND TRAINING DEPTH THERAPISTS[1]

We need to radically rethink the preparation of psychotherapists who will aid their clients in making major life changes. That work depends heavily on getting into the subjectivity of clients and thus calls extensively on the subjectivity of therapists. A key element in this is attention to the alliance or relationship, including transference and countertransference.

Education, Training, or What?

The words we use to describe important matters often reveal more than we intend. In order to highlight my view, I plan to take unfair advantage of the traditional terms we use when talking about preparing therapists.

All of the professions have committees, curricula, and programs for *training* entrants. "Training" suggests causing animals to perform certain objective actions—roll over, play dead, etc. Or getting athletes to do something essentially similar. Or skilled craftspersons also to do something similar but infinitely more complex—brain surgery, cabinet making, or cooking Beef Wellington.

Somewhat more dignified and academic is *education*. We associate education with the multiplication tables, the table of the elements, *DSM-III*, or famous European battles in the eighteenth century.

The reader will note that I have been using still another term, *prepare*. This has its own set of associations, of course. It calls to mind preparing for confirmation, for marriage, for battle, or for death. That's a better set of associations, to my way of thinking — better because these have to do with subjective readiness. If we are preparing people to conduct life-changing therapy, we need to repeatedly remind ourselves that life-changing psychotherapy is therapy addressed to the inner life of the client. And what is that?

About That Inner Life of the Client

First and foremost, we must recognize: Ultimately the client is an autonomous being. This is assumed, not for moralistic, idealistic, or democratic reasons, but out of the realistic recognition that each human being is individual, idiosyncratic. No human being can be fully known by anyone (including himself). Human beings are not passive receptacles filled from the outside only, but are, in themselves, sources of phenomena (ideas, feelings, perceptions, relations, etc.) which alter sequences of events.

I can summarize this by asserting that human beings are not objects but subjects. Thus, there is a crucial difference between *knowing* a person and *knowing about* a person. Psychotherapists who only know about their clients do well to stay with behavior modification and similar objective approaches. If one seeks to truly know one's clients, one is inexorably drawn into the subjectivity of that person.

Goals of Subjectively Oriented Preparation

What is needed in a candidate for preparation to conduct subjectively oriented psychotherapy? The list which follows is not inclusive. Instead it centers on those elements which are chiefly neglected in today's training programs. I would look for the following in selecting those to be prepared:

- A deep sense of humility and responsibility in undertaking this kind of engagement with persons.
- A disciplined compassion (that can set limits and make firm confrontations).
- A balanced appreciation for the support knowledge can provide without undue dependence on it.

- A growing capacity to recognize, evaluate, and selectively utilize the human capacity for intuition.
- A broad perspective on the human condition, on the possibilities and limitations of individuals, and on the urgencies of the broader community.
- A genuine dedication to continuing growth in all of these regards.

Methods for Achieving These Goals

These preconditions for preparation make it evident that a very different sort of program is required to guide and support the subjective growth of the would-be therapists. Currently, we know far too little about preparing the subjective, so we usually dodge the attempt, although most would give lip service to its importance.

The requirement of personal therapy has been the most pertinent recognition. Astonishingly, there are those who question its pertinence! The contradiction in requiring what needs, more than most anything else, to be elective is only one of the difficulties with this requirement. Having no completely satisfactory solution to this problem, I will content myself with listing situations which have the possibility of nurturing an enrichment of therapist-to-be's own subjectivity:

- Extensive and intensive personal psychotherapy experiences, preferably with therapists of both sexes and including group therapy.
- At least three years of life experience in which the candidate earned his own living in the larger world, outside of the mental health field.
- Clerkships in a social agency, a mental hospital where the candidate has frequent contact with a range of the major psychopathologies, a general medical hospital, *and* a public school.
- Selective and balanced study of the basics of human psychology, medical perspectives, social influences, and professional ethics and responsibility.
- Extensive reading of both fiction and nonfiction—portraying a wide range of human experiences and the great existential and philosophic issues of life, with limited reading of the literature of psychotherapy until she has at least three years' experience.
- Continuing relations with one or more mentors and models who stimulate the candidate to reflect on her experiences and grapple with them in ways which vary from fantasy to active planning and execution.
- Internships or residencies which carefully nurture the development of sensitivities and skills as well as personal innovation.

Of course, these experiences ideally would also provide opportunities for more traditional learning, but that is definitely a secondary purpose.

PSYCHOTHERAPY AS A LIFE CAREER

So many of us come to our careers in this field because we have so long and so deeply been concerned with our own inner strivings and turmoil. That is not a shameful admission; rather, it is closer to a proud boast. We chose to do something about our distresses. We saw them as circumstances which were within reach of what was known about people generally, and we went after that knowledge. We had strong hope and an acted-upon intention that we could change. And we sought to bring these learnings from our own struggles to the service of others. Indeed, a boast.

Of course, we usually have hidden away in a corner of our being a locked box in which are our residual guilt for still having a fair amount of unresolved neurosis, for having forbidden thoughts about our clients (chiefly antagonistic and sexual, of course), for the inevitable lapses of attention, and for just plain not being all that these people need—these people who trust us with so much of their lives.

Ours is a demanding, consuming, and exhausting field, for sure. Our rates of alcoholism, suicide, divorce, and disturbed offspring are much higher than average. I think these sad statistics are produced by a variety of influences, not the least of which would be how often our work falls short of what we and our clients hope for, how frequently our investments in our work give our spouses and children less than they deserve, how intensely the dramas which we daily witness make the concerns of family and friends seem pale, and how again and again—if we remain aware—our own shortcomings and incompletely worked through issues return to confront us.

Being a therapist means being a nomad, being God-like, being insufficient, being Satanic, being under threat, being intensely loved and hated, and being self-questioning. Our work's frustrations are that we are always uncertain, that always we confront resistance from those we would help, that our successes are always less than complete, that our failures may be hauntingly clear, that our best work is often invisible even to the person with whom it is done, and that we are irretrievably alone in our work even though we are with someone most of the time.

Yet all that is but half the story. We are also able to feel and see the results of our career-long personal and professional growth as new opportunities and new vistas continually challenge us. At times we know that we have really made a difference in some lives, differences that will have ripple effects and reach unknown others. There are the occasions when we feel truly seen and confirmed by some of those we serve. And over and above all else we are privileged to peer deeper into the well of mystery than do almost any others.

A PSYCHOTHERAPIST'S JOURNEY[2]

They have said that God is dead, and it may be so. But I believe that the god who is dead is the god in the cage, the zoo god. We thought to contain the zoo god by our definitions, our interpretations, our inventions of "divine laws." That god whom we captured and domesticated in our intellectual zoo of exotic concepts, that god has not thrived in captivity, and that god has died.

But the wild god, the god that cannot be captured by our wills or our intellects — the wild god who will not be domesticated — is as alive and as free as ever. He moves in the wind. She sings in the silences of the desert. It nourishes us in the sun.

The wild god is more than the god of evolution; the wild god breathes revolution as well. The zoo god could not take us by surprise; we visited him at our convenience and chiefly as children. The zoo god could not upset the comfortable routines of our lives, and he seemed — until he died — to require little feeding with anything that mattered.

Not to be so trained is the wild god, who may overturn everything as he comes into our lives. She may demand all we have as It devours our complacency and requires us to change violently, totally, frighteningly.

I think about depth psychotherapy as the search for the wild god. This work best claims the name *psycho*therapy, that is the nurturing of the spirit or soul. Here the intent is to confront and incorporate the existential conditions of our being — among which, of course, is the ultimate unknowableness of being, the inexorable coming up against our limits in the midst of limitless mystery.

Tillich[3] called the wild god, "the God above god." The wild god is the god of mystery. And mystery is a word too seldom found in psychological writing or psychotherapeutic discourses. We deny mystery; we pretend it exists only in the minds of children, authors, and mystics. And we deceive and blind ourselves when we do so.

The wild god comes upon us in ways we cannot predict and in forms we do not expect. The wild god may come disguised as a frightened and withdrawn client who awaits release to show a rich, poetic creativity. The wild god may be the client who baffles us, frustrates us, and forces us to think freshly about aspects of our work which we had felt solid and dependable. The wild god may work through our own restlessness and irritability to force us to confront long-denied inner conflicts. The wild god shakes the ground under our feet, obscures the path we follow, and makes us aware we dwell in cages that we have constructed and that we call "reality."

Ortega said it,

> For life is at the start a chaos in which one is lost. The individual suspects this, but he is frightened at finding himself face to face with this terrible reality, and tries to cover it over with a curtain of fantasy, where everything is clear. It does not worry him that his "ideas" are not true, he uses them as trenches for the defenses of his existence, as scarecrows to frighten away reality.[4]

Mystery enfolds knowledge, contains knowledge. Mystery is infinite; knowledge finite. As knowledge grows, even more does mystery grow. Mystery is the latent meaning always awaiting our discovery and always more than our knowing.

We psychotherapists can so easily be caught into a collusion with our clients, a collusion to deny mystery. In this unholy pact what is implicit—but rarely explicit—is the illusion that there is an answer for every life problem, that there is a discoverable meaning for each dream or symbol, and that rational control is the goal and ideal for a healthy psychological life.

Psychotherapists must be knowledgeable, of course, but they must be humble in that knowledge. Let's be straight about it: We never know enough. We never can know enough. As fast as we learn, just so fast do we learn there is ever more to learn. To pretend to a client that we know what the client needs, what the client should do, what choices the client must make, is to deny mystery and to betray the client. Any thorough-going therapy needs to help the client accept and confront the mystery within and the mystery which enfolds us all.

The client with whom I've worked 300 hours in deep and intensive exploration of her life still surprises me with a new aspect of her being, a different attitude, or an unexpected response—for example, if I invite that client into a therapy group. Each client is always a mystery in important ways. I must not deceive myself into thinking I know any person—including myself—fully.

But true educational preparation always makes evident the limits of knowledge. The kind of therapist I abhor is the one who seems not to recognize limitations. Such a person is a truly dangerous necromancer masquerading as a professional.

The destructive effect of the psychotherapist who does not recognize mystery is that the world-view transmitted implicitly or explicitly to the client is of a way of being in which all that is important is ultimately knowable and controllable. Thus arise expectations of oneself which are certain to be disappointed, but the client is likely to read those disappointments as due to her own failings. This, in turn, can lead to self-criticism, depression, and alienation from one's genuine talents.

The therapist who recognizes and respects the omnipresence of mystery need not take refuge in fatalism or that form of mysticism which is wispy and precious. The openness of possibility is also a powerful encouragement to reconceive the familiar, to attempt the new, and to explore with innocence of perception. Only the pessimistic see the empty canvas as meaningless; those who cherish mystery recognize it as an opportunity for new enterprise.

Psychotherapy that is truly the nurturing of the spirit or soul must be the search for the wild god, the god of mystery, the god back of god.

If we seek the wild god, we must go out into the world, out into the dangers and opportunities, go without a map, without a compass, without enough food, protection, anything. And as we seek the wild god, we may be captured by him. For mystery comprehends us; we do not comprehend it.

Suggestions for Practice

EACH OF THE 13 dimensions which have been presented will gain in meaning and usefulness if the reader supplements reading with observations and practice. For most chapters two tasks need attention: (a) developing sensitivity to the presence and fluctuations of the process under study, and (b) increasing skill in actually using the dimension in conversations. Efforts toward one of these will, inevitably, support growth in the other, but both need careful attention.

Throughout this book suggestions are made to help the therapist increase sensitivity. All else the therapist may do rests ultimately on the ability to sense where the client is subjectively, what is the general trend of the client's movement at any moment, and what is needed at that point. "Intuition" is a name for this trained and essential capacity.

Intuition certainly has an important component that is native to some individuals, as the Jungians have particularly proposed. However, it is also present in some degree in each of us (Goldberg, 1983), and it is very much a capacity which can be increased and made more accurate (Vaughan, 1979).

Most of the dimensions of therapeutic art which have been described in previous pages depend on the therapist's ability promptly and intuitively to be alert to his own and the patient's patterns. Accordingly, the most fundamental practice suggestion is to work with these dimensions as often and with as much alert intelligence as possible. In this way, and only in this way, will the therapist come to the point at which the perspectives these dimensions provide are available preconsciously but do not intrude into engagements with patients.

Opportunities for Observation and Practice

Several different occasions for observation and practice are described below. Try to use each of them frequently. Additionally, watch for other opportunities.

Disciplined eavesdropping. Listening to others' conversations is a breach of good manners at best and downright rude at worst. Nevertheless, I suggest risking these dangers—with discretion and responsibility, of course. When you are in a situation which permits unobtrusive listening and watching, make it a habit to attend to how people talk with each other. Your conscience—and mine—can be salved at least a bit if you accept this license solely for observing the *process* of the interactions while you disregard the *content*.

In a waiting room, a coffee shop, a beauty salon, or some such place, position yourself so that you can hear (and, if possible, see) two people in conversation. It is better not to try to follow the process with larger groupings, at least at first.

- Begin by noting your immediate impressions:
  Who is the dominant speaker?
  Who is most invested in their talk?
- Now ask yourself what were the cues that suggested your answers to these questions.
- Next, watch their body language, gestures, facial expressions, and all that is nonverbal. How do these confirm or modify your impressions?
- Finally, attempt to predict what one or the other will do next (e.g., if they are arguing, which one will be converted to the other's views; if they are trading anecdotes, which will change the subject).

Practice with a friend. Particularly helpful are opportunities to try out these dimensions quite deliberately and free of the professional responsibilities we feel when working with clients. These can best be had when a colleague or friend interestedly participates with you in practice interviews and you have genuine conversations (but with the understanding that they are for practice purposes). It is helpful also to take turns playing the roles of therapist and patient.

It will be helpful if you record this conversation for later review and perhaps discussion with your friend or with a coach (see below).

> *Remember: Human relationships are powerful, and that power can be used for benefit or harm. When you carry out these assignments, it is more important to keep faith with your own values and with your friend's trust in you than to foster an inappropriate level of immersion simply to practice this task. This means that if your friend becomes caught up in the talk, is truly self-disclosing, or evidences genuine emotional need, you will respond with professional discretion, maintain any confidences fully, and stay with her or him as long as you are needed to help in dealing with any emotions which may be evoked. This does not mean that you will attempt to do therapy with your friend, a dangerous and ill-advised effort. If need for such help is demonstrated, aid your friend in finding a qualified professional. No matter what your training or experience, you are not that person if this relation is truly a friendship.*

Collecting Recorded Conversations. Sensitivity to a dimension comes from observing its operations in actual conversations. Living circumstances (as contrasted with role-played or other practice) have an integrity that is elusive but important, so try to get both live and recorded samples. If facilities are available, make video as well as audio recordings. They can be used repeatedly, and indeed much will be gained from studying the same interview with different perspectives. In this way, an enriched grasp of the multifacetedness of our material will be attained. Of course, it is also helpful to collect some fresh samples from time to time.

Here are some kinds of conversations which can usefully be minded:

- Actual, spontaneous, and usual talk between yourself and others. Make a habit of recording your conversations whenever it would not be inappropriate. You can thus gradually accumulate some of sufficient length and seriousness to be productive. In collecting these, vary the kinds of persons, topics, and circumstances of the conversations.
- Deliberately planned conversations (as suggested above) with a companion who makes him/herself available for practicing the various dimensions. Again variety is desirable.
- Recordings of ratio or television interviews. Try to get an extended conversation between two people. Shows in which there is much shifting from one person and setting to another are less helpful.

Using recorded conversations. When using these recorded conversations, several guidelines are suggested:

- Take samples from several points in the conversation. Each sample should be of sufficient length (a minimum of ten responses from the person whose patterns one is studying).
- Listen systematically. Several of the chapters have observation schedules (see below) which facilitate the study. If these are available, use them; if not, try to make some record. The point is to make the listening an active, rather than a passive, process.
- Free yourself of good/bad judgments. The task is to become familiar with the processes being presented, not to grade yourself or the interviewer or therapist to whom you're listening. Stress-free study can become enjoyable and stimulating with resulting gains in sensitivity and skill that will not be present if there is a continual fault-finding atmosphere.
- Listen with a companion if you can find one who is similarly motivated, who will use the opportunity in a working but enjoyable mood, and with whom you can discuss your experiences and observations.

Using observation schedules. Some of the chapter practice suggestions call for you to use observation schedules. These are all later in this appendix so that you can experiment among them at any time.

Try to mix free uninstructed observations with times of using these guides. These are especially valuable in providing specialized perspectives from which to observe the conversational interactions. Using them, you are likely to see more than you would without them.

So will you use them? Probably not.

Often there is an inertia about using such aids as these schedules. Only the most dedicated exercise enough discipline to do so for more than a few times and to use them systematically and fully.

You're right: That's a challenge.

So what are you going to do about it?

PRACTICE SUGGESTIONS

The suggestions for the first few chapters are spelled out in some detail, while those for the latter chapters are more briefly sketched. As you get the general idea of practicing these skills, it is best for you to take on increasing responsibility for carrying the work forward in your own style.

It is very easy to glance at these practice suggestions and then move on, mentally noting "If I ever have time, I want to try some of those." If you've persisted this far, give yourself a better break, and make time to try these out and to follow through.

Chapter 2: Communication Level

Get the habit of noting the degree of involvement that you are experiencing and that your conversational partners display. This will be helpful in your work as a therapist, of course, but it may provide you useful cues when talking with a salesperson or when arguing a point with a colleague.

Disciplined eavesdropping. Use the general suggestions above, but particularly ask yourself about the people you are observing:

- What fluctuations in their levels of involvement do you detect?
- Does either or do both stay formal or at the contact maintenance levels?
- Does either get beyond the standard level? What effect, if any, does that have on her or his partner?
- Does either seem aware of any differences in immersion?

Observation Schedule 2.1 suggests ways of attending to nonverbal aspects of conversations. Sometimes you can use this unobtrusively.

Practice with a friend. With a friend with whom you have a trusting relation, engage in a meaningful conversation. If possible, record this talk. The topic can be anything appropriate to your relation, but the more personal and mutually self-disclosing the better. In this conversation you will try to aid your friend *and yourself* to get more immersed, to reach a deeper than usual level of engagement. Do not disclose this purpose until after the conversation (when the instructions below will tell you to do so).

When the discussion is completed, and assuming that you and your companion had a meaningful exchange, consider these questions (if your friend is a co-professional, you may find it useful to do this jointly):

- At what level of involvement was your friend as the conversation began? At what level were you?
- What movement to deeper levels occurred?
- What facilitated that movement?
- Was there any occasion when something occurred which acted to reduce the involvement for one or both of you? What was it? How could it have been avoided?

- How do you feel about your ability to meet your friend genuinely at an immersed level? Are you able to identify within yourself the hesitation which most of us feel about that encounter?
- Tell your friend what you have been doing and ask for his or her candid feedback on how the process was for her or him.
- Use Observation Schedule 2.2 and have your friend also use it to get at your impressions of the communications climate and levels of the conversation.

Using recorded conversations. Questions such as those suggested above can be helpful when listening to recorded conversations. Additionally, consider the following:

- When a clear change in level of presence occurred, what precursors can you now discern?
- If the change was in a direction of lessened involvement, can you now identify points at which an intervention might have prevented that loss of immersion?
- If you have a video recording, you can use Observation Schedule 2.1 to study the nonverbal aspects of the conversation.

Chapter 3: Therapist Presence and the Alliance

The instructions for Chapter 2 are applicable for this chapter also. Pay especial attention to the similarities and differences between therapist and client (or the persons in these relative roles). If you are the therapist in any of the sample interviews, can you discover when and as a result of what stimulus you are inclined to withdraw?

Other observations. Several observation schedules are available to help you practice getting greater depth and to disclose any unwitting patterns you may have picked up which interfere with your getting the depth you want. Use Observation Schedules 3.1, 3.2, 3.3 on recordings of your own interviews.

Chapter 4: Interpersonal Press

Attention to the nonverbal. Necessarily, these practice steps focus on the verbal aspects of therapeutic conversations. In written guides such as this, the words get emphasized. It is the therapist's responsibility, however, to use the words only as pointers to the total interaction with the client. Mere mouthing of words is never psychotherapy.

Using recorded conversations. Record a conversation with a friend on some topic of mutual interest (e.g., hobby or sports activity, current political issue). Try to continue for at least 15 or 20 minutes (so that initial self-consciousness will be reduced). Using Observation Schedule 4.1, "Interpersonal Press," listen to three samples of ten responses each (ten times that you speak), taking one sample after the conversation has been going about one minute (i.e., early in the talk), one sample midway, and one shortly before the end. As you listen, each time that you speak tally in the appropriate cell of the form, working from left to right. Draw a vertical line to separate the samples.

As you look at the patterns, what do you think of the way you use press?

- Do you seem to have a consistent pattern?
- How did immersion in the topic (if it occurred) seem to affect your press level?
- Do you think the conversation might have been significantly different had you used a different press pattern? What kind of difference? From what alternate pattern?

Studying professional interviewers. You can do a similar study by taping a TV or radio interview show such as *60 Minutes* or *The Tonight Show*. It is interesting to contrast different interviewers in terms of their interpersonal press styles.

Press exercises. Practice modulating interpersonal press by doing "Interpersonal Press Practice A and B" (below). Sample responses are in the last section of this appendix, but wait until you've tried your own skills before looking at them. Then contrast your responses to see whether you have been able to graduate your movement along the scale as did the therapist whose answers are given there.

INTERPERSONAL PRESS PRACTICE A

TH: *What are you thinking right now?*
CL: *I'm thinking about what I should talk about next.*
   [Phrase eight therapist responses between the response numbered "1:" and "10:" below. Distribute them evenly on the scale of interpersonal press intensity.]
   1: Mh-hmm. (Pleasant, attentive manner).

2: _____

_____

3: _____

_____

4: _____

_____

5: _____

_____

6: _____

_____

7: _____

_____

8: _____

_____

9: _____

_____

10: It's essential that you say what matters to you now. If you don't do that, there's no use in our talking anymore. Now quit stalling.

Below use Roman numerals to indicate the octave of the interpersonal press scale each response represents:

#2 _____ #3 _____ #4 _____ #5 _____ #6 _____ #7 _____ #8 _____ #9_____

How well modulated were you? Two responses in each octave?

INTERPERSONAL PRESS PRACTICE B

TH: *You're feeling a lot of pain and anger right now.*
PT: *Yes, I am. It just feels like it's too much, and I'm afraid I won't be able to take it.*
   [Phrase nine responses the therapist might make which vary on the scale of interpersonal press between the two extremes given below.]
   1: Mmmm. (Sympathetic tone and manner).

2: _____

_____

3: _____

_____

4: _____

_____

5: _____

_____

6: _____

_____

7: _____

_____

8: _____

_____

9: _____

_____

10: _____

_____

11: You haven't any choice really. This is just one of the things you've got to
face and deal with. Trying to avoid it only will mean more pain in the
long run; so hang in. I'll be with you every way I can be.

Below use Roman numerals to indicate the octave of the interpersonal press
scale each response represents:

#2 _____ #3 _____ #4 _____ #5 _____ #6 _____ #7 _____ #8_____ #9_____

Section III: Subject Matter Guidance

All chapters in this section may be practiced in the same way. Different
observation schedules are, of course, used for each:

5.1 Topical Paralleling
6.1 Feeling Paralleling
7.1 Frame Paralleling
8.1 Locus Paralleling

Look for opportunities to use each of these perspectives in different settings and with contrasting conversations. Disciplined eavesdropping, recorded conversations, and role-played practice all will afford such possibilities.

Exercises

A. Look back at Segments 2.8 (page 41) and 3.6 (page 60). Go through
these using an observation schedule (one at a time) and tallying the therapist's responses in one color and the patient's in another on the same form.
Segment 2.8 shows a therapist supporting a client's self-exploration. Segment 3.6, in contrast, demonstrates a therapist's challenging a client's resistance to involvement. Evaluate how the difference in the interaction is reflected in the paralleling processes.

B. The interview segments from these chapters have all been tallied for all four forms of paralleling. Choose several, and make the tallies yourself; then compare your assessments with the author's as the latter are shown in the third section of this appendix. Do not expect that we'll always agree completely, but take note of the direction of any consistent differences.

C. With a friend, conduct short interview segments in which you try to make as many responses as possible in one paralleling form (e.g., all responses "diverging" or emphasizing feelings exclusively or broadening the frame or directing attention to yourself). This would seldom be desirable in actual work, but it is an interesting experience to try out and to see what effects it has on your conversational partner.

Chapter 9: Objectification-Subjectivity Ratio

Ask a friend to let you record a brief segment of conversation with him or her. Promise (and follow through on your promise) that you will treat anything said in confidence. Then record the answers to one of the following questions when it is asked in the way that I will now describe:

When the recorder is started, tell your friend that you are going to ask a single question but that she or he is to keep talking in response so long as needed to answer the question fully. Also explain that you will want to continue with the conversation for a minimum of five minutes, and ask for patience to hang in for that long.

When it is clear the friend understands, ask your question. After that you are to do just two things *and only these two things*:

- When your friend pauses, thank him or her simply, and then re-ask the question.
- Confine your responses to the first (listening) octave of interpersonal press. Look again at Figure 4.2 (page 72) to be sure of the limits of your activity.

Continue the conversation for at least five minutes by the clock. If your friend wants to stop sooner, encourage him or her to keep going till the time is up.

Select one of the following questions for each person. When you use the question, do so just as it is stated here. Do not put any special emphases on the way you say it or vary the intonation and pacing with which you present it each time. A simple, direct conversational tone is what you need. (The point is to keep the "stimulus" neutral so that your friend can do with it whatever suits him.)

"Who are you?"

"Where are you going?"

"What do you need?"

If the opportunity presents it is desirable to repeat the experiment with one or more other friends (who have not heard the interview with the first respondent). You may use the same question or another, as you see fit.

Studying the results. Using Observation Schedule 9.1 and the recording of the conversation, assign each of your friend's first five responses to one of the clusters on the objectifying-to-subjective scale. Then skip ahead to about halfway through the interview and rate five more responses. Finally, do the same for the last five responses before the talk ends. Of course, you may use more than five responses at each point, the more responses you evaluate, the more you will have to work with.

- What sort of trend is evident in the movement along the scale?
- Were there points at which the work deepened and then came back closer to the surface?
- What seemed especially helpful in fostering deeper engagement?
- What interfered with engagement?
- How did the experience affect your friend emotionally?
- How did it affect you?
- How were your feelings for/about each other affected?

Chapter 11: Concern: Source of Power and Guidance

This is an opportunity to engage in a guided exploration of your own subjectivity. There is no reason you need to show the products of this exercise to anyone, and I recommend that you now plan not to do so. In that way, you may genuinely accept this invitation to be thoroughly candid.

You will find below a series of questions. Use a tape recorder if possible, if not write your answers to these. In answering be as complete and specific as needed to truly express your own feelings and views. Whenever you make a general statement, try to supplement it with one or two examples.

It will be most helpful to you if you do not look ahead to the suggestions for studying your responses until after you've finished answering the questions. If you can't restrain yourself, it won't defeat the exercise, but it will probably make it somewhat less revealing to you about yourself. (Of course, if you can't hold back, that may tell you something too.)

Getting set. When you are going to do this exercise, it is best if you arrange to have the better part of an hour in which you can work without interruption or distraction. Then, get comfortably set. Take several minutes to center yourself as fully as possible, setting aside other matters for now. Then begin with the first question and work your way through them.

1. How do you appear to those who know you reasonably well? (Not to your most intimate friends or relatives.)
2. How content are you with the way your life is going these days?
3. What are you putting off? What do you look forward to at some future time, wish you had done or could do now?
4. What's your most secret fantasy for yourself?

5. If all goes well, how would you like your life to be different in five years?
6. For how long have you been invested in being a therapist and for how long in the future do you think that investment will last?
7. What sort of situation might cause you to consider seriously killing someone?
8. What do you imagine is the most probable neurotic element in your make-up?
9. If you became psychotic (crazy) what form do you think it would take?
10. If you could make just one change in the makeup of all human beings, what would it be? (Avoid sweeping generalizations; keeping it fairly simple and direct.)

Studying the results. When your time is up or you have finished the questions (be sure to take time enough to really deal with them), set them aside for at least 24 hours. You want to come to them with a measure of freshness.

Now read each question and your answer to it. Keep a pad of paper or tape recorder handy. Muse and speculate about what you have said. How would you say it differently now? Do any answers surprise you? Make you uncomfortable? Please you especially?

Next, look back at the four aspects of therapist's concern: need, vision, presence, and sensitivity. If those answers came from a client of yours, would you feel fully concerned for that client? If you were the client and those were your therapist's answers, how would you feel about him or her?

Finally, you may want to look at your answers from the standpoint of the client's concern. How much do your answers demonstrate a mobilized and focused client concern? Have you been able to show yourself any of your pain? (We all have some, so don't cop out on that.) How about your hope for yourself? Are you really committed to your own emergence? Do you project it all onto the questions, or on me, or on something else; or are you looking inward also?

Note: If you've done this exercise seriously and come out with some challenges, you've done yourself and your clients a real service. If you had to skip over it lightly, well. . . .

Chapter 12: Intentionality and Spiritedness

This is another introspective exercise. In carrying it out, you may find there are points of convergence between what you developed in responding to the exercise for Chapter 11 and the material you will work with this time. That is appropriate and desirable. Take advantage of such linkups as they will point to important processes within you.

Values in the exercise. Most of us feel we know our own intentions very well and that it is chiefly external circumstances which keep us from carrying more of our impulses into satisfying actualization. While that is very likely true in some measure, it is also true that a really candid self-exploration of our own inner seekings will often reveal ways we are blocking ourselves. This exercise provides a way of looking into this matter, but it has no magical powers. What you will get from it will be strictly a product of what you put into it of yourself, you genuine hopes and fears, anticipations and apprehensions. Remember the computer people's "GIGO"—"garbage in, garbage out."

Collecting information. You are asked to use three steps in collecting information about your own intentions. Do each spontaneously and in circumstances which provide you with maximum opportunity to work deeply within yourself without intrusions. You will know what these are by now and not need instruction here.

1. Review the past week and think how you have used the 168 hours it provided you. Use the actual past week, not a hypothetical "better," "more typical," or other week. You can do that also, if you wish, but it's what you actually did do that is needed here. Divide the 168 hours up among all the main ways you used it.
2. Now fantasy an ideal life just exactly the way you'd like it to be if all your dreams could come true at once. Divide up 168 hours for a week of that ideal life.
3. Finally, think as realistically as you can about what you want to accomplish in the next year. What do you hope to have done, experienced, or brought about in some significant degree by one year from today?

When you have written out your answers to these three questions, set them aside for at least 24 hours. Give them a chance to marinate in time.

Studying the information. Read through your answer to the *third* question, your realistic hopes for the next year. Try to pull out and write down five to ten reasonably explicit or concrete goals that you have for your life.

Next review the intentionality sequence, Table 12.1 (page 229), and decide at what point in this sequence each of the intentions you identified is now located. It will probably be handiest if you arrange them so that the intentions are now listed under each of the steps—"wish, will, want, action, actualization."

Look next at the clusterings and speculate about their relation to the "gates" that must be passed if these intentions are to be actualized. See Table 12.2 (page 232). Are there similarities in what you need to do? Can ways be found to have some intentions reinforce each other? Do others conflict? What help would assigning priorities to the intentions give?

Now go back to your actual week (*first* question): Facing the hard facts of how your life is actually going, how realistic are your assignments of positions to your intentions? How well have you taken account of the actual impeding effects of the gates? What readjustments in the overall distribution of your energies (time, money, emotions, other resources) are indicated?

Finally, look at your dream week (*second* question): This may be a resource you can mine for renewed energy and hopefulness. The fantasied ideal is not just a superficial matter; it is your touch with deeper resources within you. If you can find ways of tapping into these, you may be able to reinforce your real intentions and move toward more truly actualizing the future you want.

OBSERVATION SCHEDULES

These schedules act as specific lenses to help their user see details not usually noticeable and to extend the possibilities for skill development. It is simple to learn to use them. One need only note a few conventions:

- The letter "Y" is used to refer to you, the therapist or interviewer, the one seeking to develop skills.
- The letter "O" refers to the other person with whom the conversation is conducted, the patient or client, the interviewee, or the friend lending him- or herself to the task.
- Many of the schedules present a grid to be checked as observations are made of the progress of the conversation. When this is the case, as in the sample below, each vertical line represents a response. Check marks in the rows indicate the nature of that response.

LISTENING				✔	✔	✔			✔	✔					✔	✔
GUIDING	✔							✔			✔	✔				
INSTRUCTING		✔	✔										✔			
REQUIRING							✔									
Key words																

Some schedules have somewhat different patterns but each will provide instructions which make it obvious what is required. The space for key words is used for distinctive words which will help to identify where in the conversation the entries are being made.

Observation Schedule 2.1: Nonverbal Communication

You are to observe both the Y and the O. Watch posture, gestures, facial expressions, movements, even tone and pacing of speech—in short, everything but the words said and their meanings. See what you can learn about the communication that exists between these two people—or about what interferes with their genuinely communicating.

Here are some questions that may suggest aspects to observe. Do not be restricted to these, but use your own sensitivity and intuition.

1. Sequences of movements or of interactions (e.g., when one leaned forward did the other usually move forward also or pull back?)
2. Which nonverbal channels did each seem to use most (e.g., hands, posture, variations in pacing)?
3. Was there a general trend in either (or both) speakers (e.g., toward the other, away, unchanging)?
4. How congruent was the verbal communication of each speaker with the nonverbal?
5. If you had seen only a silent movie of this conversation, what might you have concluded about it?

© James F. T. Bugental, 1978

Observation Schedule 2.2: Presence Levels

Answer the following questions by checking the appropriate blanks.

1. Was what Y said to O clear and understandable?
   Always ____ Mostly ____ Half ____ Seldom ____ Never ____
2. Did Y seem to understand what O had to say?
   Always ____ Mostly ____ Half ____ Seldom ____ Never ____
3. Estimate the deepest level of presence O reached:
   Formal ____ Cont. Maint. ____ Standard ____ Critical ____ Intim. ____
4. Estimate the deepest level of presence Y reached:
   Formal ____ Cont. Maint. ____ Standard ____ Critical ____ Intim. ____
5. Estimate O's most frequent level of presence:
   Formal ____ Cont. Maint. ____ Standard ____ Critical ____ Intim. ____
6. Estimate Y's most frequent level of presence:
   Formal ____ Cont. Maint. ____ Standard ____ Critical ____ Intim. ____
7. Did O seem genuinely open, accessible?
   Mostly ____ Some ____ Varied ____ Not very ____ Role blocked ____
8. Did Y seem genuinely open, accessible?
   Mostly ____ Some ____ Varied ____ Not very ____ Role blocked ____
9. Did O seem to want to put out, to express him/herself?
   Mostly ____ Some ____ Varied ____ Not very ____ Role blocked ____
10. Did Y seem to want to put out, to express her/himself?
    Mostly ____ Some ____ Varied ____ Not very ____ Role blocked ____
11. Did O have the impulse to withdraw from the conversation?
    Often ____ Some ____ Occasionally ____ Rarely ____ Never ____
12. If O did have the impulse to withdraw, did Y notice?
    Immediately ____ Later ____ Didn't seem to ____ Can't say ____
13. If the answer to 10 is yes, how did Y react to it?
    Took effective action ____ Was some help ____ Apparently ignored it ____
    Changed the subject ____ Tried to vainly to help ____
    Other _____

14. What was the general feeling of the conversation? Check as many of the
following as apply:
Friendly _____ Uneven but okay _____ Easygoing _____ Intense _____ Cold _____
Self-conscious _____ Awkward _____ Too glib or slick _____ Disorganized _____
Needing better listening by Y _____
Other _____

Observation Schedule 3.1: Exploring the Subjective

Each time Y or O speaks, tally to indicate whether the main thrust of
the comment was directed toward objective matters (B), Subjective (S), or
about evenly to both (B-S). If it is unclear, tally in the (?) column.

the "Y"   the "O"

B	B-S	S	?	KEY WORDS	B	B-S	S	?	

the "Y"   the "O"

B	B-S	S	?	KEY WORDS	B	B-S	S	?	

the "Y"   the "O"

B	B-S	S	?	KEY WORDS	B	B-S	S	?	

the "Y"   the "O"

B	B-S	S	?	KEY WORDS	B	B-S	S	?	

Observation Schedule 3.2: Responsibility for Movement

Place check marks in front of those answers which best describe the ways in which Y encouraged O to take responsibility for interview movement or interfered with the O's doing so. You may check more than one, but double check the most frequently used patterns.

Y fostered O taking responsibility by . . .

_____ adopting a waiting pace.

_____ using explicit structuring which called on O.

_____ relying chiefly on listening and guiding press modes.

_____ conveying an expectant attitude nonverbally.

_____ chiefly using wide frame questions.

_____ frequently employing parallel and developing responses.

_____ (other, specify) _____

_____ (other) _____

_____ (other) _____

Y discouraged O taking responsibility by . . .

_____ seeming impatient for response.

_____ interrupting O frequently.

_____ often changing the subject.

_____ using many narrow focus questions.

_____ having an impassive, unresponsive manner.

_____ seeming distracted or busy with own thoughts.

_____ showing little evidence of interested listening.

_____ (other, specify) _____

_____ (other) _____

_____ (other) _____

What other suggestions or observations have you that might aid Y to increase his/her ability to involve the O in an active and responsible fashion?

_____

_____

_____

Observation Schedule 3.3: Time Distribution

Keep a record of the amount of time each speaker uses. Use your watch or counting to yourself ("One, one thousand; two, one thousand;" and so on). The pattern for doing so is illustrated.

THE Y .... THE O ....

||||| |||| ____ ____ ____   XXXXX XXXXX XXXXX XXXXX _____

____ ____ ____ ____ ____   XXXXX XXXXX XXXX _____ XXXXX

|||| | ____ ____ ____   XXX ____ ____ ____ ____

||||| ||||| ||||| ||| ____   XXXXX XXXXX XXXXX XXXXX XX ____

||||| ||||| || ____ ____   XXXXX XXXXX XXX ____ ____

Observation Schedule 4.1: Interpersonal Press

Observe one conversational partner (at a time) to record the interpersonal press that person uses. Indicate which you are observing:
Therapist _____ Client _____

Occasionally note some key words to identify where in the conversation your tallies occur.

LISTENING ___															
GUIDING ___															
INSTRUCTING ___															
REQUIRING ___															
Key words															
LISTENING ___															
GUIDING ___															
INSTRUCTING ___															
REQUIRING ___															
Key words															
LISTENING ___															
GUIDING ___															
INSTRUCTING ___															
REQUIRING ___															
Key words															

Observation Schedule 5.1: Topic Paralleling

Tally in sequence below to record the degree of continuity of each response of the person you're observing with the immediately preceding response of the other person. Enter a key word or two at intervals to locate where in the conversation you are tallying.

Observing: Y _____ O _____ Both _____

PARALLELING															
DEVELOPING															
DIVERGING															
CHANGING															
Key words															
PARALLELING															
DEVELOPING															
DIVERGING															
CHANGING															
Key words															
PARALLELING															
DEVELOPING															
DIVERGING															
CHANGING															
Key words															

Observation Schedule 6.1: Feeling Paralleling

Tally in sequence below to record the degree to which the person you're observing gives the same or more or less emphasis to feelings or ideas as did the immediately preceding response of the other person. Enter a key word or two at intervals to locate where in the conversation you are tallying.

Observing: Y _____ O _____ Both _____

FEELING EMPHASIS															
PARALLELING															
IDEA EMPHASIS															
UNCERTAIN															
Key words															
FEELING EMPHASIS															
PARALLELING															
IDEA EMPHASIS															
UNCERTAIN															
Key words															
FEELING EMPHASIS															
PARALLELING															
IDEA EMPHASIS															
UNCERTAIN															
Key words															

Observation Schedule 7.1: Frame Paralleling

Tally in sequence below to record the degree to which the person you're observing broadens or narrows or stays at about the same degree of abstraction as did the immediately preceding response of the other person. Enter a key word or two at intervals to locate where in the conversation you are tallying.

Observing: Y _____ O _____ Both _____

BROADENING (WIDE-ANGLE)																
PARALLELING																
NARROWING (TELEFOTO)																
UNCERTAIN																
Key Words																
BROADENING (WIDE-ANGLE)																
PARALLELING																
NARROWING (TELEFOTO)																
UNCERTAIN																
Key Words																
BROADENING (WIDE-ANGLE)																
PARALLELING																
NARROWING (TELEFOTO)																
UNCERTAIN																
Key Words																

Observation Schedule 8.1: Locus Paralleling

Tally in sequence below to record the degree to which the person you're observing puts the chief focus on the same one of the four loci as did the immediately preceding response of the other person. Enter a key word or two at intervals to locate where in the conversation you are tallying.

Observing: Y _____ O _____ Both _____

PATIENT INTRAPSYCHIC																
INTERPERSONAL PT-OTHERS																
INTERPERSONAL PT-THERAPIST																
THERAPIST																
Key Words																
PATIENT INTRAPSYCHIC																
INTERPERSONAL PT-OTHERS																
INTERPERSONAL PT-THERAPIST																
THERAPIST																
Key Words																
PATIENT INTRAPSYCHIC																
INTERPERSONAL PT-OTHERS																
INTERPERSONAL PT-THERAPIST																
THERAPIST																
Key Words																

Observation Schedule 9.1: Objectification to Subjectivity

Assign each response to the appropriate cluster (refer to Table 9.1, page 150). It may not explicitly match the names; use implicit sense. If several fit, average. Every few responses note "key words" to show location.

OBJECTIFYING																			
TENDING TOWARD OBJECTIFYING																			
TENDING TOWARD SUBJECTIVITY																			
LARGELY SUBJECTIVE																			
Key Words																			
OBJECTIFYING																			
TENDING TOWARD OBJECTIFYING																			
TENDING TOWARD SUBJECTIVITY																			
LARGELY SUBJECTIVE																			
Key Words																			
OBJECTIFYING																			
TENDING TOWARD OBJECTIFYING																			
TENDING TOWARD SUBJECTIVITY																			
LARGELY SUBJECTIVE																			
Key Words																			

EXAMPLES OF RESPONSES TO PRACTICE EXERCISES

Chapter 4: Interpersonal Press Practice Exercise A

TH: *What are you thinking right now?*
CL: *I'm thinking about what I should talk about next.*
   [Phrase eight therapist responses between the responses numbered "1" and "10" below. Distribute them evenly on the scale of interpersonal press intensity.]

   1. Mh-hmm. (Pleasant, attentive manner)
   2. *You're uncertain what you want to talk about, eh?*
   3. *Well, just fill me in on what's important to you these days.*
   4. *What are some of the topics you're considering?*
   5. *Tell me how it feels to be uncertain that way.*
   6. *Are you aware how much you have to stand apart from yourself to make a judgment such as that?*
   7. *Detachedly trying to plan what you will say is keeping you from being into what you talk about.*
   8. *You're frightened of where your thoughts will take you and so you're trying to be very careful of what topic you pick. Well, I think it's time you risked getting into some of the tough stuff; don't you?*
   9. *Once again you're keeping yourself an object. It's as though you were the subject of a paper you're writing. You're losing your life right now as you do this.*
   10. It's essential that you say what matters to you now. If you don't do that, there's no use in our talking any more. Now quit stalling.

Below put a roman numeral to indicate the octave of the interpersonal press scale each response represents:

#2 <u>I</u> #3 <u>I</u> #4 <u>II</u> #5 <u>II</u> #6 <u>III</u> #7 <u>III</u> #8 <u>IV</u> #9 <u>IV</u>

How well modulated were you? Two responses in each octave?

Chapter 4: Interpersonal Press Practice Exercise B

TH: *You're feeling a lot of pain and anger right now.*
PT: *Yes, I am. It just feels like it's too much, and I'm afraid I won't be able to take it.*
   [Phrase nine responses the therapist might make which vary on the scale of interpersonal press between the two extremes given below.]

   1. Mmmm. (Sympathetic tone and manner)
   2. *Your pain and anger feel like they may be too much.*
   3. *How do you experience that threat in your body now?*
   4. *Can you let me be with you as you face those frightening feelings now?*
   5. *You don't have to let it all through at once. You can take it one step at a time.*
   6. *Each time we get to these feelings you have this dread that you're going to be overwhelmed. Yet, though you avoid facing them, those feelings keep coming back.*

7. *As frightening as the pain and anger are, they are only parts of you. All of you, and I, will be here to help you deal with them.*
8. *Once again you want to get away from your own feelings, and once again you're postponing what we both know you've got to face some time. You've got to realize they're not going to just go away.*
9. *Don't kid yourself, Ben, those are your feelings, and they are going to keep coming till you face them. I'm with you, but I can't do it for you. It's time you took better care of yourself and got on with the job.*
10. *Sure it's scary. I've been in that place myself, but now it's your time to look your feelings straight on. There'll never be a better time.*
11. You haven't any choice really. This is just one of the things you've got to face and deal with. Trying to avoid it only will mean more pain in the long run; so hang in. I'll be with you every way I can.

#2 I   #3 II   #4 II   #5 III   #6 III   #7 III   #8 IV   #9 IV   #10 IV

Part III: Subject Matter Guidance: Paralleling Estimates

Note: These estimates of the degree of paralleling in the responses of therapist and client are made with implicit assumptions about nonverbal accompaniments of what is said. If you rate the same responses somewhat differently, it may be that you have made different implicit assumptions. Take note of differences, try to understand them, but recognize that you may be "right" as well as I may be.

Segment 5.3 (pages 104–106)

response	topical	feeling	frame	locus
TH-1	parallel	parallel	parallel	parallel
CL-2	developing	idea emphasis	narrowing	client/others
TH-2	parallel	parallel	parallel	client/therapist
CL-3	developing	parallel	narrowing	client/others
TH-3	parallel	parallel	parallel	parallel
CL-4	diverging	feeling	broadening	client/others
TH-4	diverging	parallel	parallel	parallel
CL-5	changing	feeling	narrowing	intrapsychic
TH-5	parallel	feeling	parallel	parallel
CL-6	diverging	feeling	broadening	parallel
TH-6	developing	idea emphasis	parallel	parallel
CL-7	diverging	idea emphasis	narrowing	client/others
TH-7	parallel	parallel	parallel	parallel
CL-8	changing	feeling	broadening	intrapsychic
TH-8	parallel	parallel	parallel	parallel
CL-9	diverging	idea emphasis	narrowing	client/therapist
TH-9	parallel	parallel	parallel	parallel
CL-10	diverging	parallel	parallel	therapist
TH-10	diverging	parallel	broadening	intrapsychic
CL-11	developing	parallel	parallel	parallel
TH-11	parallel	parallel	parallel	parallel

CL-12	diverging	feeling	narrowing	client/therapist
TH-12	developing	parallel	parallel	intrapsychic
CL-13	diverging	feeling	broadening	client/therapist
TH-13	diverging	idea emphasis	narrowing	client/therapist
CL-14	developing	parallel	narrowing	client/others
TH-14	diverging	idea emphasis	narrowing	client/others
CL-15	changing	idea emphasis	broadening	client/therapist
TH-15	changing	feeling	narrowing	parallel
CL-16	developing	feeling	narrowing	parallel
TH-16	parallel	idea emphasis	parallel	parallel
CL-17	parallel	feeling	parallel	parallel
TH-17	parallel	parallel	broadening	parallel
CL-18	parallel	feeling	narrowing	parallel
TH-18	developing	idea emphasis	broadening	parallel
CL-19	diverging	feeling	narrow	therapist
TH-19	diverging	idea emphasis	narrowing	intrapsychic
CL-20	diverging	feeling	broadening	client/therapist
TH-20	diverging	idea emphasis	broadening	client/others
CL-21	parallel	feeling	parallel	parallel
TH-21	developing	feeling	narrowing	intrapsychic
CL-22	developing	parallel	parallel	client/therapist
TH-22	diverging	feeling	broadening	intrapsychic
CL-23	parallel	idea emphasis	parallel	parallel
TH-23	diverging	feeling	broadening	client/others
CL-24	parallel	parallel	parallel	parallel

Segment 7.2 (pages 126–128)

response	topical	*feeling*	*frame*	*locus*
CL-1	developing	parallel	narrowing	client/therapist
TH-2	diverging	feeling	parallel	parallel
CL-2	developing	idea emphasis	narrowing	client/others
TH-3	diverging	feeling	parallel	intrapsychic
CL-3	developing	idea emphasis	narrowing	client/others
TH-4	developing	feeling	broadening	client/therapist
CL-4	developing	idea emphasis	parallel	client/others
TH-5	developing	idea emphasis	broadening	parallel
CL-5	developing	idea emphasis	narrowing	parallel
TH-6	diverging	idea emphasis	broadening	parallel
CL-6	developing	feeling	narrowing	intrapsychic
TH-7	developing	idea emphasis	narrowing	parallel
CL-7	parallel	parallel	broadening	parallel
TH-8	developing	idea emphasis	narrowing	client/therapist
CL-8	developing	feeling	parallel	client/others
TH-9	developing	idea emphasis	narrowing	parallel
CL-9	developing	idea emphasis	narrowing	intrapsychic
TH-10	developing	parallel	parallel	client/others
CL-10	developing	feeling	parallel	intrapsychic
TH-11	developing	idea emphasis	narrowing	parallel
CL-11	developing	idea emphasis	parallel	parallel
TH-12	parallel	parallel	narrowing	parallel

CL-12	developing	idea emphasis	parallel	parallel
TH-13	developing	parallel	narrowing	client/therapist
CL-13	diverging	parallel	broadening	parallel
TH-14	diverging	feeling	narrowing	intrapsychic
CL-14	developing	feeling	parallel	parallel

NOTES AND COMMENTS

This section is organized by chapters. Reference items cited only by year date are listed under "Bugental, J. F. T."

Preface

1. 1975/76 offers a preliminary statement of the need for a psychology of the subjective.
2. See Table 1.1 of 1978 (pp. 12–13) which suggests six clusters of psychotherapies and some of the dimensions on which they may be distinguished.
3. Debra J. White of The Saybrook Institute is conducting the first longitudinal study of the development of psychotherapists. When this is completed we may know much better how to facilitate this evolution.

Chapter 1

1. See 1976, 1978, 1981.
2. Kate's experience in psychotherapy is reported in detail in 1976, pp. 237–277.
3. My three chief publications about this way of working are (1981), which provides the most comprehensive statement, (1978), which synopsizes the theory and practice, and (1976), which offers detailed case illustrations.
4. Valuable discussions of intuition and how it may be developed are offered in Goldberg, 1983, and Vaughan, 1979.
5. In personal conversations, discrepancies between what one says in words and what one conveys with body, face, gesture, and intonation usually result in the verbal being discounted. However the reverse is true in public situations—"I'm not a crook"—probably because the nonverbal is so much more transitory and resistant to clear specification.
6. See Stone (1967).

Chapter 2

1. Many of the dimensions here, as well as others, are described in 1980b.
2. A wide-ranging discussion of presence is synopsized in 1983b.
3. Rollo May (1969, page 248) says, "I now believe that one reason psychoanalysis doesn't 'take,' doesn't get to the basis of the problems of persons . . . in a certain number of cases, is that the intentionality of the patient is not reached. He, therefore, never fully commits himself, is never fully in the analysis, never has a full encounter."
4. The Victorian epoch seems to have been the high water point of formality in relating. Typical of that mode is the great motivational power of shame, which at its zenith frequently led to rupture of relations, suicide, and murder. Today shame is less obviously potent, but new formalities arise and humiliation (another form of shame) is still a much dreaded experience. The new formalities have included the ritual dress and speech of "hippies" or of the "yuppies," for examples.
5. Figure 3.1 (p. 51–54) provides a useful form for collecting such information and protecting interview time for more subjective work.
6. The contractions which are among the physical manifestations may alarm the inexperienced therapist with their superficial similarity to epileptoid phenome-

na. However, they are not necessarily evidences of deep psychopathology but may be manifestations of the bodily representation of the struggle between the resistance and the seeking toward emergence.

Watching a client writhing in these involuntary and powerful contortions, one can readily understand the idea of possession by an alien entity. Indeed, in a very real way that is the case: A splitoff subself which has been the seat of the client's way of being in the world is being "driven out" or "killed off" by the therapeutic work.

7. E. Jones, 1953, page 253.
8. This case is reported in 1986.

Chapter 3

1. Mahrer (1986) repeatedly calls for the therapist to bring her deeper sensing to the work. See, for example, pages 40 and following.
2. This form has not been copyrighted. Readers who find it useful are free to copy it, amending it as they may wish.
3. This excerpt is taken from the account of my work with Jennifer which is in 1976, pages 56–100.
4. The notion of a "dominant emotional theme" is discussed and illustrated in 1981, pages 111–114.
5. This work is illustrated in 1976, pages 159–162.
6. This is the case of Eric, 1986.
7. Maurice Friedman (1985) has written definitively in extending Martin Buber's I-Thou perspective to the therapeutic engagement and in developing what he calls "dialogic psychotherapy."

Chapter 4

1. This keyboard reads from right to left in the numbering of the octaves. This is due to the linkage of the listening mode with the treble and the requiring mode with the bass — aesthetically justified if a bit confusing to our left-to-right reading habits.
2. Rogers is identified with a perspective which holds that teaching and directing are countertherapeutic, while Ellis represents an opposing view which places heavy reliance on such interventions.
3. Such a case and its near-disastrous course is described in 1976, pages 237–277.
4. Rogers, 1942.
5. Gerald Burton was my research assistant.

Chapter 5

1. 1948, 1952. The two further papers referred to are 1953, 1954.

Chapter 6

1. If memory serves, it was Victor C. Raimy who made this valuable comparison as part of a class or seminar he conducted at Ohio State University in 1947.
2. The hackneyed question, "What do you feel?" is not solely the possession of therapists. Radio and television reporters seem to use this inquiry with a blindness that is shocking: To the mother of a child tragically killed in traffic, "What are you feeling about what happened?"

What is astonishing is how often some therapists and some media interviewers seem to feel they have received a valid answer when this question is so bluntly put without any attention to the situation or the context.

3. Increased awareness is the fundamental healing/growth process which leads to the desired outcomes of psychotherapy. See 1978, pages 119–144.

4. Ronald Laing has used the traditional Zen aphorism, "the finger pointing at the moon is not the moon," to recall us to the depths of our subjectivity. His book of "knots" is a potent disrupter of complacency in therapists who risk encountering his versified koans, Laing, 1970, pages 87–88.

Chapter 7

1. From 1976, pp. 200–201.

Chapter 8

1. Neither this book or any book can say all that could be said about the demands on therapist. The effort to make everything explicit is blind to or ignores this central reality. Sadly, many who are charged with administering psychotherapy programs or training or licensing therapists seem unaware of this, or they are so captured by the pressures for swift and simplistic approaches that they suppress their recognition of it. The current fad of creating standardized "treatment manuals" is a shocking example of this dismal situation.

2. Adapted from 1976, pp. 106–110.

3. Fromm, 1941, pages 24–39.

4. Tuchman, 1984.

5. An extreme example of this fallacy is B. F. Skinner's *Beyond Freedom and Dignity* (1971), which blithely equates *freedom* and *dignity* with the literature discussing those concepts!

6. Existential anxiety has been notably dealt with by May (1977) and Tillich (1952).

Chapter 9

1. This title is deliberately not grammatically parallel, and it is so to call attention to an important point: To objectify one's concerns is to make them and oneself into objects, things, impotent products of outside forces. To speak of one's subjectivity is to characterize a state of being, a centered perspective on one's life in which one has responsibility and power.

   It is also significant that the truest objectivity is only possible when one is totally subjectively centered. Then there is no distorting self-consciousness intruding on consciousness—the thing in itself may be observed.

2. The scale which is the basic frame of this chapter is derived from one I developed in 1974 in collaboration with William E. Bridges, the author of that excellent treatment of human change potentials, *Transitions* (1980).

3. The answer to the third puzzle is "Double or nothing."

4. I need to acknowledge that my skill with these materials is still limited. Thus I refer readers to the classical works by psychoanalysts, the Jungian analytic psychotherapists, and the more recent writing (e.g., Delaney, 1979; Rossi, 1972/1985).

5. This capability is variously named and is tapped into by various means by therapists and others.

   Freud sought to draw on it with his basic rule of "free association." Eugene Gendlin (1978) speaks of "focusing." John Welwood (1982) calls it "unfolding,"

and I—following a tradition of general psychology earlier in this century—think of it as "searching." It has been drawn on by those who practice "brainstorming" in its various forms. Whatever it is named, it is a vital and potent power which has been too little recognized and brought into play by psychology and by many psychotherapists.
6. In Andrade (1954), pages 134.
7. William Emerson, 1985, 1986.

Chapter 10

1. See Freud, 1916/17.
2. This approach to the resistance is based on psychoanalytic methodology, especially as set forth by Wilhelm Reich in his brilliant Part I of *Character Analysis* (1949). I have also been importantly influenced by Kaiser (Fierman, 1965), Kelman (1948/63), and Saul (1958). Additional discussions of my work with resistance will be found in 1978 and 1981.
3. Kelly, 1955, and my 1978 and 1981.
4. May, 1977.
5. From 1976, pages 204–205.
6. Laurence, Jennifer, Frank, and Louise are described in 1976.
7. See 1978, pp. 75–81; 1981, pp. 166–181. Also see Mahrer 1983 (pages 371 and following).
8. Frances Vaughan (1985) has given us an encompassing view of our nature which makes place for the sensual, the emotional, the mental, the existential, and the spiritual. See especially her unique reexamination and extension of the pleasure principle (page 79–92).
9. Jourard, 1963. Elizabeth Bugental and I have carried this suggestion forward in a number of papers (1967b; 1980a; Bugental, E. K. & Bugental, J. F. T., 1984; Bugental, J. F. T. & Bugental, E. K., 1984).
10. The wonderful Alan Watts quotation is from his *Nature, Man and Woman* (1970, page 181).

Chapter 11

1. From 1976, pages 22–24.
2. Adapted from 1976, pages 19–20.
3. Financial issues can be important, but they also can be ways of resisting full presence in therapy. See 1983a.
4. See 1978, pages 47–61; 1981, pages 266–268.
5. I have read the reports of people who say they would rather talk with a computer than with a live counselor, and I am vastly unimpressed by them. I suspect strongly that such putative clients either are persons who have never experienced a sincere and sensitive interviewer or they are more intrigued by the gadget than needful of help. There is a third possibility: They may have experienced the dubious ministrations of supposed counselors who had no need for them or for the work, in which case I roundly second their choice of the computer.

    Whatever the case in these barren experiments, the kind of therapy with which we are here concerned requires a motivated, invested therapist who draws nurturance of some sort from practicing her art.
6. From 1976, page 70.
7. Rogow, 1970, page 90.
8. Rogow, 1970, page 100.
9. The greater power described in this paragraph helps clients who cannot at first

risk letting their needs fully be known (e.g., Frank in Segment 8.3, pages 137–139) or who cannot penetrate their own resistances (e.g., Hal in Segments 7.2 and 10.5 (pages 126–128 and 191–192 respectively).

Chapter 12

This chapter is adapted from Bugental, E. K. & Bugental, J. F. T., 1984.

1. Allport made this observation (perhaps quoting someone else) at the First Invitational Conference on Humanistic Psychology. (See 1965.)
2. The notion of this sequence is an adaptation of Rollo May's conception in *Love and Will* (1969, pages 223–245). His treatment of intentionality is the most penetrating in our current literature, and my discussion is indebted to it.
3. See Yalom, 1980, and Farber, 1966.
4. Jourard, 1963. Also see notes in Chapter 10 about "spirit."
5. Yalom (1980) develops a valuable existential conception in which he postulates four "givens": death, freedom, isolation, and meaninglessness.
6. A remarkable corrective for any tendency to vaunt human knowledge and power is a thorough perusal of the Morrisons' *Powers of Ten*, which takes one from the outer reaches of the universe to the most minute of which we know. It is an inspiring and humbling work.

Chapter 13

This chapter is adapted from 1967a.

1. See 1981.
2. See Yalom's valuable discussion of guilt and responsibility, 1980, pp. 276–286.
3. I have twice offered "spouses groups" for the husbands and wives of people in intensive therapy. These were designed to be educational and supportive, not therapy as such. The turnout in both instances was very small compared to the number who might have taken part. Indirectly, I learned that many of the spouses feared the group was just a stratagem to get them to make some changes or enter therapy themselves!
4. See Fromm, 1959.
5. See 1968a for discussion of the psychotherapy patient as a social change agent.
6. These instances are reported in 1976, pages 14–55, and 141–189, respectively.
7. A survey of attitudes of a sample of depth therapists showed that they resisted having hard and fast limits to what they might do in a patient's behalf (1968b).
8. Pascale and Athos (1981, pages 90–91) describe an important contrast between Japanese and American managers as being that the former include in their expectancies ambiguity, uncertainty, and imperfections, while their counterparts in this country regard each of those as a serious breach of competence.
9. See Tillich, 1951, page 98.

Chapter 14

1. Adapted from a presentation made at the Evolution of Psychotherapy Conference, Phoenix, Arizona, December, 1985.
2. Adapted from 1985.
3. See Tillich, 1952, page 15.
4. See Ortega y Gasset, 1957, pages 156–157.

REFERENCES AND SUGGESTED READINGS

Andrade, E. N. (1954). *Sir Isaac Newton.* New York: Anchor.

Bridges, W. E. (1980). *Transitions: Making sense of life's changes.* Reading, MA: Addison-Wesley.

Bugental, E. K. & Bugental, J. F. T. (1984). Dispiritedness: A new perspective on a familiar state. *Journal of Humanistic Psychology, 24,* 49–67.

Bugental, J. F. T. (1948). *An investigation of the relationship of the conceptual matrix to the self-concept.* Unpublished doctoral dissertation, Ohio State University. (Also: *Abstracts of Doctoral Dissertations,* Ohio State University Press, 1949, 57, 27–33.)

Bugental, J. F. T. (1952). A method for assessing self and not-self attitudes during the therapeutic series. *Journal of Consulting Psychology, 16,* 435–439.

Bugental, J. F. T. (1953). Explicit analysis of topical concurrence in diagnostic interviewing. *Journal of Clinical Psychology, 9,* 3–6.

Bugental, J. F. T. (1954). Explicit analysis: A design for the study and improvement of psychological interviewing. *Educational and Psychological Measurement, 14,* 552–565.

Bugental, J. F. T. (1965). The First Invitational Conference on Humanistic Psychology: Introduction. *Journal of Humanistic Psychology, 5* (2), 180–181.

Bugental, J. F. T. (1967a). Commitment and the psychotherapist. *Existential Psychiatry, 4,* 13–23.

Bugental, J. F. T. (1967b). Existential non-being and the need for inspiriting in psychotherapy. In P. Koestenbaum (Ed.), *Proceedings of the San Jose State College Conference on Existential Philosophy and Psychotherapy.* San Jose, CA: San Jose State College.

Bugental, J. F. T. (1968a). The humanistic ethic: The individual in psychotherapy as a societal change agent. *Journal of Humanistic Psychology, 7,* 11–25.

Bugental, J. F. T. (1968b). Psychotherapy as a source of the therapist's own authenticity and inauthenticity. *Voices, 4,* 13–23.

Bugental, J. F. T. (1975/76). Toward a subjective psychology: Tribute to Charlotte Buhler. *Interpersonal Development, 6,* 48–61.

Bugental, J. F. T. (1976). *The search for existential identity: Patient-therapist dialogues in humanistic psychotherapy.* San Francisco: Jossey-Bass.

Bugental, J. F. T. (1978). *Psychotherapy and process: The fundamentals of an existential-humanistic approach.* Reading, MA: Addison-Wesley.

Bugental, J. F. T. (1980a). The far side of despair. *Journal of Humanistic Psychology, 20,* 49–68.

Bugental, J. F. T. (1980b). *Talking: The fundamentals of humanistic professional communication.* Santa Rosa, CA: Author.

Bugental, J. F. T. (1981). *The search for authenticity: An existential-analytic approach to psychotherapy* (Enlarged edition). New York: Irvington.

Bugental, J. F. T. (1983a). The forbidden topic. In P. S. Rappoport, *Value for value psychotherapy: The economic and therapeutic barter* (pp. v-viii). New York: Praeger.

Bugental, J. F. T. (1983b). The one absolute necessity in psychotherapy. *The Script, 13* (8), 1–2.

Bugental, J. F. T. (1985). Seek a wild god. *AHP Perspective,* March, p. 8.

Bugental, J. F. T. (1986). Existential-humanistic psychotherapy. In I. L. Kutash & A. Wolf (Eds.), *Psychotherapist's casebook* (pp. 222–236). San Francisco: Jossey-Bass.

Bugental, J. F. T. & Bugental, E. K. (1984). A fate worse than death: The fear of changing. *Psychotherapy, 21,* 543–549.

Delaney, G. M. V. (1979). *Living your dreams.* San Francisco: Harper & Row.

Emerson, W. (1985, July). *Infant birth refacilitating.* Paper presented at the Pre- and Post-Natal Psychology Association, San Diego.

Emerson, W. (1986, August). *Infant psychotherapy.* Paper read at a meeting of the International Primal Association, Elmer, NJ.

Farber, L. H. (1966). *The way of the will: Essays toward a psychology and psychopathology of will.* New York: Basic Books.

Fierman, L. B. (Ed.) (1965). *Effective psychotherapy: The contributions of Hellmuth Kaiser.* New York: Free Press.

Freud, S. (1916/17). *Introductory Lectures on Psychoanalysis, Part III. General Theory of the Neuroses.* Lecture XIX: Resistance and Repression. In *The Complete Psychological Works of Sigmund Freud,* Vol. 15. New York: Norton.

Friedman, M. (1985). *The healing dialogue in psychotherapy.* New York: Aronson.

Fromm, E. (1941). *Escape from freedom.* New York: Rinehart.

Fromm, E. (1959). Value, psychology, and human existence. In A. H. Maslow (Ed.), *New knowledge in human values.* New York: Harper & Row.

Gendlin, E. T. (1978). *Focusing.* New York: Everest House.

Goldberg, P. (1983). *The intuitive edge: Understanding and developing intuition.* Los Angeles: Tarcher.

Jones, E. (1953). *The life and work of Sigmund Freud* (Vol. 1). New York: Basic Books.

Jourard, S. M. (1963). The role of spirit and "inspiriting" in human wellness. *Journal of Existential Psychiatry, 3,* 293–306.

Jung, C. G. (1968). *Analytical psychology: Its theory and practice.* New York: Pantheon/Random House.

Kelly, G. A. (1955). *The psychology of personal constructs.* New York: Norton.

Kelman, H. (1948/63). *The process in psychoanalysis: A manual.* New York: American Institute of Psychoanalysis.

Laing, R. D. (1970). *Knots.* New York: Pantheon/Random House.

Mahrer, A. R. (1983). *Experiential Psychotherapy: Basic practices.* New York: Bruner/Mazel.

Mahrer, A. R. (1986). *Therapeutic experiencing: The process of change.* New York: Norton.

May, R. (1969). *Love and will.* New York: Norton.

May, R. (1977). *The meaning of anxiety.* (Revised edition). New York: Norton.

Morrison, P. & Morrison, P. and the Office of Charles and Ray Eames. (1982). *Powers of ten: A book about the relative size of things in the universe and the effect of adding another zero.* New York: Scientific American Library.

Ortega y Gasset, J. O. (1957). *The revolt of the masses.* New York: Norton.

Pascale, R. T. & Athos, A. G. (1981). *The art of Japanese management: Applications for American executives.* New York: Simon & Schuster.

Reich, W. (1949). *Character analysis.* New York: Orgone Institute Press.

Rogers, C. R. (1942). *Counseling and psychotherapy: Newer concepts in practice.* Boston: Houghton Mifflin.

Rogers, C. R. (1965). *Client-centered therapy: Its current practice, implications, and theory.* Boston: Houghton-Mifflin.

Rogow, A. A. (1970). *The psychiatrists.* New York: Putnam's Sons.

Rossi, E. L. (1972/1985). *Dreams and the growth of personality: Expanding awareness in psychotherapy.* (Second edition). New York: Brunner/Mazel.

Saul, L. J. (1958). *Technic and practice of psychoanalysis.* Philadelphia: Lippincott.

Skinner, B. F. (1971). *Beyond freedom and dignity.* New York: Knopf.

Stone, I. (1961). *The agony and the ecstasy.* New York: Doubleday.

Tillich, P. (1951). *Systematic theology,* Vol. 1. Chicago: University of Chicago Press.

Tillich, P. (1952). *The courage to be.* New Haven: Yale University Press.

Tuchman, B. W. (1984). *The march of folly: From Troy to Vietnam.* New York: Ballantine.

Vaughan, F. E. (1979). *Awakening intuition.* Garden City, NY: Anchor/Doubleday.

Vaughan, F. E. (1985). *The inward arc: Healing and wholeness in psychotherapy and spirituality.* Boston: New Science Library/Shambhala.

Watts, A. W. (1970). *Nature, man and woman.* New York: Vintage/Random House.

Welwood, J. (1982). The unfolding of experience: Psychotherapy and beyond. *Journal of Humanistic Psychology, 22,* 91–104.

Yalom, I. D. (1980). *Existential psychotherapy.* New York: Basic Books.

INDEX